There is no one I'd rather have a[s] ... than Heidi. Her heart, her passio[n] ... *Gonna Be Good.* My advice is to sink in and soak in every word o[f this] book. P.S. You won't regret it.

AMY WEATHERLY, bestselling author of *I'll Be There (But I'll Be Wearing Sweatpants)* and cofounder of the wildly popular Sister I Am With You

Heidi highlights the questions many of us are asking about faith and answers them by pointing us back to Truth. Through biblical story, candor, and a ton of humor, she reminds us that God writes the best stories (they're really, really good). This is a must-read for any woman wanting to see what Scripture has to say about #allthethings burning in her heart.

REBECCA GEORGE, author of *Do the Thing* and host of the *Radical Radiance* podcast

If you're facing a situation that you can't control or fighting a battle that seems hard to win, God is going to use this book in your life. With her fun and conversational style, allow Heidi Lee Anderson to get you into God's Word, remind you of His promises, and prepare you for the battle you face.

JASON STRAND, senior pastor at Eagle Brook Church

I found myself both deeply moved and equally challenged as I read *P.S. It's Gonna Be Good.* Heidi has a way of drawing the reader in with her wit and charm, and then immerses them with biblical narrative and truth. She takes questions every person has asked themselves at one point or another and draws out answers by looking at Scripture in fresh ways. Heidi is the real deal, and her writing matches her authentic pursuit of God. I highly recommend this book!

JOHN ALEXANDER, teaching pastor/executive director of creative arts at Eagle Brook Church

Each of us will reach a point in life when it feels like we have more questions than answers. The what-ifs and how-tos and why-mes can threaten to overwhelm us, especially when everything seems to be falling apart. Heidi Lee Anderson knows this well, and she also knows who stands ready to answer our questions and carry us through as we trust in Him. This delightful journey through God's Word will have you laughing, nodding, crying, and praising the Lord for His goodness! If you need some encouragement, a few chuckles, and soul-deep refreshment, then you're holding the right book in your hands.

NAOMI VACARO, founder of the Wholehearted ministry and author of *Quiet*

Powerful yet practical, Heidi has written a powerful survival guide for the seasons of questioning and doubt. This book is a road map—and a must-read—if you're anything like me and have found yourself wrestling with your faith and struggling with doubt, fear, or insecurity.

JORDAN LEE DOOLEY, national bestselling author of *Own Your Everyday* and *Embrace Your Almost*

Many times throughout our lives, we face circumstances that find us questioning. Our faith can waver, and we may wonder if God will come through this time. In *P.S. It's Gonna Be Good*, Heidi Lee Anderson invites us to face the hard stuff of life head-on and discover how a sovereign God won't only show up, but He's been there all along. With Heidi's signature way of making ancient Bible stories relate to our modern everyday lives in a very powerful and practical way, this book is a must-read!

RUTH SCHWENK, blogger, podcaster, and author of the bestselling devotional *Trusting God in All the Things*

P.S. It's Gonna Be Good is the book we all need for the real questions we face every day. Heidi is a great guide with her humor and deep understanding of trusting God through hard things. You will find encouragement and strength to press on in trusting God is always good.

ASHLEY MORGAN JACKSON

You're not the only one lying awake at night endlessly scrolling social media in an effort to distract yourself from the hard thing you're facing. And you're definitely not the only one wondering if it's all *really* going to be okay. News flash: It's going to be more than okay—it's gonna be GOOD. In the pages of this book, Heidi meets us right in the middle of life's biggest what ifs and hands us a cup of coffee with the promise that God is with us and working ALL things for our good. Get ready for your hope to be renewed and for your sides to ache—Heidi will have you laughing for days!

ABBEY CAPPA, pastor's wife

Truth coupled with laughter is a great combo and always how you bring it, Heidi! Remember: Nothing is ever truly fatal—God wins every time!

DAN STOLTZ, proud dad, president/CEO of Spire Credit Union

Do yourself a favor and get this book! With the credibility of a cancer survivor and the biblical understanding of a scholar, Heidi encourages, inspires, and gives hope. This book is for anyone who has wondered if God is really making something beautiful out of the hard stuff. Through these pages, you will feel like you're drinking coffee with your best friend and she is giving your soul a hug. Bible teaching, encouragement, and even humor—all wrapped into the pages of *P.S. It's Gonna Be Good.* Heidi's words will bless the weary heart deeply.

MOLLY DEFRANK, author of *Digital Detox: The Two-Week Tech Reset for Kids*

We've all been there. We've all had those moments (or years) of feeling down, discouraged, and just straight-up disappointed in life. We've become disillusioned in our faith and wondered where in the world God is. If that describes you at all . . . you're in the right place. Heidi has done a fantastic job of bringing biblical truth and hope to the hard places of life. This is a book every woman needs! If you desire to thrive (not simply survive), grab a copy and dig in.

BETHANY BEAL, cofounder of Girl Defined Ministries and author of *Girl Defined: God's Radical Design for Beauty, Femininity, and Identity*

The book everyone needs to read! No matter who you are or what you're going through, I promise there's something for you. Heidi not only addresses the hard fear questions we're asking—while bringing it to life with perfectly woven-in humor—but also provides a solution to each! A passionate, biblically sound pursuit of faith over fear.

ARIEL TYSON, author of *Chase the Roar*, speaker, Instagram and TikTok content creator @arielctyson, pastor's wife, entrepreneur

P.S. it's gonna be good

HOW GOD'S WORD ANSWERS OUR QUESTIONS ABOUT FAITH, FEAR & ALL THE THINGS

Heidi Lee Anderson

TYNDALE
MOMENTUM®

A Tyndale nonfiction imprint

Visit Tyndale online at tyndale.com.

Visit Tyndale Momentum online at tyndalemomentum.com.

Visit the author online at thismotherhen.com.

Tyndale, Tyndale's quill logo, *Tyndale Momentum*, and the Tyndale Momentum logo are registered trademarks of Tyndale House Ministries. Tyndale Momentum is a nonfiction imprint of Tyndale House Publishers, Carol Stream, Illinois.

Designed by Ron C. Kaufmann

Published in association with the literary agency of Books & Such Literary Management, 52 Mission Circle, Suite 122, PMB 170, Santa Rosa, CA 95409.

For information about special discounts for bulk purchases, please contact Tyndale House Publishers at csresponse@tyndale.com, or call 1-855-277-9400.

Library of Congress Cataloging-in-Publication Data

A catalog record for this book is available from the Library of Congress.

ISBN 978-1-4964-6681-5

Printed in the United States of America

29	28	27	26	25	24	23
7	6	5	4	3	2	1

To Ty, Oscar, Mabel, Hazel, and Dottie,

My literal walking reminders that God alone holds the final word

and has such good plans up His sleeve.

No matter what's ahead, always be assured:

*I love you, and P.S. It's gonna be good.**

*Unless you never grow out of toilet humor . . .
then I can make no promises.
(Mainly talking about the kids, Ty.)

CONTENTS

INTRODUCTION

What's your deepest, darkest, biggest fear of all time?

Oops, sorry. Are we not there yet? Maybe I should backtrack. Introductions usually involve some sort of surface-level pleasantry, right? "Hi, I'm Heidi. What's your name?" may have been more polite. Now that I think of it, "What's your favorite color?" would've been safe too. Mine's brown; what's yours? Is that weird? Did things just get weird again?

Forget it. I'm not here to beat around the bush or talk color palettes (although *I have heard* brown pairs well with pasty-white redheads #itme). My guess is you aren't either. We're here to talk about faith and fear and *how in the world* God expects us to choose one when the other (I'm looking at you, dread-anxiety-doubt-disappointment-and-panic) seems to always be present.

You fill in the blank: Life was all butterflies and rainbows until

_____.

Until the doctor delivered the hard diagnosis, your parents filed for divorce, that relationship fell apart, or a certain disappointment came out of nowhere. Maybe you lost a close family member, faced an unforeseen financial hardship, floundered in a dead-end job, heard the news of a miscarriage, or got blindsided by a car accident. Whatever it may be, that *thing* you faced? Good grief, girlfriend—you were thrown quite the curveball!

And as a result?

As much as you *try* to think positive, your thoughts are consumed with what-if scenarios, which only spur on more questions. You *know* the value of seeing the glass at least half-full, for sure, but you've (kind of) become a master at imagining the worst-case instead. And while a once-blank future used to be exciting, the unknown is, well, paralyzing to say the least. Let's shoot straight—if God let *that* bad thing happen, who's to say He won't allow *another* bad thing to barge on in and crash down your whole world?

I get it.

I get *you*. I know how you once felt strong, happy, and free, but now you just feel anxious and tanked. A little disappointed and unsure. Sometimes even helpless (or dare I say, hopeless?). And you're *sick. of. it.* Fed up, over it, snapping your fingers at it. While you've heard it all—"Pray about it! Let go and let God! Don't worry because He won't give you more than you can handle!"—and it all *sounds good and you want to* . . . well, you're left, blinking hard with sagged shoulders and unanswered questions, wondering HOW IN THE WORLD, THOUGH?

Because you've done that! Prayed around the clock, scattered Bible verses around your house, cranked worship music on high, and set out every day to trust the Lord with all your heart, soul, and mind . . .

Except then the doctor calls with another piece of bad news. A friend disappoints you. Your kid plunges further into depression. The government continues to pass weird laws. Your neighbor's dog acts as if your yard is his personal dumping ground. Natural disasters strike again. Racial tension and the nation's climate are not where anyone hopes them to be.

Oh, and your toddler just smeared poop all over the carpet, cut their own hair into a mullet, and dumped a bowl of Cheerios on the baby's head—all while you stepped out of the house to check the mail and found yet another unexpected bill you can't pay.

Did I mention you found a gray hair this morning? (Stays between you and me, of course.)

Let's be real: Woman to woman, WE'RE KIND OF FREAKING OUT. Instead of seeing God's hand, experiencing His peace, and feeling confident in His good plans, we see anything *but* that. As much as we *try* to choose faith above fear, doubt, insecurities, and discouragement, we're rattled again. Anxious beyond belief. Straight-up disappointed. Unsteady in our soul. Being jerked back and forth on this roller coaster of life when all we want to do is get off, find a bench in the shade, sit in some peace and quiet, and just *be free*.

> As much as we try to choose faith above fear, doubt, insecurities, and discouragement, we're rattled again.

Would it be asking too much for some cotton candy too? #tellmeyoureamomwithouttellingmeyoureamom

"Did I steal your diary" you ask? Call your mom? Hack into the government's surveillance-camera footage through your webcam, Alexa, or smartphone? *Or hoooooow do I know your life?*

Because this is *my* life. The whole reason I picked up a pen to write this book is because I've had to battle against fear, anxious thoughts, and worst-case scenarios since one particular day back in January 2012.

I'll never forget sitting on that crinkly white paper and looking over at the doctor scanning my chart. "You have Hodgkin's Lymphoma."

At age 23, with no family history of cancer (or any disease really), here I was, thrown the biggest curveball of my life. It was so unexpected that I looked over at my mom sitting in one of the chairs across from me and asked, "What even is that?" When are we too old to bring our mom everywhere we go? #askingforafriend*

I remember her nodding, explaining that it's cancer. My whole body turned ice-cold.

Have you ever been there? Not necessarily hearing a cancer diagnosis—although maybe. But have you ever found yourself in a situation far beyond your control with the future so bleak and the unknown so scary?

---

* #butreallyaskingforme

Maybe, like me, you knew Jesus as your Savior, but it wasn't until *that moment* you desperately felt in need of His saving. Or maybe you didn't know Christ, and with nowhere to go, it felt like life was just . . . over.

There I sat, three weeks out from meeting with the oncologist . . .

Did you audibly gasp too? Augh, I know. Waiting is the absolute worst, isn't it? Not just waiting to hear the cancer staging, the treatment plan, or even the prognosis, but waiting in *all of life*.

Waiting for your house to sell, a godly man to come along, your spouse to land a job after he was let go, or that positive pregnancy test after you miscarried the last time. Because it's in this place where the enemy can really pick you apart, whisper every what-if, worst-case scenario into your ear, and aim those flaming darts right where it hurts—with the intention, of course, of making you feel utterly helpless and your situation completely hopeless.

Did I mention he's cruel? (Rhetorical, but just in case: Yeah, he's pretty ruthless.)

But here's where we call a time-out—because, girlfriend? Those of us who know Jesus as our Lord and Savior are *not* without hope, and we certainly are *not* without help. This God of ours not only reigns victorious today, but can you believe it? In Romans 8:37, He deems *us* more than conquerors too! Oh, and earlier in this very same chapter, He also assures He'll work all things for His glory and our good. (Note: Not just some things or most—but *all*. #praisehandsemoji)

Sounds pretty absolute, doesn't it? No matter how many disappointing, scary, or painful fiery darts are launched into the pathway of our lives, they must still all bow in submission to God's prevailing good plans that can never be thwarted.

Oops, I just spoiled the ending! (Although the book of Revelation kind of already did that, right?)

Back to my story. In the months following the diagnosis of stage 2 cancer, with chemotherapy and radiation as the game plan, I pulled out clumps of my hair and mastered putting on a wig. I walked around with a port lodged in my chest while also going through the motions at work. I screamed in the middle of the night when treatment had an adverse effect, then met up with friends the next morning.

So my fears today? They all stem from that experience.

For instance . . . *fun fact*: With radiation to the chest, breast cancer is a common second cancer.

Want a couple more? I love me some trivia too. The warning label on one of the chemotherapy drugs said it could result in cardiac arrest or heart failure in my forties, and oh, apparently radiation kills cancer cells in the moment but tends to grow them in the future. Not to mention, if you have cancer once, you run a higher risk in general of getting it again. SUPER FUN, RIGHT? I think that was just the first page of warnings in the packet I signed in order to receive treatment. #goodtimes

While dealing with cancer—or your divorce, miscarriage, debt, or a cold marriage—in the heat of the moment is no walk in the park, the enemy doesn't stop there. He would love nothing more than for us to battle fear then *for the rest of our lives*. Because no matter how many years you're in remission from that one cancer—and no matter how much time has passed since your trauma, disappointment, or heartache— there's a whole legion of other deadly diseases knocking at the door down the road. A whole slew of opportunities for that to resurface again. I mean, Jesus HIMSELF said troubles are a-comin'.

Yikes, is this a little much? Did I scare you off?

I'm officially terrible at introductions.

Here's what I'm trying to get at: Every unknown symptom, every doctor appointment I head into (even just routine), and every mole, bump, rash, or bodily change in myself, my kids, and my husband? I overanalyze and become quite anxious over it. (Verdict's still out, but I'm unsure if Ty enjoys waking up in the middle of the night to a flashlight beaming in his face as I'm taking pictures of his moles. Obviously just to track any progress in growth, but by his reaction, he seems to interpret it differently? #hestherealMVP)

So, me? A master at choosing faith over fear, doubt, and well, ALL THE THINGS? You *must* be able to hear my family belly-laughing across the page.

But good news: This book isn't about me.

This book is about the Author of our lives, who "has given us everything we need for living a godly life" (2 Peter 1:3), including His Word, which is "useful to teach us what is true" (2 Timothy 3:16).

When we want answers to our questions, peace in our trials, hope in the unknown, confident faith in times of doubt, and rest when our hearts beat wildly, we don't have to freak out, wondering what to do next or where to go from here.

Instead, we can open up the Book of Life and hear from the Lord Almighty Himself—and when we do, we will "know the truth, and the truth will set [us] *free*" (John 8:32, italics added). Ah, yes. There it is. That one thing we've so desperately been wanting.

Freedom.

When we lie awake at night worrying, overwhelmed by the circumstances of today, haunted by the pain of yesterday, and paralyzed by the fear of what tomorrow may bring, Jesus' invitation to freedom is not elusive nor out of reach. It's actually clear as day, within arm's reach—or rather, laid out in the palms of our hands.

When we open up our Bibles and step outside of our story, immersing ourselves in *His* story, we'll not only discover the pathway He's already laid out for us to seize that promised free, abundant life. We'll in fact see how He's been offering it this entire time.

But first, you know that saying "Stop comparing your behind-the-scenes with everyone else's highlight reel"?

We might've been doing *just fine*, but then we hop on Instagram scrolling past people with their big platforms and houses, flashy jobs and sculpted bodies. While we're over here with an inner tube around our stomach, going to a job that barely pays the bills, and looking around at our messy home, messy bun, messy life . . . well, it doesn't take much or long to feel *just a tad* jealous.

But guess what? That comparison trap isn't limited to just social media, your friends, or the Joneses down the street. We can trip over the same thing every time we open the Bible.

Like when Joshua prays for the sun to stand still, and *it actually does*?

Peter asks Jesus to let him walk on water, and *he in fact gets to*?

Elijah calls fire to fall from heaven, and *he lives to tell the tale*?

Pit that against our ordinary days, and it's hard to imagine, right? While we're washing dishes, David's slaying giants. While we're grumbling over a workout, Deborah's leading a charge into battle. And while we're struggling over our kid's homework (which, P.S. Please Jesus, never take us back to the throes of distance learning), Paul's penning half the New Testament . . . in prison . . . *with JOY.* #yougottabekiddingme

I'm sorry, but THESE are supposed to be our examples? Like for regular, average, modern-day people?

Yep.

And God, all-knowing as He is, knew we'd question it. So James nipped it in the bud: "Elijah was as human as we are, and yet when he prayed earnestly that no rain would fall, none fell for three and a half years!" (James 5:17).

Here's the deal. If we took the time to become familiar with Bible heroes' backstories before zeroing in on their highlight reels, maybe we wouldn't be so surprised after all.

Maybe we would in fact recognize that same fear, doubt, discouragement, and overwhelming stress *we* feel was also felt by these Bible characters. That unknown future with the big question marks ahead? Maybe it's not unique to us but part of their lives too. And if the God who met them there, never left their side, and showered them with peace and reassurance and purpose and guidance is the same yesterday as He is today? Well then, how He used their ordinary to do something extraordinary is maybe, just maybe, what He'd like to do for us, too.

In fact, I know He would. Scripture lays it all out in black-and-white (and sometimes red)—and we will see it for ourselves in the pages ahead.

In each chapter, we're going to follow one Bible hero as if we're tagging along right beside them, stepping into their footsteps, and looking around at the scene of their stories in real time as if we were there too. We will feel all their feels, hear what God has to say, and watch how God moved. Along the way, we'll discover what He's said, intended, promised, and reassured—since the beginning of time.

Not just to them, but to us as well.

How *they chose faith* in a prison cell, in a lions' den, and at their own brother's funeral is also how *we can choose faith* while shackled in our own chains, hearing our culture's roar, and crying at the tomb of what should've been.

All in all, if they chose faith in the midst of fear, bad news, and questions pending, then by golly, WE CAN TOO. But, like . . . how? I **thought you'd never ask.** Beyond just vague inspiration or any feel-good notion, at the end of each chapter, we'll find that practical, tangible HOW principle each Bible hero shows us.

The best part? The promise of this whole book and the one overarching *His*? While we're sitting in the middle of our stories with no idea how they're going to play out, the Author of our lives has already written the ending. Someday we will see—just like these Bible heroes did—that . . .

While we're sitting in the middle of our stories with no idea how they're going to play out, the Author of our lives has already written the ending.

It's gonna be good. Romans 8:28 assures us of that, and if we truly believe those four words as absolute truth that can never be shaken, changed, or muddied regardless of what we face, well then . . . it'll change our whole lives.

Are you feeling battle ready yet? Maybe you're looking down at the same joggers you've worn for *days*, a mug of lukewarm coffee or tea in hand, and feeling far from fired up. Your motivation is completely zapped, the question marks are too much, and the last thing you want to do is muster an ounce of energy to get off the couch.

Perfect. We don't fight from our strength anyway. We, in fact, pick up the sword of the Spirit, which is the Word of God, and get to work from there—all in Christ alone.

Remember: The Bible explicitly tells us in Ephesians 6 that the very arrows shot into our lives meant to *keep us* from choosing faith can all be extinguished once we *choose* faith.

Do you see the irony there? Every last dart meant to derail your faith? Fizzles when you take up the shield of faith.[1]

So lift up your chin, sweet girl. If the Son has set you free, you're free indeed. Jesus Christ already paid the price for every iniquity, but too many of us (100% me included) have allowed ourselves to be chained back up *unnecessarily*. But Jesus came so that we may have life and have it free and abundantly (John 10:10)—*and we're going to find it.*

You ready now? Great. Pick up your sword, hold up the shield of faith, and go ahead and turn this page—all while adding another day in those joggers to the tally. #day4forme

Make no mistake: In Christ, you are *battle ready*. Want to get started? Me too. Let's do this thang, girlfriend.

Chapter 1

DID GOD REALLY SAY...?

Eve

Imagine for a second all your favorite things together in one place. What comes to mind?

Maybe, like me, you immediately picture sitting with your husband, actually drinking coffee while it's hot, with your kids giggling in the background. Maybe you hear waves crashing on the beach, feel the warm afternoon sun hitting your face, and a nap without an alarm is about to go down. Or maybe you're laughing so hard with a circle of friends that you're choking on your latte and you have to cross your legs. #iykyk

Now imagine this moment extending without end. Your coffee doesn't get cold, and your kids are never *once* tempted to pinch the underside of each other's arms. You don't have to dread flying home or groan about getting back to the grind, and you've laughed for so long that you're standing in one big puddle—from the tears, latte, or you know what. Doesn't even matter. You're RIDING HIGH on endorphins, and all is well in the world.

This is the place we're going to start. Because these moments of bliss, peace, and joy? Where we're enjoying life to the maximum, basking in the beauty of creation, totally committed and engaged in life-giving relationships, and just never wanting it all to end? This is when we get a glimpse of heaven and what the Garden of Eden must've been like.

If you love to dance? Imagine flossing without your hip popping out. #goals

Enjoy gardening? Get ready to grow broccoli the size of your face—with no fear of it rotting, dying, or drooping.

Animal lover? Gear up because it's one big petting zoo. Animals will be so tame that the leopard will lie down with the goat, and you can shove your hand into a nest of deadly snakes and walk away unharmed. (Anticipating your question: Will we actually *want* to do this? To be fair, unsure—just reiterating Isaiah 11:8. But I'm guessing those of our children who scaled kitchen cupboards and shelves without fear will find it *exhilarating*.)

And lastly but most importantly, all your fear, disappointment, and unease? Gone. Vanquished. Permanently out of sight, forever out of mind, no longer an option or temptation, and eternally overcome.

So hold on to *this* mental picture, okay? Because that's how the world began and the direction we're going too, but it's also here in this first Garden we're introduced to our new BFF Eve.

As we step into Genesis 3 and look around at everything that happened in the first week of all time, we see God already spoke the world into motion, breathed the breath of life into man, performed the first surgery, created Eve from Adam's rib, and planted a blooming garden where His image-bearers dwelled. (All within a few days' time like NBD . . . what did you do this last week? LOL.)

These two pranced around naked without the shame or annoyance of thunder thighs, a jiggly midsection, or, for the ladies, the dreaded C-section shelf. She didn't even know it yet, but girlfriend's got it *made*!

But then one day, a slimy serpent slithered onto the scene. (Psst, it was Satan.)

Notice: As part of the original creation, snakes had been around since day six. But being as shrewd as he was, he didn't slink into the picture when Eve was strolling on her daily walk around the block with God. He didn't wriggle his way in between Adam and Eve as they sat down for dinner, table for two, feasting on their prizewinning tomatoes.

No, his timing was strategic. He waited *specifically* until the woman was alone, and *that's* the moment he crawled on over.

We see the same tactic today. It has been widely observed that when young people spend too much time isolated, they experience worse mental health outcomes, increased substance abuse, and elevated suicidal ideation.[1] Swing over to the other side of the pendulum, in long-term care facilities. AARP reports, "Isolation and loneliness are associated with a 50 percent increased risk of developing dementia, a 32 percent increased risk of stroke, and a nearly fourfold increased risk of death among heart failure patients."[2]

Yet when we read all of this, we aren't that surprised, right? We don't need studies or researchers to tell us something we ourselves have already experienced. Is it too soon to talk about 2020?

Maybe you're a Christian on a secular campus and you spend many Friday nights alone in your dorm room. You know exactly how loneliness feels. Maybe everyone else has married off, and you're the last single adult in your circle. You know what isolation does. Or maybe you've recently moved to a new town with no friends or familiar faces. The seclusion is enough to make you cry yourself to sleep, and you're tempted to maul the mail carrier with a bear hug EVERY. STINKIN. DAY. (I say just do it.)

How did God word it? Oh yeah. "It is not good for the man to be alone" (Genesis 2:18), and to be clear: God wasn't calling Adam out for being thirsty! This was a blanket statement for all mankind. We weren't made to do this life alone. Quite the contrast—being made in the image of the Trinity, we were *created* for community.

Yes, even the introverts.

100% of the teenagers who slam their doors.

And believe it or not, even that friend who leaves your texts on Read but forgets to respond 99% of the time. #towhomitmayconcernimsorry

Even Jesus' last prayer before He was arrested and crucified was for all believers across all of time to be united—repeating this desire that we "may be one" just as the Father is in Him and He is in the Father (John 17:20-23).

It just makes sense then, doesn't it? If God's heart is for us to be united and in community, then the enemy's intent is to divide and isolate. And if the enemy is on the loose and described by God as a roaring lion on the prowl looking for someone to devour (1 Peter 5:8), well then, he's not going to pounce at us without strategy. He's going to hold off until we're most vulnerable . . .

He's going to wait to attack until we're alone.

I'm no zoologist, but with all the National Geographic books my son has had me read, I might as well be. Case in point: Do you know how lions hunt their prey? I'll save you the Google search. They don't burst onto the scene without planning or scheming. Known as efficient, strategic hunters, they stalk their dinner first—staying hidden *as long as possible*. As they creep closer and closer, fixating on their meal's every move, they aren't impatient, but they wait until *the most opportune time* to pounce.[3] When the prey is facing away from them and can't see the charge coming—this is when they attack.

On the other hand, how do zebras protect themselves? Their speed and bodacious legs factor in, sure—but did you know it's their community that saves them? They rely on each other's eyes, ears, and nostrils to alert one another when they sense a predator. And when they run together, the black-and-white stripes make it hard for lions to single out any individual.[4]

When you and I stand united—linking arms in truth, prayer, and faith, and living lives marked by His stripes (Isaiah 53:5)—our enemy has a harder time singling any of us out to take us down. On our own, we're an easy dinner. Together, we are a force to be reckoned with.

Oh, one more thing. Lions often follow the same hunting patterns over and over. If they're successful from the right wing once, they'll usually saunter over to the right side again when mealtime comes around.[5]

So while they're crafty, they're not necessarily *creative*.

To wrap up this bioscience lesson: As we first meet the enemy in Genesis 3 and watch this roaring lion take the form of a slimy serpent, pay attention to his strategy. He waited until Eve was alone.

Fast-forward to Matthew 4, and . . . *well, well, well,* what do we have here? (Okay, yes—the Sunday school answer works, as always. Jesus is in fact there.)

But take a closer look. Who is that slithering onto the scene as we find Jesus *alone*?

Exactly. Same lion, same hunting pattern.

Remember how he waited to approach Eve? When Jesus was in the wilderness, the devil didn't speak *a word* until after Jesus had fasted for 40 days and 40 nights. Do you know what that means? Girl, if I go a morning without my cup of coffee? If I even miss snack time, which I pretend is just for the kids? Or, worst-case, if I find my cupboards without any sign of chocolate? I'm hangry. A headache is a given, of course. But it snowballs into such a desperate, ravenous rage that I'll Pac-Man anything. Stale bag of chips? Gone. That chocolate baking bar? Chomped through like a Hershey's bar. Easter candy from who knows how many years ago? Sniffed it out in the upstairs closet, annihilated it, and my kids are none the wiser.

The tempter didn't make his move in the previous chapter—you know, that powerful moment when Jesus was baptized, heaven split open, and the Spirit of God descended and settled on Him. Not much of a temptation to prove you're the Son of God when God's voice is literally bellowing from heaven, "This is my dearly loved Son, who brings me great joy" (Matthew 3:17), right?

The devil is just as shrewd and calculated here as he was with Eve. He waits until the end of Jesus' fast—when His human body would've been most vulnerable—and goes in for the kill in this heightened moment of solitude: "If you are the Son of God" (Matthew 4:3, 6) . . . well, *prove it.*

So when *you're* alone? When your spouse is traveling yet again? Your friends just don't get it? You're staying home with a baby who can't talk back (or maybe a teenager who very much *is* talking back)? *Bingo.*

The attacks won't come in like gangbusters on your first hard day. Satan may not even utter one word in the harder weeks after that either. But when you're most vulnerable—sinking in insecurities over your marriage, caught up in the roller coaster at work, anxious over your child's future, pushing away your friends, or disconnected from a church family—don't be surprised if he slithers up behind you.

> We're actually never alone. God is with us until the very end.

But you know what's kind of fun for us who live after the Resurrection? We may *feel* left out of a conversation, like outsiders even within our own family, or like no one gets us. Our co-workers may not understand our beliefs, our friends probably make different choices, and even the people we thought were on the same page prove by a Facebook post or their actions that they just aren't. Still the truth remains: We're actually never alone. God is with us until the very end.

Yet the enemy will always hope we'll bow to the way we feel instead of standing on the truth we know.[6]

Or even better, what if he could keep us from knowing the truth altogether?

While the Bible has never been more accessible at any other point in history than it is now, what did a recent study find? "Americans Love the Bible but Don't Read It Much, Poll Shows." While 88 percent of Americans own a Bible and 80 percent even think the Bible is sacred, 61 percent wish they read more of it, and only 26 percent of Americans actually read it on a regular basis. ("Regular" meaning four or more times a week.) For the majority—57 percent to be exact? Those Bibles are touched *four times a year or less.*[7]

Doesn't it make so much sense now? No wonder anxiety is through the roof and spreading across our nation faster than any virus ever could! Too many of us are playing right into the devil's hand—being swayed by our emotions—because *we don't even know the truth to be able to stand on it.*

Does fear nag at you more than four times a year? Yeah, me too. Like, daily. Here's my Monday morning: *What's this bump on my neck? Will my child grow out of that habit? Did they pick it up at school? I WANT NAMES—WHO ARE THOSE SINNERS? Are all these Happy Meals from McDonald's slowly killing us? Will they remember me as a bad mom? Or will I die before they can even remember me? Oof, that's kind of morbid. Speaking of, are we living in the end times? WAIT, WHICH KID JUST COUGHED? TAKE A DRINK OF YOUR WATER—I CANNOT STAY HOME ANOTHER DAY.* *breathe in, breathe out*

Well, if we pick up the sword of the Spirit and see for ourselves what God's Word has to say every (gulp) single day, then when we feel alone? Forgotten? Deserted, friendless, and left to do it on our own?

We would see with absolute clarity that God Himself promised never to leave us or forsake us—not just once, but repeatedly throughout the Old Testament (Deuteronomy 31:6 and Joshua 1:5, for starters). Then flip over to the New Testament, and we hear Jesus give us His literal Word, "Surely I am with you always, to the very end of the age" (Matthew 28:20, NIV). Since the clock's still ticking, then surely, certainly, without a shadow of a doubt, Jesus is still with us.

Need a little more convincing? Oh, I'm glad because I haven't even mentioned the best part yet! Jesus specifically left this earth where He dwelled *with* us so the Holy Spirit could come dwell *in* us (John 16:7). Do we really understand the reality of that? I don't always. But Old Testament heroes would've given ANYTHING to have God's Spirit living in them, comforting them, guiding them, speaking to them. I mean, I can get winded climbing up a flight of stairs, while Moses had to climb *a mountain* to meet with God (Exodus 34). And everyone else? Waited down below for the news. So the very fact that you're sealed with the Holy Spirit who raised Christ Jesus from the dead? *Mind-blowing.*

Oh, and in case you were hoping for something a little more tangible, something you could see with your own eyes, you're also connected to and forever supported by the body of Christ—the church all around the world, currently totaling 2.3 billion people[8]—who are in this *with you.* Plus, Hebrews 12 says we're also surrounded by a great cloud of heavenly witnesses, cheering us on as if selling out the stands in a packed stadium while we're down here running the race.

So . . . "alone"? LOL. That's just what the enemy wants you to think, but we have more than enough evidence to know nothing could be further from the truth.

Let's head back to the Garden of Eden, because the serpent's about to strike. If it's really true that you can't teach an old dog new tricks, it'd be worthwhile to get to know his tactics, wouldn't it?

Surprisingly, though, we don't see him biting Eve and waiting for the venom to do its work like we might expect. He's not coiling his body around her to constrict her breathing either or crush her bones like we've learned snakes do. (Anyone have a contact with Ranger Rick?)

Why does that matter? Bottom line: He's not after our physical bodies. We must know he's out to attack our minds, hearts, and souls. **So instead of killing your oxygen supply, he's out to kill your peace. Instead of destroying your health, he's more interested in destroying your confidence in God. And instead of stealing your short life on earth, he wants to steal your everlasting faith.** My grandma was right . . . snakes are just disgusting.

But again, we shouldn't be surprised. This isn't new news here. Paul cleared it up long ago in Ephesians 6—our struggle isn't against flesh and blood. So deadly viruses and wayward political movements?

Our micromanaging boss and even more micromanaging in-laws? That mounting pile of bills, your junker of a car, or those white hairs threatening to take over your whole head? Nope, not it. As rude as all of the above are—*our own mane turning against us, the horror*—*not the real battle.*

Our fight is never against things we can see with our own two eyes, but against the evil rulers and authorities of the unseen world, against the mighty powers of darkness, and against evil spirits in the heavenly places (Ephesians 6:12). Kind of intense? A little unnerving? The stuff nightmares are made of? I know, but Paul didn't let us in on this ever-raging battle to make us *scared*. He wanted to keep us aware and alert, confident in the fight and focused on the *actual* battle.

"Did God *really say*, 'You must not eat from any tree in the garden'?" (Genesis 3:1, NIV, italics added).

Boom. Just like that, we witness the enemy's first bomb drop. Notice the ambush didn't come with a loud war cry or even a menacing voice like the Joker. He didn't roll up his sleeves, shove Eve against the garden wall, and get all cockeyed in her face either.

Rather, his strike was so subtle that it came in the form of a question. A carefully calculated, nonthreatening question from a seemingly harmless reptile who was "just curious."

Does it sound familiar? That very question he posed then is the same one he's still (*quote-unquote*) innocuously whispering today. "Did God really say . . . ?"

Did God really say He would use all things for His glory and your good? *Doesn't look that good to me.*

Did God really say He already overcame? Did He really call you more than a conqueror through Him (raised eyebrows at Romans 8:37)? *Well then, where is He? Because (no offense) you look pretty tired and defeated.*

Did God really say peace is possible? *With a chemical or hormonal imbalance, I wouldn't hold your breath. Probably best for you to accept life as is.*

I mean, did God *really* say that?

And here's the first principle, the HOW to gain from this Bible hero's story. When our minds are filled with this type of question, we must follow Eve's *initial* footsteps and go back to God's Word.

> We must follow Eve's *initial* footsteps and go back to God's Word.

"Of course we may eat fruit from the trees in the garden," Eve replies. "It's only the fruit from the tree in the middle of the garden that we are not allowed to eat. God said, 'You must not eat it or even touch it; if you do, you will die'" (Genesis 3:2-3).

So . . . she *knew* the truth. Eve heard God's Word loud and clear, and she was just fine with it *until* the serpent planted this seed of doubt and let the dirt do its work.

Is there anything you previously didn't pay any mind to—until the doctor listed potential risks, your friend dropped that side comment, or that family member questioned your faith? Then you camped out on it. Like Eve, you recognized what God had to say, but gave the devil a little more time on air.

"You won't die!" the serpent replied to the woman. "God knows that your eyes will be opened as soon as you eat it, and you will be like God, knowing both good and evil" (Genesis 3:4-5).

Important: At this time, Eve only knew good. She had never tasted death, felt betrayal from a friend, or read Facebook comments from you-know-who. By the goodness of God, He shielded His image-bearers from such evil so they could live freely, without the weight of anything wicked bogging them down and stealing their peace.

But here's a key part of the enemy's sinister strategy: He showed Eve what she was lacking, presenting it as if the knowledge of evil was *a coveted thing.*

Are you getting this? FOMO isn't new to the twenty-first century. The serpent capitalized on whatever Eve lacked and twisted it as if God was withholding something good from her. The enemy is doing the same today.

Do any of these thoughts sound familiar?

- *If I'm forever single, I'll miss out on marriage. Is God keeping something good from me?*
- *If I always battle infertility, I'll miss out on having a family. Why is God withholding a blessing from me?*
- *If I die from this disease, I'll miss out on being a part of my children's lives. How can God's plans still be good?*
- *If I took this risk but failed, I'll miss out on being successful. Why doesn't God want me to have that?*
- *Ultimately, if this bad thing happens, I'll miss out on the good parts of life. Why would He keep those from me?*

Entertain these thoughts, and it won't be long until we fall back into the original trap that led to the original sin.

But it's our choice. We can think we know it all, or we can recognize that while we only see *some* things, God sees *all* things. We can question His goodness, or we can trust that He's actually not holding out on us at all, but like with this whole evil thing, protecting us from something we know absolutely *nothing about.*

When Eve gets to this crossroads, she's "convinced" what the enemy said was true (Genesis 3:6). She's like us—once we set our minds to something, there's *no going back.* Like when "we"—er, Ty—rearranged our house 15 times the month before Dottie came home. IT HAD TO BE DONE.

In this moment, to Eve, the enemy *was* making a bit of sense. God seemed to be holding back goodness, wisdom, and life, and after all, it was just *one* apple and *one* bite.

Crunch.

Now with a mouthful, Eve makes her choice and gets exactly what she wanted. Her eyes now feast not just on the knowledge of good—but of evil, too.

Wait, what do we see her doing with her supposed newfound freedom? Celebrating with confetti? Planting a big smackeroo on Adam? Going out to explore and take in all this new insight, wisdom, and intelligence she now has?

Nope. After convincing Adam to make the same choice, these two instantly feel shame over their naked bodies, pick up needlework, throw together some makeshift leaf clothes, and hide. (Pretty impressed they did all that without Pinterest TBH.)

It doesn't sound like that coveted knowledge of evil lived up to the hype, does it?

God calls out to them, "Where are you?" To be clear, He isn't thrown off by their new camo gear, as if they're now invisible to God Himself. No, God knew exactly where they were because as hard as this is for us to sometimes comprehend, it's impossible to hide from a God who sees all things. Notice, though, that God called them out of hiding by asking a pointed question Himself. Not just where are you *physically*, but *where's your headspace at?*

You may feel lost in your own thoughts. Overwhelmed by what just rocked your world. And you're now hiding behind a facade in hopes of masking your mistake, pain, or anxiety.

While the enemy's questions are intended to drive you further away from God, His questions always draw you *nearer*. God's still calling out, "Where are you?"—not to point out our nakedness, but to restore what's been broken. So where *are* you? Where *is* your head at these days? Is your mind caught up in the never-ending cycle of worst-case scenarios? Are you sinking in your grief, shame, or insecurities? Entertaining lies and avoiding God?

As we look around the Garden, I hope you notice the enemy is nowhere to be found after that first bite. How *convenient* of him, right? But what do we expect? He entices with promises he has no intention of keeping, and once we grab the Honeycrisp, he skedaddles—because the damage is done and his work is finished.

But that's not all I hope you see. Beyond just a coward fleeing the crime scene, notice who is coming straight for Eve . . . and who's coming for us, too.

Our biggest flex is that we don't serve a distant God who gets further away the more we trip up (even though He would be right to do so). We don't serve a merciless God who leaves us in our sin (even though He would be just to do so). And we don't serve a hard, unforgiving God who puts it on us to earn our way back into His good graces and clean up our own mess (even though He would be fair to do so).

In direct contrast, we serve a personal, loving, forgiving God who comes for us in our sin, draws us to Himself, and willingly gets involved, with a plan to save *already set in motion*. He is faithful to us even when we are obviously or obliviously unfaithful to Him.

But wait, how can that be? How can we say God's so forgiving if the very next thing we see is Adam and Eve getting the boot out of the Garden? To pound the final nail in the coffin, God goes so far as to station mighty angels and a flaming sword to guard the entrance back in. No need to say more. I know when I'm not wanted!

Are you picturing it like that too? Suitcases thrown out the hedge window, their collection of fig-leaf undergarments spilling out, and a loud voice bellowing, "It's over! And don't even *think* about coming back!" With a quick turn on His heels, God shakes His head and hands as if glad to finally be rid of us, sending His rebel kids on their way with nothing more than a "good riddance!" (Too much Dr. Phil? Yeah, I kind of overdid it in middle school.)

Before we pull an Eve and jump to the wrong conclusion, camping out on a lie as if it's truth, let's rewind a tad and hear what God actually said right before this: "Look, the human beings have become like us, knowing both good and evil. What if they reach out, take fruit from the tree of life, and eat it? Then they will live forever!" (Genesis 3:22).

Do you hear the *concern in His voice*? God wanted them to live forever, yes—but not stuck in sin, eternally tainted by evil, relegated to a broken relationship with Himself. Our God is so good that He sent them out so He could later bring them (and us) *back in*—forgiven, restored, and healed through Jesus.

Speaking of, did you know the Hebrew derivative of "sent out" in Genesis 3:23 is closely related to the New Testament Greek derivative from John 3:16? "For God so loved the world that he *gave* [or "sent in"] his one and only Son, that whoever believes in him shall not perish but have eternal life" (NIV, italics added).[9]

Just as He sent out Adam and Eve with a purpose, He sent in Jesus with a purpose.

Both totally redemptive contexts. Yet at the time, would Eve have considered "banished from the Garden of Eden" her preferred choice of rescue? Did she power walk right out of that perfection, giddy over God's plan, gung ho over her new assignment? . . . I doubt it.

As you're going to places *you* don't want to go—the oncologist, your job, or into the unknown like Elsa (Sorry, I have girls, and I think even Alexa's sick of repeating *Frozen*)—you have a choice. Lemme repeat: We have a choice. We can water the enemy's seeds of doubt and become convinced God's holding out on us and has abandoned us. OR we can give God the benefit of the doubt—knowing that while we can only see some things, He sees all things—and since He only ever has pure, good, redemptive intentions, we can trust His ultimate plan to redeem and restore *all things* which includes where we are today.

If you choose the latter, lace up those walking shoes, grab your Fitbit, and flip on ahead, because God is sending us out with a purpose, withholding no good thing from those who do what is right (Psalm 84:11)—and we're bound to get our steps in.

P.S. Redemption is *coming.*

FEAR:

"Did God really say . . . ?"

THE HOW: Whenever this question rises up, go back to God's Word and confirm exactly what He said in black-and-white (sometimes red, too).

DID GOD REALLY SAY I CAN HAVE PEACE? Yes, Jesus said, "I am leaving you with a gift—peace of mind and heart. And the peace I give is a gift the world cannot give. So don't be troubled or afraid" (John 14:27).

DID GOD REALLY SAY HE WON'T WITHHOLD ANY GOOD THING FROM ME, EVEN THOUGH I DON'T HAVE WHAT I DESIRE MOST? Yes, He did say that (Psalm 84:11), and we must not fall prey to a shortsighted lie. God knows what we need, He is always good, and our story isn't even done yet. We can wait patiently and expectantly.

DID GOD REALLY SAY I CAN'T MESS UP IF I WANT TO HAVE A RELATION-SHIP WITH HIM? No, that's a lie twisting the truth. Jesus came specifically because we *do* mess up, sin, and repeatedly fall short. He died on the cross to bear our punishment precisely to restore a right relationship with us. Our relationship with God is not based on what we do, but fully on what Christ has done for us. "For by that one offering he forever made perfect those who are being made holy" (Hebrews 10:14). We are adopted into His family because, if we believe in Him, "he gave [us] the right to become children of God" (John 1:12). Nothing can separate us from His love. *fist bump*

Chapter 2

BUT WHAT IF . . . ?

Moses

I don't mean to rush you, but WE HAVE GOT TO GET GOING. The plan is to meet up with our boy Moses in Exodus 2, but before we fast-forward to his top Instagram post of freeing the Israelites from 400 years of Egyptian slavery (*tap like*), we're going to rewind to the beginning.

I don't mean back to his home birth. **Bless.** But even before Moses was living and breathing, God had established a plan. For his life, yes—and yours, too: "You saw me before I was born. Every day of my life was recorded in your book. Every moment was laid out before a single day had passed" (Psalm 139:16).

Do you know that? Not just lodged in your brain—but at the core of who you are, convinced with every fiber of your being? Before you ever faced this battle, before you ever walked on the face of the earth, before your mother ever thought about having you, God thought about you, saw you, made a plan for your life, and recorded it all in His book.

So if you're still living and breathing, that must mean there's more to your story, and while you may not know how it's going to play out, *He does.* If we know His character, that's reassuring. If our view of God is skewed, we'll still feel unrest. But don't stress if you're a little uneasy, okay? It's literally the second chapter. LOL, we're gonna get there.

Up for a quick game of Would You Rather to pass the time? Great! Would you rather be pregnant when the law demands every Hebrew baby boy be thrown in the Nile River? Or when masks are mandated in the hospital with no visitors allowed? Talk about a fun icebreaker! If you give it a go next Friday night, let me know how it lands.

Unfortunately for Moses' mom, this wasn't a silly game. She wasn't given a choice, either—the former being her reality. I can attest it's hard to stay relaxed through contractions under *normal* circumstances. I think my exact words during Hazel's birth were, "I WILL NOT CALM DOWN UNTIL THE EPIDURAL COMES." But Pharaoh had indeed given such an order, and this whole genocide thing was the reality looming in the back of her mind during labor. Can you imagine the pressure, the anticipation, and the nerves on top of WELL, THE TOTAL PHYSICAL INTENSITY? "Just Lamaze your way to a serene birth, Jochebed! Recite your biblical affirmations! Don't forget the lavender oil!" This mama's already my hero.

One last push, and there he is . . . a boy. Her dream come true and her biggest fear bundled together in one package.

As we watch her kneel beside a basket, we see the fierce love of a mother take over as she sends her precious babe down the river. With one nudge, there he goes . . . and her heart along with him. (Um, you know things are bad if the best option still runs the risk of drowning your baby. Would you rather take the chance like she did or allow your baby to be murdered? Never mind, game over . . . this went downhill fast.)

Think about it, though. Was God worried about Moses' well-being at any time along the way? Once He heard Pharaoh's order, was God frantically running His hands through His hair, heart beating fast, panicking over the future? (You're shaking your head, right?) Ding, ding, ding! Winner, winner, get this girl a chicken dinner!

And just as God wasn't concerned because He knew what was to come for Moses, God isn't worried about our life or future either. He knows what's to come and still tells us we have no reason to fear.

Hold up. You're never gonna believe it. Grab your binoculars and look down the river. Out of anyone who could've found Moses taking his scenic river cruise—the very woman bending over to pick him up is . . . yep, the one and only, Pharaoh's daughter. She not only adopts him instead of killing him, but wouldn't you know it? She needs someone to nurse Moses because formula in the Egyptian market was, well, nonexistent. And who does she recruit?

> God knows what's to come and still tells us we have no reason to fear.

Wait, COULD IT BE? Is that Moses' *actual birth mother*?

You got it! Out of millions of Egyptians and Israelites, this brave mama was seen by God and rewarded beyond her wildest dreams. Not only does Jochebed see her son live, but now she gets him back in her arms to nurse him, take care of him, and raise him until he's weaned—all without fear of a bounty hunter knocking at the door.

Couldn't have planned this better even if we tried? Exactly. We could not have planned, but God, however, always has a plan.

I think they caught us staring. Quick, brush off your knees and skip ahead to Exodus 2:11! That young man we're now looking at is grown-up Moses. I KNOW, IT GOES SO FAST DOESN'T IT? Our boy's living the cushy life, strolling around the palace and enjoying royalty status while his people are stuck in slavery. Except he's not kicking back on a La-Z-Boy, playing video games, or posting selfies poolside . . . er, riverside.

We instead see him walk out to watch his own people work. As he's taking in their poor labor conditions, it bothers him. Gets under his skin. Makes him mad. When he sees an Egyptian have the audacity to beat one of his fellow Hebrews, his blood boils. "Not on my watch!" Looks to the left, looks to the right . . . annnnnd being the murderer that he is, kills the Egyptian and hides the body in the sand.

Wait, what? Did you not expect our Bible hero to be a murderer? I know, it's quite the plot twist, and this won't be the last time God uses a very unlikely situation and an undeserving person to bring about His purposes either.

It's probably a good time to mention though that God doesn't condone sin—definitely not killing another human being made in His very own image—but we see nothing is out of reach of His grace. Not Moses' sin; not ours either. Whatever we've done, we can go to the God of grace and receive mercy in our time of need (Hebrews 4:16). Not only does He wipe our slate clean, but don't miss this: Our past doesn't disqualify us from the future He has for us. Isn't He amazing? I know. It's almost like He's perfect . . .

Oh yeah that's right, HE iS.

Back to our man Mo. He just goes home like NBD. No guilty conscience, just another day in the life of a Hebrew living as Egyptian royalty. A *little bit* of a red flag, but let's watch as he saunters back the next day. Same place, same time—and he sees another fight break out. Are you holding your breath too? Well, we can let out that air because this time it was just between two Hebrews, so he sees no reason to commit murder today. (Don't want to assume the worst, but *phew.* Felt like a close call, didn't it?)

Even still, Moses can't help but meddle, and as he sticks his nose where it doesn't belong, he finds these men know exactly what he did. They don't mind letting the cat out of the bag either. How would your daddy—you know, *the Pharaoh*—like hearing you killed one of his men . . . for one of *us*? In the heat of the confrontation, what does Moses do? Flees. And just as he runs from his circumstances, sometimes we want to run from ours, too.

When your spouse asks for a divorce, you learn your child is falling behind in school, the doctor delivers bad news, your friends betray you, your pockets and savings are empty and you get scared, where do you go?

Moses runs to Midian—what's *your* Midian? Is it your mom—do you pick up your phone right away or hop in the car to spend the night at her house? Is it Netflix—do you try to distract yourself with someone else's quintessential plot or hope to laugh at Jim encasing Dwight's stapler in Jell-O? (Please tell me you own all nine seasons.) Or is it to the freezer for that gallon of ice cream? Unrelated: Have you tried Cold Stone's dark chocolate peppermint ice cream? Maybe just showed my hand . . .

Before we look around at all that Midian has to offer, it's a good time to speed walk to Psalm 91. The writer of this piece of poetry (possibly even Moses) is looking back on his life, and while he's sifting through the memories, it seems he's learned a lesson or two about where to run.

Want to learn from his mistakes so we don't have to make them? *Same.*

When life gets hard and we're tempted to seek a quick fix of comfort, the things we typically run to—although not necessarily bad in and of themselves—won't be able to give us the peace we want and the refuge our soul is looking for. This Psalmist cracked the code: When we run to God, we find protection under His feathers, rest in His shadow, and a promised rescue under His care.

Again, it's our choice. We can flee to other people, we can flee from our circumstances, or we can flee to the presence of the Lord Almighty. Only one is the safest place to be. Where will you run today?

At this point in his story, Moses chooses Midian. Upon arrival, he somehow saves seven damsels in distress, and their father tracks him down and offers a daughter to him in marriage. You know, just your average hanging-by-a-well, stumble-into-a-marriage-proposal type thing. Has a nice Hallmark ring, doesn't it?

But this place where Moses fled to simply get away very soon becomes a long-term stay with no end in sight. (P.S. Tends to happen unless we intentionally change course.) He now has a wife and a glamorous job as a shepherd, which snowballs into children and putting down roots without his criminal record getting in the way. Seems like a good place to retire, right?

Let's do the math: 40 years old when he leaves Egypt, add another 40 as a country bumpkin—and wow, yeah, 80! If you ask me, time to sell those sheep, grab some golf clubs, and get a condo overlooking the Mediterranean Sea. Come and visit when you can, grandkids!

But like we've already seen, if we're still living and breathing, God's not done. No matter how far we run, how off-track life seems to get, or how much time has gone by, we can never outrun God and His purposes. He will pursue us even to Midian, beckon us back, and ensure His good plans prevail . . . whether we like it or not.

Time to kick it up a gear and power walk to chapter 3 of Exodus. *Pamela Pumpkin ain't got nothing on us.* While Moses was minding his own business—checking off his to-dos for the day in the family business, tending to his father-in-law's flock out in the wilderness—God met him in a burning bush. Just as Moses was tending to his sheep, God was tending to His.

BTW, that's still true today. You may feel lost. Like you've wandered off-course, unsure how to retrace your steps back to home base, and plunging further into the wilderness with every day that passes. Great news: We have a Good Shepherd who leaves the ninety-nine just to track down the one who got a little sidetracked. So even if you're straining your eyes and can't spot His rod in the pitch-blackness of your circumstances? Keep waiting with expectant hope. As I learned even after a miscarriage, while waiting for biopsy results to come back, and amid the decision of leaving a job I loved, help is *always* on the way. God will never leave you behind to figure out the way yourself. He'll follow you into the wilderness to bring you back—even if that means showing up in a burning bush to get your attention.

What if we saved ourselves a lot of heartache and tried running to Him *first* today? Since surely His goodness and love will follow us all the days of our lives (Psalm 23:6)—the correct translation of all is . . . well, *all*—we can be assured that includes even here, even today, even in Midian.

Do you hear Him? God's calling from a burning bush, "Moses! Moses!" (Exodus 3:4). Strange, right? Imagine you're in the backyard, soaking up the rays, pruning the garden, or watching the kids play, and the shrub next to you bursts into flames and calls your name.

I jump and dial 911 at the sound of creaking floorboards when Ty's gone, so I'm not sure I would survive that. (To be clear, I *dial.* I've never actually hit Send—although to any burglar reading . . . I am always only one tap away.)

But while it's easy to look for God at church, in your small group, or when you have a Bible sitting in front of you, for those who have the eyes to see, God is moving and working and speaking all around us, all the time. Psalm 19:1 relieves any doubt, "The heavens declare the glory of God, and the sky above proclaims his handiwork" (ESV).

Yet so many of us are sucked into our iPhones, the clutter of our homes, and the beckoning of our to-do lists that we don't leave any time to look up. To glance around at creation. Stop and smell the literal roses. We can be so absorbed in our own problems that we miss God's hand moving all around us. But God can show up in an *instant* while we're washing the dishes, teaching our kids, having a conversation with the neighbor, or taking the first bite of our lunch. When He does, let's be the first to respond like Moses: "Here I am."

From the burning bush, God gives Moses a full report on what's still going on back home sweet home—you know, the problem he tried to run away from—"I have indeed seen the misery of my people in Egypt. I have heard them crying out because of their slave drivers, and I am concerned about their suffering" (Exodus 3:7, NIV).

HOLD ON. Did you hear it? There it is again! More than just taking notice, we once again hear that tone of *compassion.* This God of ours— the Creator of the world, the King who sits enthroned over all—isn't distant, callous, or cold. He's not kicking back on His throne like *peace sign* "Good luck down there, kiddo!"

Rather, He's seen your misery. He's heard you crying. And He's *concerned* about your suffering and well-being. In fact, if you flip through all four Gospels, the number one emotional response Jesus showed other people isn't anger, sadness, disappointment, or annoyance (as much as culture seems to believe)—but *compassion*.[1]

So what's hurting you? Tanking you? Emptying you? *God doesn't like it either.* In due time—in the right time—we *will* see His compassion move His hand on our behalf too.

But it's important to note: The cries of the Israelites reached God because they were praying *to* Him. This may go without saying . . . but are we praying to God about our trial more than we're worrying about it? Or vice versa?

Those warning lights on your dashboard? (I know, they're very small and easy to miss.) When that low fuel light dings, it's a signal indicating it's time to bring the car to the gas station, right? The same is true for worry. **Worry isn't an indicator to keep stressing about it, but to go to God and pray about it.**

That check engine light? (Is it obvious I'm well-versed in all things dashboard?) We head to the mechanic because he or she knows the ins and outs of our swag minivan and can actually do something about it. Wouldn't it make sense, then, to take our fears and anxieties to our Maker, who knows the ins and outs of our brains and situations—and has the authority and power to heal them, restore them, and reboot them?[2]

If you're like me, though, we act as if worry is the be-all and end-all. Better dwell on it! Answer every what-if question! Prepare for every worst-case scenario! Analyze it from all angles OR ELSE . . . Well, or else we'll probably just die. #accordingtoWebMD

While worry rises up when we realize we have no control, peace rushes in the moment we remember who does. Instead of following every thought spiraling down to our demise, we can hurl every care up to the heavens. Let's watch how this plays out with Moses.

God: "I've come to rescue My people, so go to Pharaoh and bring them out of Egypt." (CliffsNotes version.)

You'd think after 400 years, this would be cause for celebration. Finally free from slavery? God Himself coming to the rescue? Woo-hoo! But we don't see Moses jumping in the air, pumping his fist like Super Mario beating a new level (#boymom). We don't even see a compliant *nod*. Instead, we watch Moses dig his heels in like, "What? You said *you're* going to rescue them. So I'm sorry, but . . . when did this become *my* problem?"

Excuse me, homeschooling? Taking care of my elderly parents? Reaching out to my lost neighbors? Giving clothes to those in need? I'm sorry—when did their problem become *my* problem?

I know. I don't always like it either. It's really easy to forget that we're God's plan A to reach this lost world—because most of the time, we have our own plan A don't we? But all through Scripture, we see when God wants to move, He moves through His people. (Oh, and P.S. *There is no plan B.*) So the question remains—are we willing? Will we let the Lord work through us in a way we may not have chosen (and probably don't want)?

You may not like needing to go to the doctor as often as you do—I get it. I talk to my doctor more than most friends, and at this point, I kind of view MyChart messages like texting. But will we allow the Lord to work through us to reach nurses, doctors, and possibly other patients or people suffering through the same condition? I remember being totally absorbed in my symptoms, unsure what they could be (but also convinced they meant certain death, you know?), when my doctor offhandedly asked, "So what's your book about?" That question snapped me back into reality, and as I talked about faith over fear and how the Bible has something relevant to say about it, I thought, *Maybe I'm here for something so much more than mere headaches . . .*

You may not delight in the state of our nation right now, but will you allow the Lord to work through you and be a bridge builder paving the way for restoration?

Or maybe you don't enjoy staying home all day, every day (#extrovertsunite), but will you allow the Lord to use this time to strengthen your family relationships, dig into some personal development, and draw you closer to Him?

> If you allow the Lord to do His thing, which is always good and restorative and purposeful, you will say yes to the best ride of your life.

There is purpose even here—even in Midian, and even back in Egypt, where you certainly don't want to go. If you allow the Lord to do His thing, which is always good and restorative and purposeful, you will say yes to the best ride of your life.

But God does ask us to move and go where He sends us. Are we willingly taking those steps . . . or dragging our feet? Trust me— there's plenty of skid marks in my past.

Moses understands this whole dilemma too. He's digging trenches with his sandals. "God, your plans sound good, but I'm out. Who am I that I should go to Pharaoh and somehow convince him to let all of his slaves go?"

Lean in as God answers, "I will be with you."

I know I'm already wearing out the pause button on the remote here, but if we could halt and really, truly grasp this? That the Lord Almighty, Creator and Sustainer of this world, is here as our personal bodyguard too? That He's always on duty in our lives and willingly takes full responsibility as our Refuge, Defender, Strength, Deliverer, and Savior? Then, whatever we face, *it doesn't hold a candle to our present God who is in this with us.*

"So . . . what if they don't believe you sent me?" Moses wonders. Roll up your sleeves and let the what-if games begin!

"What if they ask me, 'What is his name who sent you?' What should I tell them then?"

Leaving no loopholes in His plan, God gave quite the detailed response, "I am who I am. Here's what you have to say . . . <insert exact dialogue here>."

Hooooold up. You mean God lays out the plan *in word-for-word detail* down to the literal words spoken by both Moses *and* Pharaoh?

Yep (and then some): "After you say this, go assemble the elders and say this. They'll listen to you. Then go to the king of Egypt and say this. I know he won't let you go, so I'll stretch out My hand and perform all these wonders. After that, he will let you go, and also you'll plunder the Egyptians on the way out."

Like, I'm sorry, but if I could get an Exodus 3 for *my* future? If God could break it down for me *verbatim*? Complete with what I should specifically say, as well as what He will specifically do—oh, and bonus, how it will *specifically end*? EASY STREET.

But Moses shows us we'll still resist the harder path no matter how clearly God has paved the way.

"Well, what if they don't believe me? Or listen to me?"

Are you also rattling off all the what-ifs? They're never ending, and if you're as creative as I am, there will always be more. However, when we direct them straight up to the heavens like Moses did, we see just how patient God really is. He already gave Mo His Word, which yes, should've been enough, but then God takes it a step further and gives Moses something to see, feel, and do.

With the Lord's direction, Moses throws his staff on the ground, God turns it into a snake, and . . . get this . . . our model Bible hero runs from it. After a surprise visit with a local garter snake in our garage, though, I hold ZERO JUDGMENT.

But God's all like, "Not so fast." Even worse, He instructs, "Reach out your hand and grab its tail."

Say whaaat? His previous command to speak in front of a church elder board in Exodus 3:16 made sense—get their support before approaching Pharaoh. But this? Disgusting. A little weird. IMO unnecessary.

Some of what *we're dealing with*, though, can seem very unnecessary in the moment too, right? Any time we wonder, *Why am I going through this?* it's important to remember that while we can only see some things, *God sees all things*. To build on that, we learn from Moses that wherever

God calls us and whatever He asks us to do is *never* in vain or for nothing. It may be bizarre, random, and tough to figure out in the moment, but God will *always* use it for a purpose that someday we'll see.

In this case, God was preparing Moses *now* for the real performance coming *later*.

Same goes for you—I know whatever you're going through seems unnecessary, scary, and unwanted, and you'd prefer to skirt past this dress rehearsal and get on with it to Egypt. But if God's truly in control and good? (P.S. He is.) Then we can trust Him, knowing He's doing a work in us *now* in preparation for what's *later*, and just grab the nasty thing by the tail already.

Moses does exactly that. As the snake turns back into a staff in his very hand, God says, "Perform this sign. . . . Then they will believe that the LORD, the God of their ancestors . . . really has appeared to you" (Exodus 4:5). Ohhh, I see.

We good now, Mo? Ready now? Bags packed and time to hit the road? "Um . . . Pardon your servant, Lord."

You rolled your eyes too, didn't you? I mean, is this really the man for the job? Out of all the human beings in the whole wide world, is there really *no other willing vessel out there*?

Maybe, maybe not. But God already established a plan. Our days have already been ordained. So Moses? Buckle up. You have been chosen. You're the man for the job.

(Probably a good time to mention it—but girl, you too? You've also been chosen. *You're* the girl for the job. God deemed you His ambassador, daughter, and the light of the world. So whatever scary thing lies ahead—in His strength, in His power, in His name, and in His presence, you can do it. And you will do it!)

How?

Hold that thought because Moses is stumbling his way through one last line, and we don't want to miss it: "Uh, pardon me, I'm not very . . .

good with words. Never have been . . . and—and—and I'm not now. I get tongue-tied, and my words get ta-a-a-angled."

Like a ping-pong match between God and Moses, God returns with, "Who makes a person's mouth? Who decides whether people speak or do not speak, hear or do not hear, see or do not see? Is it not I, the LORD? Now go! I will be with you as you speak, and I will instruct you in what to say" (Exodus 4:11-12).

And here it's unveiled. The next step to choosing faith over fear and all the things: **It's less about us than we think it is, and it's more about Him than we realize.**

What are the what-if scenarios replaying like broken records over and over in your mind? Moses' were: *What if they don't believe me? What if they don't listen to me? What if I'm scared? What if I don't speak well in front of crowds? What if I mess it up?*

When we're faced with our fears, we have the tendency to focus on ourselves, what *we* lack, what *we're* unable to do, how this will affect *our* future. Yet as Moses went through his laundry list of all the reasons why he simply could not and should not and would not, God's response every time was not glorifying Moses' strength (which was clearly very little)—but reminding Moses of *God's*. The pathway to choosing faith over paralyzing what-if questions is to take our eyes off of ourselves and fix them on our God. Focus on His character. Zero in on His promises.

As we walk in step with these Bible characters, do you already feel a blister forming? Agh, should've warned you about that. Breaking in new shoes can be uncomfortable and painful at first. But once we put in the time and get used to the feel, stepping into these footsteps left by the Bible heroes will soon become seamless, fitting like a glove—or rather, your favorite old sneakers. Press on, girlfriend. We've only just begun, and I promise it's gonna be worth it.

P.S. Nothing a little Band-Aid can't help! Only *Paw Patrol* ones in this house, though . . .

FEAR:

"But what if . . . ?"

THE HOW: Whenever you begin to play the what-if game, stop this thought in its tracks and counter it by asking, "Who is God, and what does He say He *can* do?"

WHAT IF I'M NOT UP FOR THE TASK? You probably aren't . . . ha! But whomever God calls, He equips. As Paul put it in 2 Corinthians 12:9, "Each time he said, 'My grace is all you need. My power works best in weakness.' So now I am glad to boast about my weaknesses, so that the power of Christ can work through me."

WHAT IF I'M NOT CAPABLE? It's not about our capability. It's about our more-than-capable God, who does great things through us. "For we are God's handiwork, created in Christ Jesus to do good works, which God prepared in advance for us to do" (Ephesians 2:10, NIV). He not only planned our next step long ago, but He also prepares us to move into it.

WHAT IF I'M NOT LOVABLE? When we were at our lowest, most unlovable point—as God's *enemy*—Jesus willingly died for us. "This is real love—not that we loved God, but that he loved us and sent his Son as a sacrifice to take away our sins" (1 John 4:10). Because God is love, He gets to define love—and "he loved us first" (1 John 4:19), knowing full well who we are and what we've done.

Chapter 3

WHY AM I OFF-COURSE?

The Israelites

(yep, God's very own people)

This is NOT how it was supposed to go:

- This relationship was supposed to end with a *ring*—not a nasty text and a breakup.
- This appointment was supposed to hold *good news*. Why do things keep getting worse?
- This month was *finally* supposed to bring that positive pregnancy test . . . where are the double lines?

Want to add anything else to the list? You know, that spot you're in that *you didn't want* with circumstances *you didn't choose*?

While you *thought* you were going in the right direction and you *thought* God was leading the way . . . now you're left staring up to the heavens, with sagging shoulders, a mascara-stained face (**reminder: switch to waterproof**), and a shaky prayer. "All due respect, God, but . . . where you at? Just looking for an ETA?"

Most 20-year-olds feel like they have their entire future ahead of them, and I was no different. I was going to make it BIG as a blogger. Maybe sell my calligraphy as artwork, travel the world—or you know what? WHY NOT BOTH? I planned to get married, probably buy an old farmhouse on some land—complete with a wraparound porch—and have three kids and a cat (but never, ever, heaven forbid a dog. Y'all still picking up feces with a plastic bag and carrying it around on walks like a clutch? LOL, I cannot.).

All in all, I was going to grow old with the man of my dreams, maybe write a book or two, and pass away peacefully in my sleep with a big ol' smile on my face the day I turned 125 years old (to break the Guinness World Record, of course).

But when I waltzed into the doctor's office at 23 years old and the doctor dropped the bomb that I indeed had Hodgkin's Lymphoma, all those dreams crumbled right before my eyes.

I no longer felt like my future was a blank canvas ready for me to splash as many colorful strokes of paint across the fabric as I wanted. Rather, my beloved future was now split in half, thrown in the trash. As I looked ahead at a backdrop I neither wanted nor chose, I shook my head with little hope and a *Now what?* prayer to the God I knew was listening . . . yet I didn't understand where He was or why He let this happen.

Let's rewind to the Israelites: Moses delivered them from Egyptian slavery. (P.S. This was after 400 years of slavery. Our reaction after just *ONE YEAR* of unanswered prayer and unfortunate events involves hands thrown up in the air, a forceful tapping of the shoe, and a very irritable "HOW LONG, O LORD?" mentality. No . . . just me?)

After all this time and with the clear destination of the Promised Land ahead, you'd think God would get the show on the road and lead the Israelites down the quickest, shortest route, right? I mean, they've had to wait *four centuries for this moment,* so no need to hit up the back roads and waste another minute taking in the scenery. It's time to go HOME.

Flagged for importance: We're not just talking about civilized adults making the trek. There were *children* present. (And all the mamas and grandmas just took a sharp inhale.) I'm cringing too.

Every October, our family makes the same road trip to the next state over. A car ride totaling a mere 3 hours and 38 minutes. Mind you, this is a trip fully equipped with unending snacks, a stack of books, backpacks of toys, a stop (or two) at McDonald's, and a movie cued up in the back seat for when we (children and parents included) start to lose it. Yet the *one time* we took the back roads? The *one time* Ty asked to stop at a historical marker and read the plaque? (He wasn't joking. #bless) That was the *one time* a certain child decided to wet their pants, while the other kicked the back of the seat, causing tears from that passenger in front of them, and another went full-on opera and could not (refused to) hear us begging PLEASE USE YOUR INDOOR VOICE. Oh yeah, and the DVD player broke.

Well, every fall since, no one even has the nerve to *look* in the direction of those back roads as we pass. Hi, we are the Andersons, and we are officially freeway-for-life people.

So consider the Israelites' expedition, without modern amenities— no screens to entertain the children, no freezers to pack the good snacks in, no playgrounds along the way to release the kids' abounding energy, and worst of all, no answer to "Are we there yet?"

This is where they're at. As Moses leads the way and they're confidently walking in a direction that makes sense, he takes a quick turn and starts to off-road it. In their minds, he steers them on a detour that is neither necessary nor wanted.

> Maybe you see where you want to go, but God's taking you down a detour.

Maybe, like them, you see where you want to go, but God's taking you down a detour too. This miscarriage was not in the plan. Your change in career was not anticipated. The hiccup in your education, family, or health was not requested, and as far as you know, *definitely not needed*.

With this in mind, now we can step into the shoes (er, sandals) of the Israelites and actually empathize. "When Pharaoh finally let the people go, God did not lead them along the main road that runs through Philistine territory, even though that was *the shortest route to the Promised Land*" (Exodus 13:17, emphasis added).

Now why in the world would God do that? What reasons could He possibly have for avoiding the freeway and taking them down the *desert* road? THERE'S NOT MANY MCDONALD'S OUT THERE. *What should we do without sunscreen SPF 100? What if we need to refill their sippy cups? Will there be shade for a proper naptime?* GOD KNOWS SLEEP-DEPRIVED TODDLERS ARE NOT IDEAL TRAVEL COMPANIONS.

There were at least two reasons why God led them the roundabout way (seeing now with the gift of hindsight), which might give us a hint why He's taking us down the back roads too.

1. They didn't know Pharaoh had turned on them. Last they heard from their old slave driver, he was quite clear, "Get out! Leave . . . go" (Exodus 12:31-32). Yet God knew something they did not. Pharaoh had in fact changed his mind and ordered his troops to bring the Israelites back.

Have you considered God knows something you do not?

Maybe your previous company will soon fold, but instead of keeping you there through the process, He's bringing you down a path where you'll be covered by severance while looking for something new. Or maybe your boyfriend is far from God, so the Lord stopped the relationship from progressing since you were unequally yoked— which would only amplify in the years ahead. Or possibly you'll meet nurses and doctors far from God, and He wants to use you to plant seeds of faith.

I'm simply guessing because we don't *yet* have the gift of hindsight like we do with the Israelites' story, but remember: At the time, they didn't either.

However, instead of assuming the worst . . . what if we gave God the benefit of the doubt? Trusted in His character and protective hand? Remembered that He promises to take care of us, give us the things we need, and flip everything for our good and His glory?

Because the truth of the matter is, **someday we will see,** and when we get to that day, will we regret doubting or exhale in joyful relief that we held on in faith? Like the Israelites, even when the desert feels hard, we can trust God is protecting us from unknown circumstances and a harder alternative.

In this case? If the Israelites hopped on the freeway going full steam ahead, they would've come face-to-face with a fully armed enemy, and God knew how that would go down. "If the people are faced with a battle, they might change their minds and return to Egypt" (Exodus 13:17). Boxed in on both sides would not have been ideal for these weary travelers. And God, as all-knowing as He is, led them down a path *knowing what they could and could not handle.*

The desert may still seem like too much to bear. But just like God guided with a cloud by day and a pillar of fire to give them light by night, He will never abandon us—but will faithfully lead us down the pathway He knows is best.

Will you believe God may be protecting you from a harder battle? One you may be too weak to withstand? It's a thought worth entertaining and may be a mercy we don't realize until later—on this side of heaven or when we finally go home.

Hoooold up! As we're faithfully falling into step with the Israelites, following that cloud and fire, Moses gets a change in GPS. "Tell the Israelites to *turn back* and . . . encamp by the sea. . . . Pharaoh will think, 'The Israelites are wandering around the land in confusion, hemmed in by the desert'" (Exodus 14:1-3, NIV, emphasis added).

Um, excuse me . . . Pharaoh *will think we're wandering confused? LOL. How about WE WILL THINK we're wandering confused?*

Pause. You may not see an obvious enemy in your own life, and therefore miss the correlation here. But the truth is: You have an enemy on your tail too.

He may not be obvious like an entire town armed against you, and he may not be loud like the pounding hoofbeats of Pharaoh's army stampeding behind you. But he's the same enemy Eve faced in the wilderness, and he's been working full-time since to derail you in your faith, plant seeds of doubt in your mind, and get you to fixate on all that's going wrong instead of lifting your eyes expectantly to a God who, with certainty, will someday make all things right.

I wouldn't look back if I were you, but can you still hear their wheels churning and hammering down the dirt road? Keep in mind Pharaoh just lost two to three *million* of his workers, and with the fury of a dad who also lost his son because of *their God*, well . . . he pulled out all the stops and sent out plenty of men to herd the Israelites back. We're talking 600 of his best chariots, to be exact, "along with all the other chariots of Egypt, with officers over all of them" (Exodus 14:7, NIV).

But yikes. If you aren't one of the brave souls looking back, you must be looking forward, which, um . . . it's not like things look great up there, either. The not-so-tiny Red Sea lies ahead, and if you were to google modern-day measurements (I did), then your eyes are bugging out over the 190 miles wide of water with a maximum depth of roughly 10,000 feet. Suffice it to say . . . the doggy paddle would be inadequate.

The Israelites were facing what looked like a dead end. Impossible to cross. Trapped on both sides. Do you feel just as trapped? Cornered by the circumstances of your life? Looking behind at a past that haunts you? Looking ahead at a future just as bleak?

When the doctor listed off all the possible worst-case scenarios of chemotherapy, radiation, and cancer itself, let's just say I wasn't pumping my fists in the air like SURELY, THE LORD IS IN THIS PLACE.

No, the possibilities felt grim. The environment was dreary. And the forecast looked gloomy.

"As Pharaoh approached, the people of Israel looked up and panicked when they saw the Egyptians overtaking them. They cried out to the LORD, and they said to Moses, "Why did you bring us out here to die in the wilderness? Weren't there enough graves for us in Egypt? What have you done to us? Why did you make us leave Egypt? Didn't we tell you this would happen while we were still in Egypt? We said, 'Leave us alone! Let us be slaves to the Egyptians. It's better to be a slave in Egypt than a corpse in the wilderness!'" (Exodus 14:10-12).

Do you hear your own cries amid theirs? "Why did you bring me here just to die? Why did you allow me to get pregnant only for it to end in a miscarriage? Why did you cross my path with that guy only for him to break my heart? Why did you give me that job only to later take it away? Why did you give me that role model only for her to pass away far too early and way too suddenly?"

I was better off before *this*!

Yet we know just as well that the Israelites had actually longed to leave Egypt and finally be freed up to lead their own lives. As for us, we wanted that positive pregnancy test too. We were lonely and prayed for a special someone. We worked hard to get that job. And the moments we had with that loved one, although not long enough, are irreplicable and forever cherished.

No, as much as we don't like it *here* facing enemies on both sides, things weren't perfect back in Egypt, either. We weren't content. We dreamed of the next season—and no one, except ourselves, made us step forward into the possibility of change. We're just disappointed how it played out, right?

Good news: God shows us His goodness on the brink of the raging waters, and for those who wait expectantly for the Way Maker to show up, we will "see the goodness of the LORD in the land of the living" (Psalm 27:13, NIV) for ourselves as well.

Yep, you read that right, girlfriend! We don't have to wait until heaven to see His goodness. The land of the living is in this world, in our lives this side of the grave, the territory God has already prepared as our inheritance. It may not look as we pictured it—and, like the Israelites, maybe right now we can't even imagine it! But the truth remains: God is good, and He *will* work all things for His glory and our good (Romans 8:28).

Hooooow did He do that for Israel though? Back to the waters. As Moses is holding up one of those "Keep Calm" signs downloaded off Pinterest, the Lord says, "Why are you crying out to me? Tell the people to get moving! Pick up your staff and raise your hand over the sea. Divide the water so the Israelites can walk through the middle of the sea on dry ground" (Exodus 14:15-16).

LOL, I'm sorry, but "why are we crying out to God?" Maybe because we've done all that we could and have literally reached the end? And, by the way, isn't this what we're *supposed to do* anyway? Pray to *Him for help*? Be still and know that *He is God*? Be confident He will fight *for us*?

Yes. But that doesn't mean that's the only thing we need to do. We should 100 percent lean on God for help, acknowledging that He alone has the power to make a way, and take the time to recognize His sovereignty over our situation.

As we see with the Israelites, though, there is always one other thing we can do—move forward in faith. Even when the job search appears fruitless, keep moving forward in faith. Even when that loved one has passed, move forward in faith. Even when our journey is taking a detour we don't understand or like, we must still move forward in faith— knowing He will make a way along the way and He still has a purpose for our lives (Psalm 138:8).

Moses lifts up his staff. Stretches his hand out, and I'm not kidding you, THE WATERS PART. Never before seen, never before done, and never before imagined, God uses the wind to literally divide the seabed. With now walls of water on both sides, the Israelites shuffle down the middle without needing Crocs or rain boots BECAUSE THE GROUND IS DRY, Y'ALL.

I need a minute.

BUT WE DON'T HAVE ONE because the Egyptians are chasing us down, and their faster chariots are closing the gap. "The LORD said to Moses, 'Raise your hand over the sea again. Then the waters will rush back and cover the Egyptians and their chariots and charioteers'" (Exodus 14:26). Blow out that air. We can finally breathe again! Even better, this is also where we see the purpose. This is when we catch a glimpse of God's reasoning.

> What the Israelites viewed as the dead end was *the very thing God used to wipe out their enemy.*

2. **What the Israelites viewed as the dead end, the stumbling block, the impossible feat keeping them from the Promised Land, was** *the very thing God used to wipe out their enemy.* Because He did it this way, they wouldn't have to live constantly looking over their shoulders, fearful of being hunted down at any moment, uneasy for the rest of their lives.

No, **God made them free.**

And, girlfriend? That's His trademark; that is just what He does. For "wherever the Spirit of the Lord is, there is freedom" indeed (2 Corinthians 3:17).

Life may not be easy, and sure, it can *feel* like we're taking the round-about way. We know of a path that's—*in our humble opinion*—quicker, shorter, better. But what if we learned from the Israelites and instead acknowledged God *must* know something we don't?

"When my glory is displayed through them, all Egypt will see my glory and know that I am the LORD!" (Exodus 14:18). And that they did. Also, how interesting that "moving forward in faith" and "letting the Lord fight for you" proved to be one and the same.

The same could be true for you. Wherever you feel off-course, choose to "trust in the LORD with all your heart, and lean not on your own understanding; in all your ways acknowledge Him"—and you know what?—"He *will* make your paths straight" (Proverbs 3:5-6, BSB, emphasis added).

My favorite part? Even when it doesn't make sense today, one day we will stand on the other side of our own Red Sea, and like the Israelites, be "filled with awe before him" (Exodus 14:31). We'll realize then what was always true . . . He didn't forsake us—not even for a second.

P.S. This story ends with the Israelites "[putting] their faith in the LORD" (Exodus 14:31), but let's not wait until after the miracle to do that, okay, girlfriend? It's easy to praise God after the gift comes, the explanation shows up, and His power obviously unleashes in our life, but we can save ourselves *a lot* of wasted time if we put our faith in the Lord *today*.

You up for it? Me too. From here on out, we'll wait expectantly (with thankful hearts for McDonald's on our every road trip).

FEAR:

"Why am I off-course?"

THE HOW: God knows what you don't, so when things don't make sense, choose to trust in the Lord with all your heart, and lean not on your own understanding; in all your ways, acknowledge Him, and He will make your paths straight (Proverbs 3:5-6).

WHY DID HE BRING ME OUT HERE? There's more to the situation than just what meets the eye. So while you may not know WHY today, know that "the Lord will fulfill his purpose" for you (Psalm 138:8, ESV). Give God the benefit of the doubt and wait to see what He's up to.

WHY DID YOU MAKE US LEAVE EGYPT? TO DIE? The truth of the matter is God doesn't want anyone to be destroyed, but wants everyone to repent (2 Peter 3:9). This is why the Father sent Jesus, so anyone who believes in Him could be forgiven and would never have to face death—because He took the punishment we all deserved, and He conquered the grave! So would He be so cruel as to lead you down a path of destruction? No, He is kind enough to guide you "along right paths, bringing honor to his name" that always results with *life* and *purpose* (Psalm 23:3).

BUT WHAT IF I BELIEVE I WAS BETTER OFF BEFORE ALL OF THIS? Like the Israelites thought they were better off as a slave in Egypt than as a corpse in the wilderness (Exodus 14:12). No, we know that isn't true. Rather, we're better off as a slave to the Lord, set free from sin (Romans 6:22), following Him wherever He leads, because His ways and commands always lead to freedom. When you do, it won't be long until you can declare along with the Psalmist, "I will walk in freedom, for I have devoted myself to your commandments" (Psalm 119:45).

Chapter 4

WHAT IF I DON'T HAVE WHAT IT TAKES?

Gideon

What makes you want to hide under your covers all day long?
Is it the curriculum your school district just passed or the
diagnosis a family member received? Maybe it's certain laws the government is proposing to enforce, the challenges of a newfound allergy, or
the inadequacy you feel in your job. Or, let's be real—quite possibly, it's
just your kids' ever-changing moods, how you feel pulled in a million
directions you can't keep up with, and the lack of privacy as you're . . .
you know, trying to take care of business . . . THAT JUST MAKES
YOU WANT TO RUN FOR THE HILLS.

Cue the Israelites. By the time we get to Judges 6, the Midianites
were being *so cruel* to God's people that the Israelites literally made a
run for it. They carved out hideaways in mountains and caves in hopes
of remaining unseen, but this enemy still came after them in hordes,
destroyed their crops, took all their sheep, cattle, goats, and donkeys,

and stayed until the land was stripped bare. "So Israel was reduced to starvation by the Midianites" (6:6).

This is where we meet our soon-to-be-bestie Gideon. Like all the other Israelites, he's hiding, but we don't see him cowering under a blanket, biting his nails, or texting his friends the latest "Did you hear what happened?" No, our Gideon is a doer.

Are you the same way? When you're stressed, you kick into ACTION, deep clean all the bathrooms, power through your inbox and to-do list, and reorganize your kids' sock drawers (twice over) even though they're seventeen? (Just kidding, that's not reorganizing; that's investigating, *and I stand with you.*)

But watch as our man Gideon gets to work threshing wheat *inside*. (Maybe you already spend most of your days removing seed heads with a flail, so no explanation is needed. However, if, like me, the closest thing you can imagine is serving store-bought wheat bread in your Threshold pan from Target? Well then, lemme break it down for you.)

Just like gardening is usually done outside instead of down in your dimly lit basement, threshing wheat was usually and preferably an *outdoor* activity since the breeze could blow the chaff away naturally. But down at the bottom of a winepress? Not exactly normal. Yet here's Gideon because he's terrified to go out in broad daylight and face his life. *We're with you, bro—this world is getting weeeeeeird.*

Get ready, though, because at this point, an angel appears and says, "Mighty hero, the LORD is with you!" (Judges 6:12). Gideon doesn't give a "hello" back or "put 'er there!" handshake. He doesn't even appear to be fazed that a supernatural being just miraculously popped in for a visit. Instead, he rolls up his sleeves and gets right down to it: "Sir, . . . if the LORD is with us, why has all this happened to us?" (6:13).

I'm not the only one who still has yet to master exchanging pleasantries . . .

Yet are our questions much different from Gideon's? "If God is with me, why am I still struggling with infertility? Why have my kids walked away from the church? Why all this cultural pushback against our convictions? If God is with us, why did He allow this evil to happen?"

Gideon isn't done. "And where are all the miracles our ancestors told us about? Didn't they say, 'The LORD brought us up out of Egypt'? But now the LORD has abandoned us and handed us over to the Midianites" (6:13).

Translation: "I know God blesses people. I've heard stories of people healed from cancer and chronic illness. I know preemies have survived and rebellious kids have returned to church. I've listened to podcasts of people climbing out of mountains of debt, and I've read posts about couples defying the odds and working through an affair. That whole 'God brought us up out of Egypt' thing? *Must've been nice for them.* I've heard the stories, but if the Lord really was with *me*, why has all this happened? I'm sorry, but . . . God hasn't been good to *me*. I haven't seen Him move in *my* life like He has for so many others."

Ever thought any of this? Gideon (and I) can't really be the only ones, right?

Now, on one hand, we might just be comparing apples to oranges here. Because in the Israelites' case, God made it CLEAR that they shouldn't worship the gods of the Amorites. Yet what did they do? *insert cringe-face emoji* Built an altar to Baal and an Asherah pole to consult the Canaanite fertility goddess.

So this invasion of the Midianites? Well, they knew full well it was a direct consequence of their willful disobedience.

I don't know about you, but my DIY skills are relegated to in-home manicures, baking cookies from scratch, and gluing googly eyes on foam cutouts for my kids. All impressive, I know, but I'm just saying I don't run the risk of building ornately constructed altars in my backyard. My guess is you don't either. But we don't need a hammer and nails to build ourselves idols. Most days, we can just pick up our phone instead of the Bible, prioritize our kids' sports over church, and recite affirmations to manifest our destiny instead of reciting the Word of God to learn the will of God.

Good news: God repeats Himself throughout the Bible—for instance, flip over to Joel 2:13, Zechariah 1:3, Job 22:23, and BEYOND—saying that when we return to Him, He will have *compassion* on us, receive us *graciously*, show Himself *abounding in lovingkindness*, wipe out *all* our transgressions, and *restore our souls*.

But it's your call—choose your allegiance.

Unfortunately, when we meet Gideon, the Israelites have made their choice . . . and it wasn't the Lord. As a result, they've faced seven hard years of living under Midianite rule being ruthlessly bullied, their livelihoods stripped away, reduced to starvation and grinding poverty. Yet even when a prophet was sent to warn them against carrying on with this idolatry—what do we see? Their idols all remained intact.

> Let's not waste unnecessary years of heartache by living a life apart from God.

But don't miss it: *The moment* they decided to cry out to God for help—*this* is when the angel came to visit Gideon and the plan of rescue was set in motion. Lesson learned: Let's not waste unnecessary years of heartache by living a life apart from God, deal? DEAL.

Rub your hands together because now we're getting to the good part: "Then the LORD turned to him and said, 'Go . . . and rescue Israel from the Midianites. I am sending you!'" (Judges 6:14).

Gideon's looking around at this point, confused to say the least. Like *Sorry, God . . . you may not be familiar with this area, but I come from the weakest family in this whole clan. In fact,* I am *the weakest in my family, the runt of the litter, the shrimp of the bunch. So, uh, yeah . . . you've got the wrong guy.*

Where do you feel inadequate? You know, that thing you want to do SO BAD, but at the same time, you shake your head like *Pfff, never going to happen . . . don't have what it takes.* Maybe you want to apply for a certain job or lead a class, but you don't have the training. You want to write a book, but you don't know where to start. Or you want to talk about Christ to your friend, but you barely know the Bible yourself! Or maybe you're like me: I want to be a good mom, but whenever I let impatience get the best of me, I shake my head like I blew it and have now scarred my kids beyond irreparable damage. Do I live by extremities? Yes . . . yes, I do.

So what do we do in these moments when doubt and insecurity rise? We can indeed focus on ourselves and our limitations; that's always an option.

Or we can listen to God tell us who we are.

Now, remember: We didn't meet Gideon standing on the front lines, face painted and battle ready. No, this supposed "mighty hero" was hiding out, cowering from the enemy, and had already resigned himself to defeat. Yet while Gideon saw himself as the weakest and lowest, God still called him *mighty* and *warrior*.

Here's where the next principle comes into play, the HOW to gain from this Bible hero's story: **We are not who we think we are.** We might *assume* we have a good picture, but **we are *always* who God says we are.** When our inner selves voice inadequacy, God—as our Creator who knows us better than we know ourselves—always sees more. It changes the game when we *actually believe Him.*

Take Peter. He was swayed by peer pressure, denied knowing Christ, and made the same mistakes over and over again. But Jesus saw a rock that could not be moved.

David was an overlooked little shepherd boy. Samuel considered all his other brothers before landing on him, but God saw David's heart and called him to become king.

And while others viewed Rahab as simply a prostitute, God saw her as a woman whose heart would be changed, and His Son would later come down her family tree.

Do you see the common thread in all of these people's stories? **God knew what they would become well before they ever did.** It certainly became evident to everyone else *later*—when Peter boldly proclaimed the gospel and called for repentance from the crowd who persecuted Jesus. When David wrote much of the Psalms, singing to, dancing for, and worshiping his God—a man after God's own heart. When Rahab, a prostitute and idol worshiper, turned woman of faith (Hebrews 11:31). They could've remained focused on their inadequacies, limitations, and sinful pasts and remained stuck in that identity, but they listened to God instead—and their stories were *forever changed* because of it.

While it is all too easy to identify ourselves based on our past or current set of circumstances—like "I'm *just* a stay-at-home mom wiping butts and floors all day" or "I'm *just* a single girl unsure what I even want to do with my career" or "I'm *just* an empty nester with little influence on my kids today"—too many of us are entertaining the lie that we can't be used by God because of what we've been through or where we are today.

But Jesus did not come to this earth, carry our sin on His shoulders, die a painful death in our place, defeat death (and with it, the punishment for our sin), come back to life, and send His Holy Spirit to dwell within us today . . . just so we can continue to live with regrets, be defeated by our past, sink low because of our circumstances, and essentially live life as if He did none of those things *at all*.

> When we go to Jesus and offer Him what we have, it does not MATTER what we lack.

No, like the little boy with the bread and fish, when we go to Jesus and offer Him what we have, it does not MATTER what we lack. Colossians 2:10 affirms we are complete in Christ. He will never turn down a couple of fish even when *you* are convinced it's not enough . . . because He is enough and can multiply your little lunch box to host a whole fish fry for thousands more.

He just wants your offering.

So how *does* God see you? In Christ, what *does* God call you? For starters, here's 10 of my favorites:

1. Protected and upheld (Psalm 3:3; 55:22)
2. Strong (Psalm 28:7)
3. Bold and confident (Psalm 138:3)
4. Friend of Jesus (John 15:15)
5. Redeemed (Romans 3:22-25)
6. More than a conqueror (Romans 8:37)
7. Loved (Romans 8:35-37)
8. Free (2 Corinthians 3:17)
9. His work of art (Ephesians 2:10)
10. A fearless powerhouse (2 Timothy 1:7)

The choice is ours: We can either focus on our limitations, wave off our new God-given identity, and essentially reject who we are in Christ. Or we can set our gaze on our Savior, listen to the only Voice that calls us by name, believe Him and His promises, and watch how they unfold and come to fruition in our lives—just like they did with Gideon.

If we choose option B, we'll realize it does not matter all that we lack; *He is* whatever we lack. "For by that one offering he forever made perfect those who are being made holy" (Hebrews 10:14).

Back to the bomb God just dropped on Gideon. "You know those people you're afraid of? Yeah, the ones that have taken everything from you? Driven you out of your house, still terrorizing you today, and the sole reason you're hiding out right now? Okay, go. I want you to fight them."

HA.

Wait, He's serious?

Don't forget—Gideon's faith in God *IN GENERAL* was on shaky ground seconds before this conversation—and now he not only has to come to terms with (1) who God is, (2) who he is in God, but (3) he's got to turn right around and slaughter an entire army on top of it all? LOL, and we're nervous to ask for volunteers in the church nursery!

But think about it for a second. Answer those questions above quick. If (1) God is the Lord of Heaven's Armies here with us (Psalm 46:11) and (2) "we are more than conquerors" and "he trains [our] hands for battle" (Romans 8:37; Psalm 18:34), then (3) maybe this *isn't* that big of an ask. Maybe it actually *makes sense*—that a God who's already overcome the trials of this world would ask His people—who are more than conquerors—to go out and fight the battle. #foodforthought

So who or what are the Midianites in your life? What makes you most afraid? Who or what has taken everything from you—your joy, your peace, your future—and driven you out of the land that in Christ rightfully belongs to you?

No matter the form, that's what fear does. Tried and true, it always pulls us away from our God-given territory.

Watch it happen: Because of this diagnosis, we aren't so certain God's protecting us anymore—*one step out*. In light of current events, we aren't that sure He has good plans for us anymore—*another step away*. Throughout this wild-goose chase of a job search, we're kind of doubting He even cares. How could He flip this thing for our good and His glory? It's hard to see His blessings when our life is so full of trials.

Now all of a sudden, yet not so suddenly, we've found our feet planted in a place we were never intended to be—hiding in mountain clefts, caves, and strongholds rather than standing on the promises of God.

Yet just as God commanded Gideon to go fight this enemy, our God demands the same of us today.

You think my face is red now? That's just my complexion. #redheadproblems But catch me at a playground with some punks teasing my kids, and lemme tell you, I RISE UP.

Even better, God refuses to stand idly by watching His own kids taunted by the enemy, hunted down while trying to plant seeds of faith, and invaded point-blank by the evil rulers and authorities and powers of this dark world. No, Jesus paid a mighty high price to give us life to the full, and He's not about to witness His own people robbed of it. In the words of Joe Fox (or *The Godfather*, depending on your loyalty to *You've Got Mail*), it's time to go to the mattresses.

But first, let's clarify: God never said to Gideon, "Go fight. I'll just be up here—report back when you're done. Best of luck!" No, when Gideon was overwhelmed with the HOW, God simply said, "Go in the strength *you have.* . . . Am *I* not sending you?" (Judges 6:14, NIV, emphasis added).

In other words, "**Do what you can do, and trust I will do what only I can do.**"

Which, P.S. In Gideon's case . . . that was actually a lot. He recruited thousands of willing men to go to battle. He stockpiled an inventory of trumpets and torches, so they were armed. And he planned strategy, educating his army as a military leader would. I mean, *that's quite a bit of prep work* when (spoiler alert) they didn't actually end up fighting.

Personally, I don't looooooove all the wasted time and effort, but, then again, if we look at it from a different angle, we realize none of it was really wasted. God wasn't trying to build up the Israelite army—**He was out to build up their faith.**

This is where you may be today. You're putting in the work. You're planning strategy, equipping yourself with the armor of God, and moving forward in the strength you have.

Good news, girlfriend: You can wait expectantly. Not impatiently, in panic or alarm over the looming question marks ahead. But "those who wait for the Lord [who expect, look for, and hope in Him] shall change and renew their strength and power" (Isaiah 40:31, AMPC). Psalm 25:3 takes it even further: "Indeed, none of those who [expectantly] wait for You will be ashamed" (AMP). Don't you love the absolute nature of those promises? I KNOW, ME TOO.

I repeat, this is not a drill: When we do what *we can do*, and then bank everything on God to do what *only He can do*? We can move forward in confidence knowing that our God will surely show up.

P.S. Help is on the way.

FEAR:

"What if I don't have what it takes?"

THE HOW: You probably *don't* have what it takes. (Ha! Try that for your next #mondaymotivation), but in Christ, you are complete (Colossians 2:10). He is whatever you lack.

HOW DO I STOP MY DOUBTS AND INSECURITIES IN THEIR TRACKS? Ask yourself, "Am I focusing on God or myself?" Whenever we fixate on our limitations, we're just making it all about ourselves, and we miss the point. But when we turn our attention back to God, we'll hear Him say to us—just like He did to Gideon—"Am I not sending you?" It's actually less about us than we think it is, and more about God than we realize. Shift your focus.

WHAT IF I'M A PLANNER AND I GET STUCK ON THE "HOW"? Remember Gideon, who repeated the same question—"How can I rescue Israel?" Let his story remind you that you can't execute any of God's plans in your own power. But when you go forward in the strength you have, God will show up for the rest. Do what you can do—start there—and then expect Him to do what only He can do.

HOW DO I ESCAPE MY NEGATIVE THOUGHT PATTERN? Instead of hiding like the Israelites did, God wants you to take refuge in Him. To find your life, joy, peace, and contentment in Him. When you stop building castles of sand with your hands and kneel before the one true God, who offers a firm foundation, then you can repeat Psalm 16:8: "I keep my eyes always on the LORD. With him at my right hand, I will not be shaken" (NIV). You may have Him at your right hand, but your eyes may sometimes be fixated on something else. Not today. Today, this is the day the Lord has made, so you can rejoice and be glad in Him—in Christ alone (Psalm 118:24). Turn your gaze up and taste and see for yourself that He is good (Psalm 34:8).

Chapter 5

WHAT IF I WANT TO RUN AWAY FROM THIS?

Jonah

Life was so much simpler before _____.

Something came to mind right away, didn't it? Life was so much simpler before Dad passed away, we had kids on social media, this chronic illness creeped into the picture, that unforeseen accident (with a heaping pile of bills) turned our lives upside down, or that *awful* fashion trend made a comeback. #LEARNFROMOURMISTAKESCHILDREN

Every now and then, Facebook resurrects old posts at the top of our feed, so as soon as we log in, we take an unexpected walk down memory lane, you know? Sometimes, it's fun—like oh yeah, I *did* play college ball! I used to get out *past 9 p.m.*! We crazy college girls *did* collect piles of our hair for months, and one day, our brother hall woke up to our knee-deep accumulation! Weirdest prank of my life.

But sometimes, it's cringy—like, I actually *wore that*?

Other times, it's sad—I'm not friends with that person anymore, or my kids have grown up *way* too fast.

My feed just refreshed to a picture taken mere days before I found out I had Hodgkin's Lymphoma. I had both arms around my grandparents, smiling ear to ear, naive over what was to come, and ready to dive into an indoor water park in the middle of January *because that's just what you do to stay sane when you live in the tundra* (aka the Midwest). As I stared at that face, tears formed in my eyes and I wistfully thought, *I wish I still lived in that kind of bliss.* Back before I had long-term side effects looming over my future. Before I had annual appointments and scans. Before I felt the constant need to check for lumps and stay ahead of every worst-case scenario.

For you, when did life feel so much simpler? Lighter? Better?

Now's the perfect time to meet Jonah. Boy had it *made* in Israel. Among God's people, it was a comfortable place to teach His Word, and as a prophet, he was both recognized and respected. kinda the 775 BC Billy Graham. For all we know, Jonah could've stayed put in that place, his old stomping grounds, kicking back until it was time to retire.

But right before Jonah could hit "Continue Watching" on Netflix to roll over to the next show (why do they still have to ask?), God's ready for Jonah to get off the couch and get on mission: "Get up and go to the great city of Nineveh. Announce my judgment against it because I have seen how wicked its people are" (Jonah 1:2).

Hold up, go to *Nineveh*? The capital of Assyria, a feared world powerhouse? This city was not only massive (you'd have to set aside three travel days just to circle around it) and strong (their military was unmatched), but . . . they were known for being ruthlessly violent. We're talking the equivalent of modern-day terrorists.

In fact, archaeologists have discovered carvings that show exactly what the Ninevites did to folks from outside of town. It's a little much, so let me give the PG-rated version. To start with, they violated women, did away with the children, and exfoliated men's skin . . . if you catch my drift. From there, they either left them on stakes or buried them alive in the desert. Should we go back to Would You Rather? Oh, also, they built monuments out of their skulls . . . a unique choice in architectural design to say the least.

In conclusion, Nineveh wasn't *exactly* the top tourist hot spot. The book of Nahum describes it this way: "The city of murder and lies! She is crammed with wealth and is never without victims. Hear the crack of whips. . . . See the flashing swords and glittering spears. . . . There are countless casualties, heaps of bodies—so many bodies that people stumble over them. All this because Nineveh, the beautiful and faithless city, mistress of deadly charms, enticed the nations with her beauty" (3:1-4).

Yet *here* is where God calls Jonah? LOL, no wonder he's hesitant!

Like, *I know you know all things, God, but . . . you do realize you're sending me to certain death, right? We're both well aware what the Ninevites do to anyone who even* looks *at them the wrong way, yet you want me to waltz right in like I own the place and straight-up call them out on their wickedness?*

Just out of curiosity . . . *are we expecting this to go well?*

"Imagine God sending a Jew to Germany in 1941 to confront the Nazis, and you start to get a feel of what God is asking this prophet. *But He spoke clearly.*"[1] The assignment was go preach to people who may very well kill you.

Jonah *certainly* did not choose this path, and maybe you didn't sign up for yours, either. You could've done without that unexpected move, your kid's diagnosis, or being out of a job for as long as it's been. It's hard to understand why God would ever point your feet in that miserable, barren, good-for-nothing direction.

It's here, standing alongside Jonah, where we reach a crossroads with only two choices available: (1) walk away from God or (2) follow where He leads.

Jonah gave the first option a test run: "But Jonah got up and went in the opposite direction to get away from the LORD. He went down to the port of Joppa, where he found a ship leaving for Tarshish. He bought a ticket and went on board, hoping to escape from the LORD" (Jonah 1:3).

Maybe you've already tried the first option too. God says don't give up meeting together, but we'd rather keep our weekends free, thank you. Sure, God says forgive, but man, He must not have been talking about *my* situation! I'll put up boundaries instead. He heals, yeah . . . but not this. This is just how I am, and this is just how it is. And I know, I know, Jesus came not to be served, but to serve—however, this is the year I'm prioritizing self-care. Maybe dying to self can be next year's resolution?

All along the way, we've set sail to Tarshish when God has always called us to Nineveh.

However, it's impossible to flee from God by boat when He's the One who created the seas. So while our kids may think they're running from God, the truth of the matter is His eye hasn't left them for a moment. And if our in-laws criticize our faith and seem so far gone, God still hasn't given up on them (and P.S. Neither should we).

Ultimately, no matter how many steps we track on our Fitbit headed in the opposite direction of God's commands, His mercy still tracks us down. He is characteristically, historically, disproportionately faithful even when we are faithless.

Drip, drop. Drip, drop.

Do you see the dark sky? Lemme pull up the weather app because those clouds do not look good.

Update: The hour-by-hour forecast doesn't look any better, and I hate to point any fingers, but . . . it's (kind of) all Jo's fault. Jason Strand puts it this way: "Sin always has a storm attached to it,"[2] and in Jonah's case, this Mediterranean cruise he hopped on to escape the storms of life certainly brought on a whole new monster of an actual storm. "The LORD hurled a powerful wind over the sea, causing a violent storm that threatened to break the ship apart" (1:4).

Look into the faces of the desperate sailors. While Jonah's taking a catnap below deck, they're fearing for their lives, terrified their ship is about to break into pieces, and shouting at each other to toss everything overboard. In a frantic panic, they throw all cargo—their most prized possessions and savings included—into the water, and then you hear it . . . prayers.

Every last sailor is shouting to his gods for help. "Do you hear us? Can you save us? Please rescue us!" Out of the corner of our eye, we spot the captain marching down into the hold of the ship, and as we follow him down the stairs, he shouts to Jonah, "How can you sleep at a time like this? Get up and pray to your god! Maybe he will pay attention to us and spare our lives" (1:6).

Not the first time Jonah's been told to get up, and it's not the first time he doesn't pray in response either.

Pull up your binoculars, because this is crucial: When *you're* being rocked back and forth by the waves of life, don't lose sight of the fact that others are in the boat watching you. They may be facing the exact same thing, and they've seen cancer steal someone's future, infertility steal a woman's hope, and this setback turn someone into a bitter cynic. So why would you be any different?

Well girls, *we are different* because, like Jonah, we know the one true God. WITHOUT EXCEPTION, He will never leave us nor forsake us, and He holds *all* power to redeem our situation.

But when all eyes are on us, giving us the opportunity to share about the hope we have (1 Peter 3:15), what do we do? Declare who our God is or remain silent?

Jonah's lips still remain tightly sealed . . .

But here we have it, the moment of truth: The sailors press Jonah, "Who are you? What is your line of work? What country are you from? What is your nationality?" (Jonah 1:8). As our eyes bounce back and forth between the men punting these questions and Jonah staring right back, are you holding your breath too?

"I am a Hebrew, and I worship the LORD, the God of heaven, who made the sea and the land" (1:9). Uff da Jo, YOU REALLY HAD US IN THE FIRST HALF.

Even on the run heading the wrong way, Jonah turned his allegiance back the *right* way—and literally and figuratively, this is when everything began to turn around.

"Throw me into the sea," Jonah said, "and it will become calm again" (1:12), and as hesitant as you would be hurling a grown man overboard into a hurricane without floaties or a life preserver, desperate times call for desperate measures, and that's exactly what they did. Oh, and wanna guess if Jonah's prediction was right?

YOU GOT IT. The storm ceased. The waves calmed. I feel it's too late, but . . . we probably could've just turned the boat around, no?

Before we join Jonah floating in the water though, what God's doing back on the boat is not something we want to miss. Those unbelieving shipmates—the ones who, mere moments before, were crying out to other gods—"were awestruck by the LORD's great power, and they offered him a sacrifice and vowed to serve him" (1:16).

Never forget it: As much as WE JUST WANT OUT of our storm, we must not forget to declare about our God in the midst of it. The course of the lives of those watching may be changed for all eternity—and that alone may be worth the time we spend in the storm.

Are you sick of hearing about my health history yet? Me too. For years, I pushed aside every memory of cancer. Because really, why drag up that pain? Especially when hearing about someone else's diagnosis sent me reeling backward, scared of a recurrence myself. But then messages like these came pouring into my inbox: "My friend was just diagnosed . . . My husband's scan had some red flags . . . We got the news today . . ." and I realized there are people sitting in the seat today that I sat in 10 years ago, looking for reassurance. More than anything, they're desperate for *hope*.

So I share today not because it's my preference, comfortable, or in any way fun, but because the God of all comfort who comforted *me* in my troubles calls me to turn right around and extend that same comfort to *others* (2 Corinthians 1:4). I'm still in the thick of scans these days, and I just want OUT of the doctor's office, OUT of these plaguing symptoms, OUT of these fearful trials . . . but every thought in this book was birthed from those moments, and in that way, I see the redemption rolling out. Keep sharing in the middle of your storm, and with certainty, you'll get a front-row seat to God's redemption at work too.

Back to Jonah. The still water starts rippling, and it's not from Jonah's butterfly stroke or us jumping in alongside him either. There's something beyond him creating the waves. Something . . . bigger and unlike anything he (or we) have ever confronted. As much as we try to dodge out of the way, the dark shadow of a fish seems to be barreling right toward us, rising higher, getting closer—and before we know it, a large mouth rises out of the water, engulfing Jonah on his way down and sinking us all into the depths of the sea along with it.

Where are we?

What's that slapping us in the face? Smells fishy . . .

Is that seaweed stuck on our foreheads?

And what is with the HUMIDITY? This does *nothing* for my smooth blowout. Does anyone happen to have some anti-frizz, humidity-shield, finishing hair spray on them? No? We're stuck looking like the Lion King? Great.

I guess we have bigger problems on our hands, though, because it appears we are . . . dare I say it . . . inside the belly of a huge fish. I know, I know; it's taking Jonah a bit to wrap his head around the situation too.

What are the odds? Great question—let's do the math. The annual risk of dying from a vending machine accident is roughly 1 in 112 million, and the risk of dying from being a left-handed person who misuses right-handed products is approximately 1 in 7 million people. But the risk of being swallowed by *a giant fish*? It's so low Google doesn't even provide a statistic in the results.

So wait, maybe the death risk calculator we use every time we scroll WebMD doesn't accurately predict our future? Yeah . . . maybe. Ha! Who would've thought? (Well, to be fair . . . Ty, who, for all copyright purposes, coined the phrase "Google is a liar," indeed already thought.)

Even though it's pitch black inside this fish, though, we can hear Jonah breathing—in and out as he treads water. But . . . he's quiet. He keeps to himself for what seems like hours, maybe even days. Personally, I think it's rude, because *hello?* This whole inside-of-a-fish thing is *kind of* a new experience, and we could really use a good heart-to-heart right about now. And I don't want to point any fingers, but it's kind of *his fault* for getting us into this mess?

At the very least, though, if not us, you'd *think* Jonah would be on talking terms with *God* by now, right? Didn't we learn our lesson and get over disobedience when the storm blew over?

Nope. I mean, I guess not because it took *three days and three nights* of the waters closing in on him, the darkness surrounding him, and the fish plunging deeper into the depths before Jonah decided it was time to pray.

Men. Not interested in pulling over to ask for directions when lost since the eighth century BC. Old habits die hard.

But lo and behold, the guy did eventually surrender, "I cried out to the LORD in my great trouble, and he answered me. I called to you from the land of the dead, and LORD, you heard me!" (Jonah 2:2). We can climb the highest mountains, sink down to the lowest depths, and run as far away from God as we possibly can. Yet even still, even there, the *moment* we cry out to God, He hears us. For "even the darkness is not dark to [God]" (Psalm 139:12, ESV).

As we see with Jonah, sometimes God allows us to take the initiative. "GOD hasn't moved . . . his holy address hasn't changed" (Psalm 11:4, MSG). We're the ones who have moved. When the doctor delivered a devastating diagnosis, we called our spouse first instead of calling upon the name of the Lord; our iPhone made that pretty easy. Or when the teacher broke the news that our child was behind the curve, we sent a group text to our friends—not a prayer request to our God. And when we came home after a long day, we walked straight to the couch for a show instead of straight into the presence of the Lord for rest.

And it's here, in the belly of a fish, in the middle of our scroll, or with the remote in our hand, that we learn the HOW to choose faith when all we want to do is run away from our circumstances. The choice is, once again, ours: **When we get scared and it's fight or flight, we can run from the Lord or to the Lord.**

If we choose to follow the footsteps of Jonah, we shouldn't be surprised when a storm or a whale halts our path. God is too good to give up on us now.

But if we run to God first? Save ourselves the 2,500 miles off the beaten path to Tarshish and choose to boldly walk the 550 miles to Nineveh with our Lord? Then, no matter what is darkening our door, dimming our vision with fear, or shadowing our faith with doubt, we can rest in the shadow of the Almighty, who is neither straining His eyes to see into that pitch-black obscurity nor confused about where to go next. To Him, darkness and light are the same, and "the night will shine like the day" (Psalm 139:12, NIV). So we can call out to God, anytime and anywhere, and be confident He *hears*, is full of mercy, and will once again prove that "salvation comes from the LORD alone" (Jonah 2:9).

It's no coincidence that after this prayer, when Jonah finally laid down his plans and opinions that he was previously clenching to so tightly and ran back to God in praise, that "*then* the LORD ordered the fish to spit Jonah out onto the beach" (2:10, emphasis added). As a person who pulled a muscle *while sleeping* (#thisis30), it's hard for me to imagine Jonah cartwheeling back to shore and living to tell the tale after this kind of physical roller coaster. But we've already defied the odds being eaten by a fish, so VAULT HANDSPRING, here we go.

As we then watch Jonah bravely march into the 15 gates of Nineveh—and as you also courageously put one foot in front of the other toward your own dreaded Nineveh—let's keep in mind what happens next.

Miraculously, once the king heard Jonah's message from God, he commanded everyone to earnestly pray. Did we read that right?! Yep. The entire wicked city *actually* listened, and they proclaimed a citywide fast, dressing in burlap to show their repentance (Jonah 3:5-9). Like watching casinos down the Las Vegas Strip turn into houses of worship, Jonah saw with his own two eyes why God sent him there.[3]

> If you trust in Jesus, that means God Himself has already deemed you an ambassador of Christ.

Sometimes, we may feel like we're wandering aimlessly—unsure why we're in this job, dealing with that neighbor, or suffering through another doctor appointment. But if you trust in Jesus, that means God Himself has already deemed you an ambassador of Christ (2 Corinthians 5:20). Like with Jonah, He is not thoughtlessly dispatching you into places or aimlessly crossing your paths with certain individuals—without reason, without purpose, without a plan.

No, if—like Jonah—we submit our plans to the Lord and trust that His ways are higher and better, then it won't be long until we realize He is the One who sat us down next to the kid in science class who's depressed, crossed our paths in the break room with a co-worker going through a messy divorce, or brought us face-to-face with an atheist client. It is no mistake the nurse who wheeled herself over to inject the chemotherapy drugs into my port knew Jesus and went to my church. She was undeniably God-sent, and the places He sends us are also just as unmistakable.

So we've got to stop for a moment. Look around. What do we see? God has strategically placed us around lost people, and P.S. He doesn't just want us to talk about the weather, our kids, or politics. He wants us to share His saving message: That all who turn to Christ can be saved, healed, and restored forevermore.

But the temptation will be to run from it, and like Jonah, become so inwardly focused on what *we want* that we miss it altogether. You are not primarily a mom, co-worker, or neighbor though. At the top of the list, you are an ambassador of Christ, and God put you there with a high responsibility and an eternally weighty calling. In His power and armed with His salvation, **He wants you to reach them**.

So keep your eyes on the mission, girl. In the end, we just might see a whole family, city, and nation turn back to the always-present God.

FEAR:

"What if I want to run away from this?"

THE HOW: Running to God instead of away is the only way to peace, purpose, and clarity.

BUT WHAT IF NOTHING ABOUT IT LOOKS GOOD? It may not, but since we don't have an eagle's-eye view of the situation nor the gift of hindsight, we can trust God, who knows all things and is leading us in that direction anyway. In the end, it has to be good, for He will work all things for the good of those who love Him and are called according to His purpose (Romans 8:28).

WHAT IF I'VE RUN FOR TOO LONG AND GONE TOO FAR? No one is ever out of the reach of our God, and no one is ever too far gone. Jesus Christ came to earth to save even the people we may consider the worst of sinners (1 Timothy 1:15). If He was still pursuing the Ninevites after all the sins they'd committed, He's still pursuing every single human walking the earth today (including you and me).

BUT WHAT ABOUT ME? WHEN WILL I START TO SEE SOME BENEFITS?

God wastes nothing, so anything we face, placed in the hands of our Lord, will assuredly be used to refine, strengthen, and purify us. But also . . . maybe it's not *just about us* either. Maybe there are Ninevites in your neighborhood, workplace, family, and nation—metaphorically speaking, of course. Let the record show I'm not calling your M-I-L a terrorist—and *just maybe* God has called you to shine His light in their darkness, breathe His hope into their weary souls, and show them the way home. Maybe, like Jonah, it's time to put aside what we want for a hot minute, and get up and *go*.

Chapter 6

WHAT ABOUT WHEN THE WORLD GOES CRAZY
(AND I'M KIND OF TEMPTED TO GO CRAZY TOO)?

Daniel

Rewind *just a few* years back. What was life like when you were growing up?

Maybe you actually had to *call your friends* to see what they were doing instead of sending a double-chin selfie on Snapchat. Or maybe you raced to Blockbuster to pick out a movie before they were all gone instead of streaming whatever you want whenever you want it. Is it true you also hopped on a bike and rode down your neighborhood without Mom anxiously watching from GPS tracking back home? (Don't tell the children.) Oh, and just a stab in the dark, but there were a bunch of Johns, Katies, Matthews, and Nicoles in your class, weren't there? Instead of you know, Gravity, Luna, and Pilot. #toinfinityandbeyond

The landscape of our world has always changed from one generation to the next. It's guaranteed with new advances in technology, new leadership sworn into office, new fashion trends, and new beliefs, opinions, lifestyles—and, well, just new *everything*.

Let it be known: I'm not a complete hater. I'm a big fan of modern medicine (*cancer survivor here!*), and it is not lost on me that I can barely keep up with laundry as it is—yet if I had to *individually scrub* each article of clothing *with a mere washboard*? *#bestillmysoul* No, I will be the first to admit that living in this day and age when Ty can just walk downstairs to join us for lunch because he works remote is a BLESSING, and the fact that I can brew a mocha in my own kitchen while sending an email and bouncing a baby, well . . . I say full speed ahead for these types of cultural advancements! Don't take me back to dial-up internet PLEASE.

But . . .

It seems as if someone stepped down on the accelerator these last few decades, doesn't it? The values that were once commonly embraced now no longer align, and the issues the majority of us tended to agree upon are now incredibly divisive. No matter our opinion on sexuality, parenting, education, aliens, when it's permissible to start listening to Christmas music (*after Thanksgiving*), if pineapple belongs on pizza (*it doesn't*), and whether or not the game is actually Duck Duck Goose or the obvious Duck Duck *Gray Duck*, we're guaranteed to be met with raised eyebrows, a fierce Facebook thread, and vocal—even violent—opposition. (*While on topic, it's also pop, not soda . . .*)

Sure, we all know the only thing constant is change, but the enormity and velocity of all of this change is kind of, well, startling. So much so that some of us are living in culture shock *in our own culture* and we'd give just about anything for Christopher Lloyd to come onto the scene and take us back a few decades, amiright? *They just don't make movies like that anymore. #thingsmygrandpausedtosay #thingsinowsay*

We're not just imagining things either. While a baby's gender was once an unquestionable fact, now it's up for debate. Instead of "be home by dinner," parents won't take their eyes off their kids—even in their own yard—for fear of predators, kidnappers, and sex traffickers. When once marriage was only ever between a man and woman, now there are homes with two dads or two moms. And where religious values were once culturally widespread—Gallup found in 1963 that only "1 percent of respondents said they did not have a religious preference"[1]—in 2021, "eighty-two percent of U.S. adults now say religion is losing its influence . . . with increasing numbers of U.S. adults, particularly young adults, lacking a religious affiliation."[2]

Add on racial tension, political unrest, social media, conspiracy theories, and that lady at the grocery store who pulled you aside to let you know—even though you were fully aware—that your child's sock is missing? Well, it's enough to paralyze even the most savvy food blogger who indeed enjoys fruit on her pizza. (BUT HOW COULD YOU?)

Here's the ultimate question: When the world goes mad and it feels like people are losing their minds and pushing us (and our kids) to do things we know are wrong . . . *what do we do?*

Dan's the man when it comes to culture shifting. Let's fall into his footsteps at the very beginning of Daniel 1, when King Nebuchadnezzar and the Babylonians took over Jerusalem. Charged with the task of bringing back home the brightest of the bright, the chief of staff must have remembered the king's words as he surveyed Israel's royal family and nobility. "'Select only strong, healthy, and good-looking young men,' [the king had] said. 'Make sure they are well versed in every branch of learning, are gifted with knowledge and good judgment, and are suited to serve in the royal palace'" (Daniel 1:4).

Basically, all the men you'd swipe right on Tinder? Yeah, haul them back to Babylon . . . just not exactly for dating or marriage purposes. More like an intensive bureaucratic training camp.

Daniel made the cut.

The plan? Indoctrinate them with Babylonian culture, teach them their new language, assign specific reading, and portion out particular food and wine for three years.

The hope? At the end of all this brainwashing, they'd no longer be faithful to Yahweh, their God, or stuck in the ways of their homeland but devoted to Babylon and its myriad of gods, and be in a good position to enter the Babylonian government and royal service.

. . . Sound familiar?

We may not have a crown and our family may not address us as queen (although if they started, we wouldn't be mad about it?), but our culture is certainly teaching a new language around pronouns, gender identity, and sexual orientation. Sure, we're out of school, but today's assigned literature is often our scroll on Facebook and Instagram. US adults use media an average of 12 hours and 9 minutes *per day* and counting.[3] We're being fed whatever is most popular on our feed. And we may not be taken from our homes, but when life is tough and the day is long, the Mommy Wine Culture has indoctrinated us to find relief by pouring that glass FULL—instead of "[pouring] out [our] complaints before him and [telling] him all [our] troubles" (Psalm 142:2).

Essentially, we can be so immersed in the norm around us, gorging in its feast, being caught up in our scroll, speaking the lingo, and regurgitating the next trendy saying that we forget our homeland. We rarely think about our King. Our citizenship in heaven slips from our mind because our identity in the world is so predominant—and let's be real, more convenient.

This is the lure, the indoctrination plan, the enemy has had all along.

The trouble? Daniel was immersed in this program for three years; most of us have been on Facebook *for decades*. Pit all these hours logged scrolling against the one hour a week we set aside for church? The five minutes we spend skimming the Bible? The two minutes before meals and bedtime we concentrate on prayer? Well, we can see why King Nebuchadnezzar chose the plan that he did. Why the enemy is commandeering this same ruse. It's awfully hard to allow God to renew our mind when the majority of our days are spent conforming to the pattern of this world.

WHAT ABOUT WHEN THE WORLD GOES CRAZY?

But what did Daniel do? What can *we* do?

"Daniel was determined not to defile himself" (Daniel 1:8). Instead of being modified by culture, he remained persistent in his convictions, stubborn in God's ways, and single-minded toward his King.

Yeah, yeah, yeah, but *HOW?* The enemy attacked him in three ways, and he responded each time. Here's what it looked like:

> Instead of being modified by culture, he remained persistent in his convictions, stubborn in God's ways, and single-minded toward his King.

1. The first attack from Daniel's enemy came in the form of assigning him a new name. Daniel was instructed to take on and answer to the name Belteshazzar. Easy to dismiss this as yet another unique celebrity invention of a name, but let's pull out the hefty baby-name book and take a closer look. In Hebrew, Daniel means "God is my judge," and it was intentionally chosen by his parents and his God. A strong declaration that he would answer to God and *Him alone.*

What does Belteshazzar mean? "Lady, protect the king!" Lady was a mythological wife to their deity, Bel, as if Daniel should be married to this concept of their gods.[4] Tack on "protect the king," and the Babylonians made it clear his attention should no longer be on his God, but now on the king and the king's interests.

We still see the same strategy being carried out today; an attack on a person's God-given identity has always been a top maneuver from the enemy's playbook. Without taking PTO, the deceiver works full-time to turn our attention away from God and distract us from the mission He's (rather seriously) entrusted us with—by sucking us into the world's interests. With his first attempt, Satan and his evil army try to rename you. Slap a label on you that God *never* put on you and get you to believe this new, distorted, corrupted identity.

For instance, feeling afraid is different from being afraid. Instead of merely *feeling* scared and *struggling* against anxiety, the enemy hopes we accept these things as *who we are* and begin to see ourselves as anxious people. "That's just how I'm wired!" would be music to his ears.

But tell that to the Creator of our personalities, bodies, and souls. God makes it clear that He did not give us a spirit of fear, "but of power, love, and self-discipline" (2 Timothy 1:7), so *fear* isn't a label we need to wear, but a struggle we will—in due time, in light of His resurrection, in the perfected-yet-being-made-holy stage of life (Hebrews 10:14)—overcome.

What labels are you wearing? What does your *Hello, I'm* _____ name tag read? We've got to get clear on this, because the enemy has his Sharpie poised, and like a toddler flying through a sticker sheet, he wants to decorate you head to toe in tacky adhesive.

Hi, I'm Sick. Forever Doomed. Beyond Help. These are some of the names the enemy continually tries to slap on my chest. "You've heard bad news once from the doc, and *you were only 23*! Ha, good luck living the rest of your life with a clean bill of health! This is just your cross to bear, Heidi. Cancer is probably growing in your body as we speak, and it's probably going to be too late next time, when not even God can save you. You are hopeless. Your body is condemned. And your future is ill-fated."

Your lie detector's going off, right? Good, because personally, my blood pressure was climbing off the charts through that exercise—but this is where we can use our emotions to our advantage. Back to those warning lights flashing on a dashboard (I'm up to five. What's your tally at?), God created us with an amygdala that activates the fight-or-flight mode whenever things feel off.

When we're tempted to wear the label *Hello, I'm Alone*, we can allow that awful feeling of dejection to alert us to the fact that we're indeed believing a lie since our God is ever present. When we feel weak, may that blinking Check Engine light drive us back to the God who makes us strong (Psalm 18:32). When we look around at our mundane life and our heart sinks at the thought of it all being purposeless, we can heed that Low Fuel light, fill our gas tank back up with God's Word, and be reminded that *we are* created with purpose and *He will* fulfill His purposes for us (Psalm 138:8).

Clear distinction: **The enemy will always want you to feel hopeless and helpless, but the Hope of the World, Jesus, and the Helper, the Holy Spirit, will always assure you of the opposite.**

This groundwork takes time, intention, and perseverance, but girlfriend, you and I have GOT to know who we are. Just as the enemy uses culture to train us to accept his lies, God gives us His Word to train us in godliness so we can embrace the truth that sets us free.

> Girlfriend, you and I have GOT to know who we are.

Notice this, though: Both require *training*. "Physical training is good, but training for godliness is much better, promising benefits in this life and in the life to come" (1 Timothy 4:8). Who are you receiving instruction from, and where are you getting your labels? The enemy and culture, or God and His Word?

2. The next attack came in the form of food, which *seems* harmless, but it was purely an invitation from the enemy for Daniel to go against his convictions. Daniel's staring down at a royal feast, and he passes on the filet mignon and Juicy Lucy—not because it doesn't sound good, but (1) it goes against the dietary laws God gave to Israel and (2) it wasn't farm-to-table but idol-to-table and Daniel didn't need the FDA to know that wasn't approved.

Instead he opted for the vegetable sides, and after 10 days of careful surveillance, what did the Babylonian attendant find? "Daniel and his three friends looked healthier and better nourished than the young men who had been eating the food assigned by the king" (Daniel 1:15), and later, "Whenever the king consulted them in any matter requiring wisdom and balanced judgment, he found them ten times more capable than any of the magicians and enchanters in his entire kingdom" (1:20).

What do you know? God's way actually *proved* to be best, and if we also follow His commands and wait for sex until marriage, give the first 10 percent of our paycheck to our church, and I don't know, *not murder anyone*? We might come to the same conclusion ourselves. Wow, no STDs? No criminal record? Maybe God, the Creator of this world and everything in it, *actually did know* what He was talking about . . . and maybe His commands aren't just better—but *exponentially* better. We may not see that in the (literal) heat of the moment or the second after we make out that first check to the church, but make no mistake—His "promises have been thoroughly tested . . . your instructions are perfectly true" (Psalm 119:140, 142). When we walk down the road of obedi- ence, God Himself sees to it that "none of [our] steps shall slide" (Psalm 37:31, AMPC).

Daniel being case in point. He continued to prove to be a worth- while investment, so "the king appointed [him] to a high position and gave him many valuable gifts. He made Daniel ruler over the whole province of Babylon, as well as chief over all his wise men" (Daniel 2:48). Man, things were sure looking up for our guy, right? He had the king's ear! Acted as judge over all the people! More than just a pretty face, Daniel *was* the face of the kingdom, representing the king himself!

But then King Nebuchadnezzar lost his mind, his son took over the family business, and after a swift murder investigation, we find King Darius the Mede reclining on the throne instead of the aforementioned son . . . suspicious? I think so.

No time for a game of Clue, though, because the last flaming arrow is being hurled onto the scene this very moment. Watch as Daniel's position—once esteemed and viewed as the prize and pinnacle of his career—is now the catalyst to the very threat that painted a target on his back.

Under the scrutiny of the public eye, Daniel finds himself with plenty of jealous enemies—but since he was an honorable businessman serving the Lord in his position, "they couldn't find anything to criticize or condemn. He was faithful, always responsible, and completely trustworthy. So they concluded, 'Our only chance of finding grounds for accusing Daniel will be in connection with the rules of his religion'" (6:4-5).

3. When the enemy can't get you to question your identity in God or go against your convictions, his last-ditch effort will be to influence and position culture against you and your God.

Surprise, surprise. A law is passed that puts Daniel in quite a tight spot—you can either pray to your king and be safe, or pray to your God and be thrown in the lions' den. Would you rather?

Okay, let's reason here. On one hand, it's just 30 days. After a month is up, we can go back to church! Pray to whomever we want! Read our Bible in peace! Tell others about our God in freedom! If we can stick it out for 30 days, we'll still have our job, health, wealth, and place of influence. We'll even still have a spotless reputation, which means we can be a better witness, and we'll have respected the government too! Win-win, *right?*

See how effective this tactic is? How easy it is to rationalize, and thus, fall prey to the lure? No wonder the enemy's still running the same play today.

Our logic: "I need this job to support my family. What would we do without my income?" **God's logic:** "Look at the birds. They don't plant or harvest or store food in barns, for your heavenly Father feeds them. And aren't *you far more valuable* to him than they are?" (Matthew 6:26, emphasis added). He "will supply all your needs from his glorious riches, which have been given to us in Christ Jesus" (Philippians 4:19).

Our concern: "I don't want to ruffle any feathers or put my reputation on the line. That could actually discredit my witness!" **God's response:** "Are you now seeking the approval of man or of God? If people-pleasing is your goal, you would not be Christ's servant" (see Galatians 1:10). "Blessed is the one who is not offended by me" (Matthew 11:6, ESV).

Our self-preservation: "But this would be unsafe! It puts my future on the line! My life could be ruined! I could DIE!" **God's reassurance:** Don't be afraid of whoever or whatever can merely kill the body; "they cannot touch your soul. Fear only God, who can destroy both soul and body in hell" (Matthew 10:28). On that lighthearted note . . .

All in all, Daniel's dilemma—and ours as well—isn't packaged as a simple "Honor God or worship the devil" type decision, or it would be easy to choose God every time. Satan doesn't play—he frames these kinds of choices as God vs. this world PLUS the things you value and fear losing most. But honor God *first*, "seek the Kingdom of God above all else, and live righteously, *and he will give you everything you need*" (Matthew 6:33, emphasis added).

Daniel was our living example. He chose God, bowed down in prayer, and was thrown into the lions' den because of it. But what did God do?

"Very early the next morning, the king got up and hurried out to the lions' den. When he got there, he called out in anguish, 'Daniel, servant of the living God! Was your God, whom you serve so faithfully, able to rescue you from the lions?'" (Daniel 6:19-20).

And out of the dark opening of the den, when chances of survival were a mere 0 percent, and not one person expected Daniel to come out of this alive, we hear the strong voice of our hero shout, "Long live the king! My God sent his angel to shut the lions' mouths so that they would not hurt me, for I have been found innocent in his sight" (6:21-22).

You honor God first, girlfriend? Obey His commands above others' commands? Believe His Word, which stands forever (1 Peter 1:25), over the word of culture, which is fickle and ever-changing? Refuse to be defiled by culture even when it may cost you *everything*?

Just like Daniel, you'll be found innocent in God's sight, and P.S. In the end, you'll see for yourself that His ways indeed prove **BEST**.

It's up to you. Will you change the world, or will the world change you? Instead of reflecting the culture, you can help set the culture,[5] and as you let your good deeds shine out for all to see, may everyone turn and praise our heavenly Father (Matthew 5:16).

This world may be going mad, BUT GOOD NEWS: WE DON'T HAVE TO—for our God has given us a *sound mind.*

FEAR:

"What about when the world goes crazy (and I'm kind of tempted to go crazy too)?"

THE HOW: When others are copy-and-pasting the behaviors, customs, and beliefs of this world, we can instead be transformed by the renewing of our minds by knowing, believing, and living out His Word (Romans 12:2).

WHAT IF OTHER CHRISTIANS ARE LIVING IN WAYS THAT ARE CLEARLY AGAINST GOD'S COMMANDS? Out of all the men recruited for King Nebuchadnezzar's training camp, we only read of Daniel and three other friends sticking to the vegan diet. God has "[made] known to [us] the path of life" (Psalm 16:11, ESV), but "only a few ever find it" (Matthew 7:14). Not everyone will be found faithful in the end. But as we stand firm in the Way, we can't look away with raised eyebrows or turn our backs on our brothers and sisters. God calls us to "gently and humbly help that person back onto the right path" (Galatians 6:1) and "[win] that person back" (Matthew 18:15). His heart is always for the lost to be found, and He wants us to join in that mission.

WHAT ABOUT PERSONAL CONVICTIONS THAT DIFFER BETWEEN BELIEVERS, BUT ARE NOT CLEARLY ADDRESSED IN THE BIBLE? The Corinthian church wondered this same thing. It was ingrained in Jews that ham was a no-go, but Gentiles were scarfing down BLTs and pulled-pork sandwiches left and right—made from meat offered to idols, no less! *What gives? And who's right?* Paul gave a nod of approval to *both* meals, though—how? Since these believers were living under the freedom of Christ who fulfilled the law, it was no longer the specific meal that mattered, but their *conviction* about the meal (Romans 14:22-23). You can follow where God's leading you while simultaneously respecting the consciences of other believers. **Stay united.**

Chapter 7

HOW CAN I HOPE
FOR A GOOD FUTURE
WITH MY PAST?

Naomi

How do you picture God?

I'm talking this very moment, as you look up to the heavens and imagine the Lord locking eyes with you—what do you see?

A heavenly Father with arms stretched wide, a pleased smile, eyes attentive, and hands completely trustworthy? An angry Man with a hard glare, foot tapping in impatience, head shaking in disgust? A lofty King, seated on a high throne, coolly watching your life play out, out of reach, out of touch, out of the picture? Or a God who is good to others, but not you? A God who is known for His miracles, but there's no evidence of that in your life? A God who allowed that terrible tragedy to happen yesterday, and now you're facing a hard reality today or looking ahead at a grim tomorrow?

Have you met Naomi? She's that stay-at-home mom in Judah, dressed in a "Raising Boys" block-letter sweatshirt, facing a severe drought, and forced to pack up for a cross-country move.

Listen on as she tells her two teenage boys to say goodbye to their friends, their predictable school schedule, the spot they worked so hard to earn on the basketball team, and that girl they've been eyeing for quite some time now (but you brought it up, so of course, they deny every last bit of it and turn completely unfeeling).

Watch as Naomi packs everything they own in a way that shouts, "This girl *slays* at Tetris." Don't miss how she kisses her boys' heads on their way out of town and faithfully follows her husband, Elimelech, who's leading the way. And then keep tabs on her as they haul up and down a mountainous strip of rugged terrain in Jordan—unclear what lies ahead, uncertain whether there will be enough food when they get there, and unsure where they will settle . . . all somehow without SORELs and with, I repeat, *two teenage boys*.

The girl's already our hero, right?

Going full speed ahead, this family rolls out the "Welcome (but did you call first?)" doormat in front of their new house in Moab, but within a matter of *one verse* (Ruth 1:3), we see Naomi wearing black, standing beside a grave, her two sons next to her—all missing Elimelech. (Warning: Pull out the tissues . . . the saga continues.)

Hit fast-forward on your streaming device, and now a decade later, Naomi's once again wearing black (1:4). Yet this time, she's looking at two freshly dug graves. In place of her two sons, we see two daughters-in-law huddled around Naomi. A sad trio of faces twisted in agony, sorrow, and grief. "This left Naomi alone, without her two sons or her husband" (1:5).

Doesn't your heart just break? Only 10 years ago, she had her whole future ahead of her, hopeful this new adventure would set up her family well, and most importantly, she was surrounded by the people she loved most. Life was tough, sure, but she had a husband she loved. Kids she adored. And as long as they were together, she could handle anything!

But now . . . they weren't together.

As a widow with no sons, her future was now more uncertain than ever before, and her financial security was one big question mark.

Beyond just *feeling* lonely and alienated without her people, as a Hebrew, she *was* a foreigner, an outsider in this land of Moab. Our girl was in a tough spot, dealt a hard hand, and as optimistic as we'd like to be . . . well, how could she ever rebound? What should she do now?

Maybe you've packed up everything you know and love, and walked bravely into a new season with all the hope in the world—but you've been met with nothing but high hurdles and rugged terrain.

Maybe you were trudging along behind your husband, wistful over what you were leaving behind, unconvinced this was the next right step for your family.

Or maybe you've stood beside the grave of a dream lost, a hope dashed, or a loved one who passed, and now your OOTD will forever be black.

Whatever your circumstances may be, you're racking up cards that make you want to fold, but there doesn't seem to be a discard pile on the board, and the Dealer doesn't look interested in a reshuffle either.

This is why I love Naomi and her story. I didn't ever want to step foot on the uphill battle of cancer, and my guess is you could've done without the harsh terrain of your own mountains. I could've gotten along just fine without waving goodbye to a clean medical history, setting up a tempo-rary camp in oncology, and facing an uncertain future with potential long-term side effects—and you could've made do without the uneasiness of your own trials. And now, years into remission, still battling against health scares that bring me right back to those first days, I echo the same questions Naomi must have asked: "How can I ever rebound from this? How can I be hopeful for a good future when *all that* happened? Where do I go from here?" Maybe some days, you wonder the same thing.

Time to go home, girls.

As Naomi packs her bags, leaving behind her "Boy Mom" crewneck but wrapping her "World's Best Mother-In-Law" mug in a scarf, she sets off on a journey she never dreamed she'd take. Back to Bethlehem—this time without her better half, without her babies bickering in the back-ground, without any hope for anything better.

With plenty of time to think on the road trip, Naomi stops dead in her tracks and turns to her two daughters-in-law, Ruth and Orpah. "Go back to your mothers' homes. And may the LORD reward you for your kindness to your husbands and to me" (1:8). As much as she'd love their company, Naomi realizes her plight doesn't have to mar their future. Living up to the title on her mug, she sends them back in hopes they remarry, have arms full of children, and ultimately have the future she could not and will not ever have again.

Incredibly selfless, incredibly heartbreaking.

We can't help but stare as all three women break down in a puddle of tears (1:9) and the girls shake their heads vigorously, wanting nothing but another goodbye—revealing just how close they all became in those 10 years together.

But Naomi held her ground. "Things are far more bitter for me than for you, because the LORD himself has raised his fist against me" (1:13). And with that, we watch as Orpah kisses her mother-in-law goodbye, takes one last look behind her, and retraces her steps back home to familiarity and possibility.

Ruth, on the other hand, refuses and, clinging tightly to Naomi, takes her own stand, echoing the words God spoke to Moses long ago.* "Don't ask me to leave you and turn back. Wherever you go, I will go; wherever you live, I will live. Your people will be my people, and your God will be my God" (1:16).

This is where we see Naomi hadn't just taken Ruth under her wing as her very own daughter, but she introduced Ruth to *her God*. Where Naomi saw a desolate, hard road ahead, Ruth now saw it as the road to restoration—the only route that led to life, the direction to take to honor her God.

Interesting how we can walk along the same paths as others yet come to very different conclusions, isn't it? One wife sees open kitchen

---

* "I will claim you as my own people, and I will be your God. Then you will know that I am the Lord your God who has freed you from your oppression in Egypt" (Exodus 6:7).

cabinets, quietly shuts them, and goes about her business. Another rages at the sight and slams them shut to GET HER POINT ACROSS AND HOPE SOMEONE TAKES THE HINT. Purely circumstantial. #iknownothingaboutthis

More seriously, one person goes through infertility, chemotherapy, or a furlough at work with total fear and signs off in defeat. Another? Strangely hopeful, somehow filled with peace.

Our plight may not be that different from others', but our response certainly can be.

Beyond the same dusty road ahead, Naomi's and Ruth's situations were very similar. Their husbands had passed, no other family members were around, and no source of income was streaming in. With no real future determined, they both decided to leave everything, move, ready to start over, all in hopes of creating a new life.

> Our plight may not be that different from others', but our response certainly can be.

Yet that is where the similarities end.

When they finally reach Bethlehem, the whole town is buzzing with excitement, and all Naomi's friends come running the second they hear the news. "'Is it really Naomi?' the women asked" (1:19). *Is it really our long-lost friend?* POP THE CONFETTI.

"'Don't call me Naomi,' she responds. 'Instead, call me Mara, for the Almighty has made life very bitter for me. I went away full, but the LORD has brought me home empty. Why call me Naomi when the LORD has caused me to suffer and the Almighty has sent such tragedy upon me?'" (1:20-21).

Aaaaand . . . cue the sound of a balloon deflating.

Yeesh, talk about a buzzkill. Instead of a sweet reunion, everyone's now just twiddling their thumbs, trying to hide the welcome home cake, and nudging each other like, "No, *you* say something . . ."

As we look over and study Naomi's face, we see what we missed before. All those years away have done more than just callous her feet—they've hardened her heart. Instead of living up to her name, which means "pleasant," we instead see a self-proclaimed very bitter woman.[1]

This is where we come to a crossroads. Jesus assured us long ago that every single person would face trials in this world (John 16:33), so trouble and sorrow weren't limited to Naomi—they're a guarantee for every human being who walks this earth.

Yet while we may not be able to avoid hardships or pick the ones we face, we're always able to choose our response. We can either (1) jump to the conclusion that God has failed us, is no longer good, and is against us *or* (2) hold on in faith that our God never fails, is always good, and is for us.

The enemy will try to convince us it's not so black-and-white, but **it really is one or the other.**

Naomi shows us what happens when we choose option 1. When we allow our circumstances to define God instead of allowing God to define our circumstances, our thoughts sound a lot like: *If God were good, then He wouldn't have let my husband die. If God were kind, I wouldn't be struggling with unemployment, wrestling with infertility, left floundering in the wake of a dysfunctional family. If He was really for me, He would've intervened by now. If He really holds all the power, then He's cruelly holding back from helping me. God is still God, sure, but He's raised His fist against me. I still believe in Him, but it's hard to believe He's kind or good in light of* _____.

The moment we allow our circumstances to shape our view of God, we step onto a slippery slope. Like Naomi, it won't be long until our experiences then mold how we see ourselves and become our source of identity as well. Because we're the ones that gave it the trump card, it's now the filter by which we choose to see all of life.

Naomi no longer wanted to identify as Naomi—but Mara. In her eyes, with her circumstances as king, she was now the one whom God had afflicted, and this bitterness ruled her words, her interactions, and her heart.

We can go down that same path and allow the curveballs of life to define who God is and who we are.

Or we can shift our focus onto Ruth, who chooses to bank every-thing on what's behind door number two. Projecting God and His promises onto our circumstances looks a whole lot like: *Since God is good, I know in due time He will flip the script for His glory and my good* (Romans 8:28). *Since God is kind, He will see me through, heal my broken heart, and do immeasurably more than all I ask or imag-ine* (Ephesians 3:20). *Since the Lord Almighty is for me, whatever was intended to harm me, God intends it for good* (Genesis 50:20), *and I will live to see His redemption win in my life. Since He holds all the power, I wait expectantly for my God to take care of me, provide for me, and faithfully lead me on* (Philippians 4:19). *For if I am loved, called, redeemed, His treasured possession* (1 Peter 2:9), *then surely He will not abandon me now.*

Ruth shows us this lens is not only possible, but essential. Even when her closest family member and friend sets off in one direction, she chooses another—and we can too. **We can keep the faith even when others don't.** We can trust God's sovereign perspective over our limited earthly frame of reference. And we can wait out our circumstances, knowing His sov-ereignty and kindness will always mark the end of our story.

Oh, look! Barley season is here, and wouldn't you know it? Ruth *just so happens* to be working in a relative's field—and not just any relative, but a handsome-single-man kind of relative with pockets full of dough AND a reputation of integrity AND faith in the Lord . . . ahem, HELLO MEET-CUTE.

It gets better. This heartthrob struts onto the scene to oversee the operations of his harvest, yet stops dead in his tracks. Spots Ruth across the field (Ruth 2:4-5). They make eye contact, and (although the Bible doesn't *explicitly* state this much) we can assume there was a cinematic crescendo of a symphony in the background, everything turned slow motion, and those cartoon bubble hearts were floating all around.

Of course, being the sensitive, noble hero that marks every good romantic drama, Boaz sees this damsel in distress, orders the other men not to touch her (#shesmine), makes her lunch (AND HE COOKS?), and sends her home with enough barley to make any carb lover's heart soar. Oh, and—as Ruth later tells Naomi—"Boaz even told me to come back and stay with his harvesters until the entire harvest is completed" (2:21). ICING ON THE CAKE.

What are the odds, huh? The luck of the draw? A mere random coincidence?

Hmmm, nope. Not with a God who holds all our times in His hands (Psalm 31:15).

Fast-forward to the end of this fairy tale, and we see a proposal, an engagement, a wedding, and finally, a *SON*. Not that pink confetti at their gender reveal would've been a bummer, but speed up to the New Testament, when Jesus comes on the scene and well, DON'T SKIM OVER THE ANCESTRY. #iknowyoubecauseiknowme

Fine, skip past Matthew 1:1-4, but park it on verse 5, okay? "Salmon was the father of Boaz. . . . Boaz was the father of Obed (whose mother was Ruth)."

NO WAY.

Sure, Ruth and Naomi saw blessing after blessing in their lifetime, but now we see what they simply could not. Not only did Ruth get a family and Naomi receive redeemed standing in society, both with a secure future—but this baby boy would become the grandfather of King David and the great-great-great-great- (technically 41 "greats" belong here, but I'm already over word count) grandfather of Jesus Christ, the Messiah, God incarnate Himself.

How REDEMPTIVE is this story? Yet again, we see how God indeed "is able to do immeasurably more than all we ask or imagine, according to his power that is at work within us" (Ephesians 3:20, NIV).

Before we tie a pretty bow on this chapter, though, pan back to Ruth's M-I-L. While she didn't choose her circumstances, we also see she didn't need to have a story shaded by anger or darkened by bitterness, either. That was what she chose, but P.S. *We don't have to.*

When we find ourselves in the famines of life, we can save ourselves a lot of heartache, hassle, and resentment if we cling to this truth: **His purposes and plan for our lives will *always* prevail** (Proverbs 19:21). As with Ruth, where we are today is *no mistake.* Our God has not misplaced us, and His ways are never arbitrary. Rather, He *always* provides for His people, which means there is *always* a field of grain at the end of our hunger and pain.[2]

It wasn't until things got better that Naomi realized what (she thought) was God's hand against her was actually His hand for her[3]—and this is when our girl started responding to the name Naomi once again. But I repeat: We don't have to wait for our circumstances to change like she did.

We can instead live like Ruth, head held high, absolutely *convinced* that our God is faithful, and He is about to turn our tragedy into triumph—*because that is just what He does.*

> Our God is faithful, and He is about to turn our tragedy into triumph—*because that is just what He does.*

Sometimes we see and hold those redemption stories today, and sometimes they aren't fully revealed until long into the future. But no matter the time frame, the ending is inevitable: God redeems *all* things. He is the God of hope who longs to fill *you* to overflowing with confident hope through the power of the Holy Spirit (Romans 15:13). Will you take Him up on His offer?

Wait out your circumstances in faith, and you too will see God is both sovereign AND kind.

FEAR:

"How can I hope for a good future with my past?"

THE HOW: Before jumping to conclusions, you can recognize you're still living in the middle of your story. No matter what plot twists you face, the end has already been written, God's redemption is assured, and you will someday see Him turn your tragedy into triumph.

BUT WHAT IF THIS LOOKS LIKE THE END? While some seasons come to an end—such as Naomi's marriage—if you're still living and breathing, God's not done with you. Rather, you can be *"certain* that God, who began the good work within [us], will continue his work until it is finally finished" (Philippians 1:6, emphasis added). For God's people, what may look like a dead end is always the setup for a new beginning. Hang on, girl. Holding on to hope *will always* be worth it.

BUT WHAT IF IT'S HARD TO BELIEVE GOD IS KIND? In these moments of doubt, ask yourself, *Am I allowing circumstances to shape my perspective of God? Or allowing God to shape my perspective of circumstances?* God's character will always prevail. In the end, His sovereignty AND loving-kindness will be evident to all. But in the meantime, it's your choice. Choose faith—which means trusting in the unseen—and like Ruth, you won't be disappointed.

IT'S COOL IF MY FAITHFULNESS BENEFITS SOMEONE ELSE DOWN THE ROAD, BUT I'M SORRY . . . WHAT ABOUT ME TODAY? Sigh. You stole my journal, didn't you? Because this is MY EVERY CRY. I know better than anyone how easy it is to live shortsighted (and if we're being honest, to live selfishly). But we're not simply living for our own kingdom, you know? The reality is, our life is but a mist (James 4:14)—but if we dedicate it to God's purposes? The ripple effect lasts for eternity, and the treasure that awaits us in heaven will far outweigh any of today's rewards on earth. Pinkie promise. As much as it goes against the grain #hadto, keep living for God.

Chapter 8

WHAT IF I DON'T KNOW WHAT TO DO?

Jehoshaphat

Ever woken up to something you didn't want and *certainly* didn't choose?

Every Wednesday, a recycling truck makes its way down our street. Pretty standard, right? Well, *it would be* if it came at 9 a.m. or 1 p.m. But our small town's hearty crew wakes up while it is still considered night to folks with a sound mind, and we must be their first stop . . .

At 5:00 a.m.

Of course, waking the baby. You better believe rousing already-sleep-deprived kids.

I mean, it's one thing for their gigantic fork to scrape the ground as they pick up our recycling bins; it's another when you hear a loud KABOOM as it pounds against the back loader. Did I mention metal crashes as the compressor does its thing? Oh, and we can't forget the hydraulics, which lower the bin to the ground with a heavy CLANG.

Coming from years of experience, people. And the icing on the cake: To reverse out of every driveway, an automatic signal sounds *beep, beep, beep.*

That's just one side of the street. A half hour later, they come traipsing back unashamed, unrepentant, and borderline satanic.

All in all, I have yet to find a sound machine, heavy-duty fan, or earplugs to drown out this jolting Wednesday-morning wake-up call, and while I am pro—reduce, reuse, recycle, I gotta admit . . . some weeks, I stand at the top of my driveway tempted to just wheel down the trash and leave the recycling behind.

THERE, I SAID IT.

I'M SORRY.

(CAN I OPT OUT?)

Maybe for you though, the situation is a bit more serious. You woke up to a phone call you'll never forget or an empty bed you expected to be occupied, and as you look at the day ahead, you wonder, *Where do I go from here?*

Whether you're stressed over recycling trucks or your marriage, sleep schedules or the passing of a loved one, it's high time you get to know our hero from 2 Chronicles.

Like an unwelcome alarm, a messenger races into Jehoshaphat's room with some bad news: "A vast army from Edom is marching against you from beyond the Dead Sea. They are already at Hazazon-tamar" (2 Chronicles 20:2).

Whoa, whoa, Jehosha-*who*? I know, it's a little bit of a mouthful, isn't it? Somehow, this guy has flown under the radar in many pastors' sermons, but he is *100 percent* worth following. In the midst of a bad slew of kings, this young buck, at age 35 (currently 35 and still *very much* in my youth, thank you . . .), takes the throne over Judah and this is where we step into the story. While still in our jammies, we look over his shoulder as he scrambles to the window and peers out from behind the blinds.

One army would've been more than enough to handle, but beyond the Moabites, we also see two other armies clanging in their armor. From the looks of it, both the Ammonites and Meunites have joined in the cause, and Jehoshaphat is terrified. I don't want to be a downer, but I would be too . . . *things were not looking good.*

Pause. Flip a chapter back, and the scene before this onslaught might surprise you.

Good ol' Jehosh is on the road, touring from Beersheba down in the south to the hill country of Ephraim up north, and urging all his people at every stop to return to God. Sounds like a pretty noble king, amiright?

But there's more. Beyond just talking to regular old joes, he diligently sets out to appoint judges in each of the fortress cities, as well as raise up priests, all with a specific charge: "You must always act in the fear of the LORD, with faithfulness and an undivided heart" (2 Chronicles 19:9).

Um, can we get some candidates like this on the next election ballot? THEY'D HAVE MY VOTE.

After generations of so much wrong, here we *finally* have a king set on making things right. So what's next? Blessing upon blessing upon blessing? Peace and prosperity? A safe and protected reign? Well, flip over to the next page, and *screeeeeeech*.

Back to Jehoshaphat crumbling under the news of enemy attack.

Hold up, are we missing something? Maybe another story in between?

Nope. Jehoshaphat gets off the tour bus, heads straight for his king-size bed, ready to sprawl out across his silk sheets . . . and the next thing we know, the nations surrounding Judah have declared war, sending our man into a frenzy.

What do *we* do when problems are pressing in on all sides? How do we respond when we're facing enemies we weren't expecting? What's our next move when we feel pushed beyond our limits, stretched beyond belief, way in over our head, and surprised by bad news? Submerged in panic, King Jehoshaphat shows us an example to remember:

1. He scrambles straight into the throne room of God and immediately begs Him for guidance. *round of applause* Most kings would've summoned their top military leaders without delay, raced into strategy meetings pronto, and trusted in the might of their armies to see them through.

Not our guy. Take a look at Jehoshaphat's track record, and the word *seek* continually defines his reign. When King Ahab previously asked for his help to conquer a land, Jehoshaphat's knee-jerk reaction was, "Why, of course! . . . But first let's find out what the Lord says" (2 Chronicles 18:3-4).

Fast-forward to this surprise attack, and we see the same automatic response. Not only does Jehoshaphat seek the Lord in prayer, but he directs all the people of Judah to begin fasting too.

Hang on a minute—command a whole nation to give up their queso and mochas for the day, and come together to pray instead? The nerve! The audacity! To be so forward and bold and impose his beliefs on others!

Yeah . . . don't you just love the guy?

He knew what a weapon prayer is, yet all too often prayer can be our last line of defense, can't it? You've heard it too—when we're at our wits' end, out of ideas, and have done all we could, we've mistakenly dropped this line one too many times: "Well, I guess all we can do now is pray." Imagine God hearing that come out of our mouths.[1] The Lord over all things, who holds all power in heaven and on earth, waiting at the ready to help His people, able to rain manna down from heaven and move mountains, empower us through the Holy Spirit, and still do miracles among us today . . . listening to that statement spoken as if it's an insufficient consolation. A meager offering. Something to shrug our shoulders about. As if we long for more.

Jehoshaphat undoubtedly knew what we fail to remember: Because we have inexhaustible access to the Lord Almighty Himself and prayer is *all it takes to get to Him*, this direct line of communication we've been given should never be our last resort but always our "first line of offense."[2]

"Shhhh!"

I'M SORRY, did someone just *shush* us? How *rude*. Who do they think—

Oh. Jehoshaphat is praying. No better than my 10-year-old self chatting it up in the back row. Old habits die hard, y'all. Let's bow our heads (and zip our lips) to join him: "O LORD, God of our ancestors, you alone are the God who is in heaven. You are ruler of all the kingdoms of the earth. You are powerful and mighty; no one can stand against you!" (2 Chronicles 20:6).

2. While some may wait until they see an answer to their prayer before praising God, Jehoshaphat shows us a better way.

Even when our enemies are getting closer, time is running out, and nothing seems to be changing, we can still raise our voice to our faithful God. Even when that relationship continues to crumble, our health takes one step back, and our spouse feels just as cold as yesterday, we still have every reason to sing His praises.

> Even when nothing seems to be changing, we can still raise our voice to our faithful God.

Just like the barren woman in Isaiah 54 was still commanded by the Lord to break out into a loud and joyful song, we can belt out a hallelujah too—simply because we know who our God is and that He alone holds the final word. Our enemy is out to steal, kill, and destroy, sure— but that does NOT mean we have to let him steal, kill, or destroy our song. Instead of wallowing over uncertainty and allowing bad news to paralyze us, we can decide to trust that God must know what He's doing and SING.

That's what our guy did. Jehoshaphat basically went live on Instagram with his thousands of followers as he stood before the entire community of Judah and Jerusalem with a prayer to pray and a message to declare: "We can cry out to you to save us, and you will hear us and rescue us. . . . O our God, won't you stop them? We are powerless against this mighty army that is about to attack us. We do not know what to do, but we are looking to you for help" (2 Chronicles 20:9, 12).

Even when we don't know what to do, we don't have to fear. Literally just texted Ty, "WHAT IF THIS IS A BRAIN TUMOR? I'M SO SCARED." So um, again . . . I'm preaching to myself here too. But our powerlessness is never the final nail in the coffin, and our instability does not have the capability to bring the house down either. That's just giving ourselves and what little control we have *way* too much credit.

No, true strength and wisdom is radiating from King Jehoshaphat here at the Temple of God as he stands in the front of the courtyard before his people—purely on the ground of God's faithfulness. And this can be true of us, too.

When no options are left, we've reached a dead end, and we can't quite figure out our next step, we can immediately seek God, recruit others to pray, declare His goodness to anyone who will listen, and stay put in the presence of the Lord with eyes fixed on Him, declaring, "He alone is my refuge, my place of safety; he is my God, and I trust him" (Psalm 91:2).

3. Lastly, Jehoshaphat and His people waited expectantly. After this prayer, all the men of Judah and their wives and children stood there with eyes fixed to the heavens and—I'm not kidding you—*waited.*

Literally.

Anyone else have to wait around at the doctor's office? From our pediatrician to my oncologist, there I sit in the lobby for minutes on end as if I didn't have a time slot assigned to my name, and you better believe I alwaaays peek down the hallway like clockwork every five minutes to see if the nurse is coming. Sometimes every three minutes.

Well, probably more like one.

But I know the nurse is coming. I've never sat in the waiting room unsure if I'll have to walk back out that day unseen and sent home without help. No, eventually, in due time, I *know* I'll see the doctor.

In the same way, these people of God were *sure* help was coming. They didn't know when or how, but eventually, in due time, they knew God was on the way.

So there, in the lobby of life, they stood and waited patiently for their appointment to come. "You could have heard the sound even of the wind among the trees at the time, for they were as hushed and as quiet as you were just now" (Spurgeon).[3] Side note: How did they teach their children the art of silence? I DON'T SEE THAT IN THE TEXT, and I feel like that's a big miss. MOMS AROUND THE WORLD WOULD'VE LIKED TO KNOW.

Breaking through the stillness, "the Spirit of the LORD came upon one of the men standing there. . . . He said, 'Listen, all you people of Judah and Jerusalem! Listen, King Jehoshaphat! This is what the LORD says: Do not be afraid! Don't be discouraged by this mighty army, for the battle is not yours, but God's. Tomorrow, march out against them. . . . But you will not even need to fight. Take your positions; then stand still and watch the LORD's victory. He is with you. . . . Do not be afraid or discouraged. Go out against them tomorrow, for the LORD is with you!'" (2 Chronicles 20:14-17).

Gotta love a man who excessively uses exclamation points. I thought it was just us millennials who retrace our emails and substitute half our exclamation points (!!!) with periods to look just *a tad* more composed and, well—sane. SOLIDARITY, BROTHER!!!

I'm unsure exactly how long the moms were able to enjoy some peace and quiet before this answer came, and I'm not totally sure how long you'll have to wait for your answer either. But if you wait on the Lord, girlfriend, He will not leave you hanging. We so often rush to get our problems answered, solved, fulfilled—but this waiting-on-the-Lord thing seems to be a call on every believer, from David in the Psalms, to

Jeremiah in Lamentations, to Isaiah, Hosea, and Micah, as well as here with Jehoshaphat.

Feels like a hate crime, I know, but we've got to understand waiting in this context was never intended to be passive. It doesn't mean twiddling our thumbs, kicking back on the couch, or huddling in our room until the Rapture hits.

No, God wants us to take a posture of leaning forward on the edge of our seat *knowing* something's about to go down. Confident He *will* answer. Certain He's on the move *NOW*.

We also see the people of Judah weren't expected to keep chilling in Jerusalem and remain in prayer. No, God commanded them to move this party over to the battlefield, and like in the passage, He's directing us to roll up our sleeves and show up to our war zone too. Waiting expectantly often involves marching back into the circumstances of our lives, taking the position of wife, employee, mom, or friend, and preparing to go face-to-face with our enemies as well.

> Waiting expectantly often involves marching back into the circumstances of our lives.

But when we do, we know we're not being sent out as defenseless, vulnerable sitting ducks. Rather, we're God's people, walking boldly with faith-filled deliberation, believing fully in His promises, and standing firm on the battleground with the backing of none other than the Lord Almighty Himself. More than the watchmen wait for the morning, completely sure the sun will rise, so we live our lives waiting confidently on the Lord to deliver us (Psalm 130:5-6).

Now Jehoshaphat could've sent his best warriors to the front lines, but who do we see assuming the position? Walking with sure steps to the forefront? Boldly occupying the most dangerous post? *Worshipers* armed with . . . get this . . . *a song of praise.* "Give thanks to the LORD; his faithful love endures forever!" (2 Chronicles 20:21).

That's . . . new. Not the most intimidating military strategy I've heard of, but maybe they weren't going for threatening? Perhaps they believed the weapon of praise was more powerful than any sword or chariot could ever be. We can take up the same arms with the same sure confidence today too.

Believe you me, I've spent many evenings that started out with crying in complete overwhelm upstairs in my bedroom while folding laundry. But the nights that ended with a calm spirit and peace (even though that pile of mismatched socks remained)? I cranked my worship playlist on loud, lifted my voice, and saw for myself how God is "enthroned on the praises of Israel" (Psalm 22:3). May we never underrate or forget how He inhabits the praise of His people.

Oh man, get out your iPhone and swipe left to launch the camera app—you're gonna wanna get this on video: "At the very moment they began to sing and give praise, the Lord caused the armies of Ammon, Moab, and Mount Seir to start fighting among themselves. . . . So when the army of Judah arrived at the lookout point in the wilderness, all they saw were dead bodies lying on the ground as far as they could see. Not a single one of the enemy had escaped" (2 Chronicles 20:22, 24).

Are we getting this? God's people were trudging an uphill climb, unsure what they'd see when they got to the top, but expecting the horde of their enemies nevertheless. Yet when they finally came over the rise, instead of fighting as they were bracing themselves to do, these children of God found the battle *already won*. God had taken care of the fight, and all that was left for them to do was to go out and pick up the plunder.

Imagine the scene: A whole fleet of men bent over to collect equipment left behind. Some are scooping up clothing, while others gather valuables. But all around, everyone is smiling ear to ear, amazed at the Lord's provision, exclaiming in awe as they're holding the evidence of His promise fulfilled in their hands. After three full days of carting home the spoils, God's people did what God's people should always do. They came together and thanked their faithful God (and P.S. threw an exuberant parade, which we in the Midwest know is really the only rightful way to celebrate—with a whole fleet of marching bands if possible).

"When all the surrounding kingdoms heard that the LORD himself had fought against the enemies of Israel, the fear of God came over them. So Jehoshaphat's kingdom was at peace, for his God had given him rest on every side" (2 Chronicles 20:29-30).

Don't miss that: Where once Jehoshaphat felt *literally pressed on every side* of Judah, God came through and saved the day, giving him *rest on every side*.

Do you want rest? To live in peace? To have victory over your 99 problems? His invitation still stands: "Come to me, all of you who are weary and carry heavy burdens, and I will give you rest" (Matthew 11:28).

Go to your God, pick up your arms in praise, and see for yourself how He indeed is still mighty to save.

FEAR:

"What if I don't know what to do?"

THE HOW: Pray immediately, declare God's greatness, and surrender with the declaration "God, I don't know what to do, but my eyes are on you." Then wait expectantly. God is *certainly* on the move.

HOW DO I MAKE PRAYER MY FIRST INSTINCT INSTEAD OF MY LAST RESORT WHEN I'VE BEEN BURNED BY UNANSWERED PRAYER IN THE PAST? Girl, just you wait until chapter 11. We're GETTING TO IT soon, but here's a sneak peek: Prayer is more than just demanding what you want from God. It's communicating with the Lord Almighty! The Savior of your soul! He wants to transform you from your old sinful self into His glorious image (2 Corinthians 3:18)! Just like with your spouse, kids, or friends, spending time together is *important* and praying builds that relationship with Him. Also, while, yes, God tells you to ASK because He loves to give good gifts to His children (Matthew 7:11), if you trust His character, His "no" still has goodness written all over it. So in the words of Jesus, "Keep on asking . . . keep on seeking . . . keep on knocking. . . . If you sinful people know how to give good gifts to your children, how much more will your heavenly Father give the Holy Spirit to those who ask him" (Luke 11:9, 13).

WHAT IF I'M HAVING A HARD TIME PRAISING GOD EVEN THOUGH I KNOW I SHOULD? If all God did was send His one and only Son to die a painful death on your behalf, so you could be forgiven, freed from sin, and saved for all eternity? Well, that alone would be enough to fill your days with song. So if your circumstances are difficult, try to leave them at the door and praise God for *who He is and what He's already done.*

HOW CAN I WAIT EXPECTANTLY WHEN OTHERS HAVE FACED MY SAME TRIAL AND IT TOOK THEM DOWN? You really want to skip to chapter 11, don't you? DON'T, THOUGH, OKAY? It's coming! In the meantime, remind yourself that you're not waiting on a certain answered prayer—but pray with the Psalmist, "I wait for the LORD, my whole being waits, and in his word I put my hope" (Psalm 130:5, NIV). Since "no one who hopes in [God] will ever be put to shame" (Psalm 25:3, NIV), fix your focus not on what you want, but on the Lord your God.

Chapter 9

WHICH VOICE SHOULD I LISTEN TO?

Caleb

Iread an article called "Everything Gives You Cancer."[1]

It was just as encouraging as it sounds.

I mean, sure, I could've guessed drinking artificial flavors, taking deep breaths of petroleum, and basking hours upon hours in the blazing sun might put us in the red zone. But did you know vegetables and fruit considered healthy and good for you—say, broccoli, apples, onions, and oranges—actually contain acetaldehyde (which is, *of course*, a known human carcinogen)?

I KNOW.

"Okay, well, I'll just order a mixed salad of lettuce, kale, and celery for lunch. Nothing dangerous about a bowl of fresh greens, right?" HA, think again! Those green superstars all contain nitrates, which—I hate to break the news—can be converted to carcinogenic compounds. While, yes, this choice may be better than that greasy cheeseburger your daredevil of a friend is chomping into across the table, you're still reckless, girlfriend! Living life on the wild side along with Popeye.

111

"This is why we buy organic." LOL. GOOD ONE. Almost had me there! The label "organic" doesn't mean pesticide-free though! In fact, the US Department of Agriculture actually gives a long list of permissible pesticides, which—did you not know? It's the *pesticides* that can kill you!

"I'll just stick with water, then . . ." Cue the buzzer! WRONG CHOICE. Did you know there are some carcinogens *specific* to tap water? It's basically one big cesspool, so don't you DAAARE turn your faucet on and expect to live. Wait, YOU ALREADY GAVE THIS TO YOUR CHILDREN? (Psst, me too.)

Was this not the most stressful page you've ever read in your entire life? *Tell me about it.* It was not a very good article to read home alone with nothing but poison in my refrigerator. 0/10, do not recommend.

But here's my point: There are so many voices telling us the healthiest, best diet to follow—Whole30 or Paleo, keto or low-carb, counting macros or focusing on just eating whole foods—and they all conflict. While one generation was told to avoid bacon grease, the next drips it all over their breakfast plate. Remember growing up on bologna, white bread, and Kraft singles? Talk about a daily dose of artificial ingredients . . . but WHO KNEW? No one at the time! (Except your friend's crunchy mom who never had sugary cereal in the pantry and refused to put jam on her wheat peanut butter sandwiches. But did her kids not raid the rest of our pantries like no tomorrow? LOL, can't win 'em all, Karen. #butreallywhoskaren)

And that's just our health, right? Around the clock, we hear opposing stories on the news, contrary reports on which medicines are (or are not) safe, clashing opinions on which form of education is best for our children—and even within the church, we're faced with inconsistent interpretations of Scripture that leave us wondering . . .

WHO IS RIGHT?

How do we know what's *true*?

Ultimately, what are we going to believe?

(And is Miracle Whip out too?)

Picture the Israelites in Numbers 13. They've just been rescued from slavery in Egypt, witnessed the Red Sea part before their own eyes, turned around to watch God wipe out their enemies, and now anxiously await their grand entrance into the Promised Land. TIME TO GO HOME, BABY!

It's a highly anticipated moment to say the least. All they need now is the green light to enter in, so a handful of willing men were sent like secret agents to scope out the territory.

A commotion breaks out: "THEY'RE BACK." Women scoop up their children, men race to the meeting spot in the wilderness of Paran, and the whole community buzzes with excitement. "WHAT WILL THE SPIES SAY? CAN WE GO NOW? I CAN ONLY HANDLE SO MANY MORE 'ARE WE THERE YETS'!"

But the closer we get to the 12 spies, the more we notice their demeanor. A couple of them match our bubbling excitement—they have a skip to their step and a big ol' grin splashed across their faces. Others are walking back slowly, eyes down with furrowed brows.

What could it all mean? Everything seems to be in slow motion, but as soon as the last stragglers finally get to the gathering place, the spies fess up and give the play-by-play of their 40-day excursion into Canaan.

The men with somber faces take the mic first, and their tone is very grave. "We entered the land you sent us to explore, and it is indeed a bountiful country—a land flowing with milk and honey. . . . But the people living there are powerful, and their towns are large and fortified. We even saw giants there!" (Numbers 13:27-28).

Gasps.

Cries.

With blood draining from their faces, everyone's shoulders slump. Hands start trembling, and the crowd looks around at each other with wild panic.

Like the beginning of a ping-pong match, Caleb speaks up on the other side. He's standing next to another dude, jumping up and down, waving his hands, trying to get the people to SIMMER DOWN. "Let's go at once to take the land. . . . We can certainly conquer it!" (13:30).

"Are you kidding me?" Our eyes bounce back to the grim-faced majority. "Did you not just see what we saw? We can't go up against them! They are stronger than us! The land we traveled through and explored will devour *anyone* who goes to live there. All the people we saw were huge. I repeat: We even saw giants there!" (see Numbers 13:31-33).

Like a great chorus, *the whole community* begins bawling and wailing aloud (14:1). From the most stoic of men who reject all emotion to the most introverted of women who normally keep their cards close to their chests, everyone breaks down sobbing, reaching for a tissue.

The only people who stand apart from the uproar are two of the original spies: Caleb and Joshua. These men blink hard, shocked at the swift turn of events.

Rewind to the beginning of Numbers 13, and we see God was the One who instigated this whole scouting mission in the first place. "The LORD now said to Moses, 'Send out men to explore the land of Canaan, *the land I am giving to the Israelites*'" (13:1-2, emphasis added).

Wait a second. This was already a done deal? God had already spoken and promised this land overflowing with milk and honey was theirs *for the taking*? All the Israelites had to do was go in, look around at the gift that was now rightfully theirs, and come back in awe over all that God had provided?

Exactly, and Caleb and Joshua understood the assignment. They were men of faith, who took their God at His Word. When they came back from their 40-day expedition, they were more sure than ever that God had given the green light for them to finally enter their home, roll out the welcome mats, and settle in. Ready to see your Dream Home Pinterest board come to life? YOU GOT IT.

The two of them make a last-ditch effort to reel God's people back in: "The land we traveled through and explored is a wonderful land! And if the LORD is pleased with us, he will bring us safely into that land and give it to us. It is a rich land flowing with milk and honey. Do not rebel against the LORD, and don't be afraid of the people of the land. They are only helpless prey to us! They have no protection, but the LORD is with us! Don't be afraid of them!" (14:7-9).

Notice: All the spies came back with the same details in their scouting report:

1. **The land was lavish, abundant, plentiful**—overflowing with milk, honey, good soil, and juicy fruit. To prove it, the spies cut down one branch with a single cluster of grapes, and it was "so large that it took two of them to carry it on a pole between them!" (Numbers 13:23). *A far cry from my Aldi bag of seedless reds.*

2. **The people living there were giants, and their walls were large and fortified.** The height difference was a fact—Caleb didn't disagree. In their own power, the Israelites certainly would not defeat these enemies.

Same details up to this point, but when opinions and feelings come into play, we hear *far different conclusions*:

The Majority: We can't attack those people! That land swallows people whole! "Next to them we felt like grasshoppers, and that's what they thought, too!" (13:33).

Except, wait . . . no, they didn't.

No actual conversation happened between the giants and the spies about their size and who they thought was bigger.[2] *(That would kind of defeat the whole stay-undercover, remain-covert kind of thing, you know?)*

No, this was assumed, then it was spoken, and ultimately, this "bad report" spread throughout the Israelite camp (13:32). Without even giving a second thought to what God had said, the people succumbed to their fear and "cried all night" (14:1).

For the record, there was no need to pull an all-nighter and lose sleep over this. To state the obvious, it was called the Promised Land because the land was *already promised to them*. But fear has a way of obscuring sense, and it always dismantles faith.

So I gotta ask, what things are *we* losing sleep over? What's keeping us up at night? What are we so worked up about that it's caused us to drench our pillow with tears and roll out of bed in the morning with bloodshot eyes?

Related: What has God already promised us?

Personally, I can get so scared of dying young when my kids are little and leaving them motherless. How would they cope? Would they be okay? Who would take care of them when they desperately need *me*? (Besides, you know, Ty. LOL)

And sure, it's only right and natural to want to be around for our kids as they navigate middle school, consider which college to attend, get ready for their wedding day, and have babies of their own. Nothing wrong with wanting to be the first call they make when they're mad at their boss or confused about something in the Bible. And the good Lord knows *somebody* needs to lead our kids back to reason when crop tops regretfully circle back again.

But the truth is: I cannot add a single hour to my life by worrying (Luke 12:25), so why do I fret as if I can? God already stated through Job that the length of my life has been decided: "You know how many months we will live, and we are not given a minute longer" (14:5). So why do I waste the time I have to live stressing over the time I'm set to die?

Furthermore, who will take care of my kids? Well . . . the Lord Almighty—that's who. If I'm not here to give them guidance on where to go to college (P.S. No thought needed, Andersons: Our blood runs purple and gold #UNWSP), who will? The Wonderful Counselor—that's who. And if I'm not here to be their helping hand while they raise *their* kids and navigate *their* careers and honor *their* marriages, well then, who in the world will? The Helper, the Holy Spirit, Jesus Christ, their

Savior will. God *will* be faithful to carry His work to completion in our lives AND in our kids', too.

What about you?

Maybe you're exhausted at work, at home, or in your marriage, and you've been telling yourself, *I'm tired. This is too hard. This is as good as it gets.*

Well, just to be clear—*you're* telling yourself that. God didn't say that. Rather, He explicitly said, "Come to me, all of you who are weary and carry heavy burdens, and I will give you rest" (Matthew 11:28) and "[You] can do everything through Christ, who gives [you] strength" (Philippians 4:13).

Others of us are lonely, and in the darkest of nights when we're huddled in our beds, we're thinking, *Everyone has let me down. No one gets me.* But let's get this straight—that's not what God says. In fact, He left no wiggle room, but definitely said He "will neither fail you nor abandon you" (Deuteronomy 31:6), so how can we say we're alone when He is right there?

A whole bunch of us have experienced something that sucked the air right out of us—along with all the hope in us too. In its wake, we're shaking our heads, already resolved in defeat, *All hope is lost. This is too much for me to handle. There's no way to rebound from this.* Well, yes, we can say that, but if we want to listen to what God says, we'll hear quite the opposite. "No one who trusts in [Him] will ever be disgraced" (Psalm 25:3). "God causes everything to work together for the good of those who love [Him] and are called according to his purpose" (Romans 8:28). And He promises that He will restore every lost thing (Joel 2:25).

> Is all hope lost? Not when you know the Hope of the world.

So is all hope lost? Nope, not when you know the Hope of the world.

Yet here on earth, there will always be voices countering God's Word. Some of those murmurs belong to us—and we then have every opportunity to camp out on those thoughts all day long. Other times, those rumors are vocalized by people around us.

Whose voice will you listen to?

Caleb is all ears on what the Lord has to say: "If God says He will give us the land, then He'll give us the land. They may be mighty, and those giants may be bigger than us—but compared to our God? They are only helpless prey, and *we'll eat them for lunch*! Against our God? They have no protection. We have all we need going for us because the Lord Almighty is on our side. Do not be afraid of them!" (see Numbers 14:7-9).

Say it louder for the people in the back? "DO NOT BE AFRAID OF THEM."

Caleb unlocks the question we need to ask ourselves: **Who are you comparing your plight to?** Your disadvantage or God's advantage? Your wavering strength or God's firm hand over your life? Your ability (or lack thereof) to protect or the faithfulness of God's sheltering wings (Psalm 91)? Your shaky power to provide or the sure promise from your God that He will meet all your needs according to the riches of His glory in Christ Jesus (Philippians 4:19)?

Perspective matters—will we focus on ourselves or focus on God?

POP QUIZ (I know, sorry, I hated those too, but I gotta be real. It's kinda fun being the one to dish it out): Who did the Israelites listen to? Which words did their leaders, Moses and Aaron, hang on to? Which perspective won out?

Answer: The supposedly realistic outlook of the majority.

Here we witness one of the saddest decisions in human history: *Millions of people* were influenced by the opinions of only *10* fearful individuals.

The same people who witnessed the miracles of the Red Sea parting, manna dropping from the heavens, and a pillar of fire and cloud leading them by day and night forfeited what God had already set aside for them . . . because fear is contagious and can easily be masked as the more reasonable option.

Giants don't just come in the form of Anak's descendants. There are more walls in the world than Jericho's, and we've seen our own set of Exodus miracles. So when we face obstacles today and come up against a brick wall in our own lives, it's wise to pause and call it out: Who's influencing *us*? Which voices are *we* taking into serious consideration? Are they from God . . . or not?

Other voices will convince you to bow out in fear; God's voice will *always* call you to rise up in faith.

We will all *feel* fear, but IMPORTANT CLARIFICATION and the HOW behind this Bible hero's story: **God didn't say don't *feel* afraid. He just said don't *be*** (Deuteronomy 31:8). This means:

1. **We can feel fear**, dwell on the worst-case scenario, and assume it will happen. We can let it consume us, dictate our actions, and spread like a bad report throughout our mind and life.

OR

2. **We can feel fear**, take that panicky thought captive, and make it obedient to Christ (2 Corinthians 10:5) in a way that says, "Yeah, this giant IS huge . . . but my God is bigger." We can move forward into the Promised Land—the free, abundant life Jesus came to give—that very next moment.

The next step is yours to take. Which pathway will you choose?

The Israelites picked the first option, and God did not hide how He felt about that. "Not one of these people will ever enter that land. They have all seen my glorious presence and the miraculous signs I performed both in Egypt and in the wilderness, but again and again they have tested me **by refusing to listen to my voice**" (Numbers 14:22, emphasis added).

Here is a staggering truth I'm challenged with *on the daily*: Listening to fear is in turn dismissing the voice of God.

> Listening to fear is in turn dismissing the voice of God.

I hate that. Don't you? But I've learned the hard way that if we don't call out fear for what it is—a spirit not given from God (2 Timothy 1:7)—then we'll only reason with it, tolerate it, and someday roll over and accept it. By doing just that and listening to another voice above God's, the Israelites didn't seize the territory God set aside for them and (the kicker) the land God *wanted to give them.*

Don't do the same and forfeit the land that rightfully belongs to you and the place ahead that God longs to give you.

Jesus already paid for us to have a free, abundant life. The moment we put our faith in Him, *it's ours for the taking.* So, girlfriend, let's take it! Whenever we face giants in our health, relationships, job, or finances? Whenever the challenges ahead feel far greater than we can handle, the walls far bigger than our heart can take? And whenever the next step seems like way more work than we even think we have left in us?

This is our time. This is the moment of truth. Will we learn from the Israelites' mistake and choose faith over fear? Or will we let fear pull us into the wilderness instead?

I'm gonna shoot straight with you: The stakes are high, and it matters what you decide. If it didn't, the Israelites would've entered the Promised Land at this point regardless—so the difference is between being stuck in the wilderness, always looking off into the horizon at a land you desperately want but *voluntarily surrendered,* or stepping foot into the Promised Land, gulping down cups of milk and honey, and resting in God's provision and good plan.

P.S. Thanks to Jesus, it's never too late. The voice you entertained yesterday can be squelched today. The fear you gave in to a minute ago can be submitted to God in faith right now.

So make your decision (yeah, like this very second) because if we wait to make up our mind until we're cowering in the shadows of the giants towering over us, our fate won't look so different from these

WHICH VOICE SHOULD I LISTEN TO?

Israelites'. But if we choose our allegiance now, ahead of time, our footsteps will have the same imprint as Caleb's. Repeat after me:

> I will keep moving forward in faith even when my hands are shaking and I don't know how it's going to pan out. Because I *do know* my God has already gone before me, He *will* fight my battles, He *will* use ALL THINGS for my good and His glory, and He knows how my giants are going to come down.

GOODNESS GRACIOUS, did you just hear yourself? If I didn't know any better, I'd say you sounded a whole lot like our man Caleb! Way to go, girlfriend! Go ahead and pack your bags, because it's clearly time to put this forlorn place behind us and move ahead, ~~freely~~, into our own Promised Land.

FEAR:

"Which voice should I listen to?"

THE HOW: God didn't say don't *feel* afraid; He just said don't *be*. The voice to reject will tell you that you have every reason to panic, doubt God's promises, and bow out in fear. In direct contrast, God will always remind you of His sure promises and call you to rise up in faith.

STRENGTH IN NUMBERS! WHAT IF THE MAJORITY OPINION LEANS ONE WAY? Just because more people agree with one opinion does not make it true. A small minority of the Israelite spies—just Caleb and Joshua—were telling the truth, and they were right! Don't forget, "narrow [is] the road that leads to life" (Matthew 7:14, NIV).

HOW DO I KNOW WHAT GOD HAS PROMISED ME? The Bible, girlfriend. It's chock-full of promises: God will never leave us, He will always provide a way out of every temptation so we can endure it (1 Corinthians 10:13), and if you ask Him for wisdom, He will give generously without finding fault (James 1:5). The more you familiarize yourself with the pages of God's Word, the more clearly you will hear His voice.

WHAT IF I'M STILL HAVING A HARD TIME DISTINGUISHING WHICH VOICE IS COMMUNICATING GOD'S TRUTH? Ask yourself: What is being said about God? In the scouting report of the majority, not once did they mention God. Not once did they consider what God had to say about their plight, and not once did they mention His presence, power, or promises. Yet skim through Caleb's account, and he compares everything to God—referring to what God has said, what God can do, and how God assured His presence. Whatever you face, whatever you're considering, whatever you're up against, filter every thought and voice through this question: What does God say about this situation, and in light of that, how must I view it? P.S. We can safely assume whatever God is asking of us and wherever He's sending us, like with Caleb, **faith will be a requirement**.

Chapter 10

WHAT IF GOD'S PROMISES DON'T LINE UP WITH MY REALITY?

Joshua

Have you hit a wall too?

You've clocked into the same dead-end job for years now. With no sign of change on the horizon, you can't help but wonder, *Is this all there is for me?*

Maybe you've tried *so many things* to address your child's behavioral issues, but they only seem to be getting worse and worse (and worse). At the end of the day, the frustration brims over, and you just shake your head. *Is it going to be this bad FOREVER?*

Or, more than anything, it's just one particular relationship. While you've done all that *you* can do (**applause emoji**), *they* don't seem to care or put in any effort to make amends themselves (**side-eye emoji**). You're about ready to throw in the towel. I mean, what more are you supposed to do when they don't even *TRY?*

Name your wall. As you've surveyed the scene, scanning up, down, and all around—looking for the silver lining or even a window slightly cracked open—hope has been slipping away. No matter the details, this obstacle is too great, too hard, too insurmountable, and it seems impossible to get around.

PERFECT. Remember the guy who stood beside Caleb as they gave a rundown of their scouting report? Yeah, the one *so confident* in God's plan to give them the land overflowing with milk and honey? The brother who wasn't JOSHING AROUND about facing the giants and seizing their Promised Land? Ty's dad jokes are rubbing off on me.

You got it! We were there when Joshua had every ounce of faith to possess the Promised Land the *first* time around but was forced to leave his dream behind and subjected to life in the wilderness—not as a result of *his* disobedience, mind you, but because of the lack of faith that paralyzed the rest of God's people. TALK ABOUT ANNOYING RELATIVES. Toxic friends! Relationship drama!

While we realize it would only be natural for Joshua to grumble against the Lord, hold a grudge against his peers, and sink into a "woe is me" black hole, we see that decade after decade, Joshua did no such thing. He held on to faith as a young thirtysomething—trusting in God's prevailing justice and care—and fast-forward to now, we watch as this seventysomething hero, still standing strong in faith, finally gets to witness the harvest of his persistence.

I have to ask . . . HOW IS THERE NO WRITTEN RECORD OF A WIFE AT THIS POINT? Was he the *true* first Bachelor in Paradise? Too far? I wondered . . .

Back to Joshua. With fists clenched, we can't help but scream on the inside and strain forward like an excited racehorse because God gave the go-ahead! After 40 long years of being held back in the wilderness, our guy's dream is *finally* coming true. It's time to enter the Promised Land, and we get to march alongside him!

WOO-HOO.

Except . . . one (minor) problem: Instead of the gate swinging wide open with a clear path paved before us, we come face-to-face with a stationary wall. Well, technically, *walls* that were known to be impenetrable for a reason. The outside fortification stood 11 feet high and 14 feet wide; then to heap on the intimidation, a stone slope angled "upward at 35 degrees for 35 feet, where it joined massive stone walls that towered even higher."[1] This created the illusion of a fortified city nearly 10 stories in height from ground level.[2]

It's here, as we look up at these gates securely barred and the unconquerable city of Jericho protected behind it, that we hear "the LORD [say] to Joshua, 'See, I have delivered Jericho into your hands, along with its king and its fighting men'" (Joshua 6:2, NIV).

"See"?

I've had LASIK, and I don't mean to brag, but my vision isn't just 20/20 . . . your girl has 20/15. *Blowing onto my nails* YOU READ THAT RIGHT. But as I'm standing next to Josh, all I see is still that great big wall. Sure, their king and fighting men are probably *behind* it, but they're not walking out with hands up in surrender. So . . . sorry, God, but all due respect . . . could you point again? Maybe this time, gimme something I can actually see with my (overachieving) eyesight?

That's what we want, right? We'd like to *see* the positive pregnancy test, the clear scans, and the date on the calendar when we'll just so happen to cross paths with our future spouse. *I PROMISE I'LL ACT SURPRISED, GOD. Move forward with boldness and confidence! Give you all the glory and honor and praise!*

Except "faith is . . . the certainty of what we do not see" (Hebrews 11:1, BSB), so that would mean having assurance in the seen isn't faith . . . like, at all.

WELL, THAT'S JUST ANNOYING.

I know. Choosing faith is often terribly inconvenient and downright challenging, but it's also what we signed up for with the whole serving-an-unseen-God thing, you know?

> Choosing faith is often terribly inconvenient and downright challenging, but it's also what we signed up for.

The path to follow is found in the footsteps of Noah *who by faith* "built a large boat to save his family from the flood" when there was no rainfall in the seven-day forecast; Abraham *who by faith* "obeyed when God called him to leave home" and go to some unknown land; and Sarah *who by faith* "was able to have a child, though she was barren and was too old" (Hebrews 11:7, 8, 11). These men and women believed their reality was more than what meets the eye, and this call is no different than what God expects from us today.

Swing back to the Israelites twiddling their thumbs. What did God say again? Oh yeah, "I have *delivered* Jericho into your hands" (Joshua 6:2, NIV, emphasis added), like *past tense.*

As a mom, I know the importance of proper verb tense. "I'm going to poop, I'm pooping, and I pooped" are all very different situations that compel very different reactions—a quick sprint to the bathroom or a hose-down in the shower.

So I can imagine the Israelites scratching their heads to this. With Jericho's people safely tucked inside those walls, I can't help but join in their confusion too. "Correct us if we're wrong, but we're still on this side of the fence? Maybe a minor detail, but we need to be, you know, *on the other side.*"

But our God doesn't misspeak. He spoke in past tense for a reason. In fact, if we rewind a bit, we'll read God already gave this assurance—"I'll give you the land"—to His people *14 different times.* So in His eyes? **Jericho's defeat was as good as done.**[3]

Pause. We aren't that different from the Israelites, are we? There are things God has told *us* over and over again in His Word—past tense, as if these promises have already come to pass:

- **"We are more than conquerors through him who loved us"** (Romans 8:37, NIV). More than *conquerors*? I can barely tackle HALF my to-do list today. My boss and clients walk all over me. Last time I checked, my health was failing. Oh, and I've been overruled by the opinions of my kids' friends, and the dog stole my side of the bed too. But overwhelming victory is *mine*? Pardon me, but . . . I just grunted. #unladylikeiknow

- **"We know that in all things God works for the good of those who love him"** (Romans 8:28, NIV). We *know*? Um, this kind of seems like a wrong assumption—because I actually *do not* know. From what I can see, none of what's going on in my life is good. The doctor doesn't think so. My lawyer said it doesn't look promising. My employees are starting to lose heart, and my family has already given up.
- **"Anyone who belongs to Christ has become a new person. The old life is gone; a new life has begun!"** (2 Corinthians 5:17). Wait a second, the old life is gone? Finished? Behind us? Then why do I still lose it with my kids? Obsess over what I don't have on Amazon? Rage on the freeway when someone cuts me off and then turn worship music on like NBD? If the old life is truly *gone*, then . . . why do I still sin?

When we take a step back and inspect these walls, it's easy to wonder, *How in the world is this going to work out? How could these sturdy bricks ever come down? How could God* possibly *use this for my good? What if God's promises don't line up with my reality?*

Important: While we can't read their minds, nowhere is it recorded that the Israelites actually voiced any hesitation, fear, or doubt. Even more surprising, the Lord assures Joshua the walls are coming down after seven days, but when Joshua turns around to his fighting men, he doesn't relay the entire message. He commands his soldiers to march and the priests to blow their horns and everyone to zip their lips until they could twist and shout, *but he left out the whole timeline bit.*

Do you love a good countdown as much as I do? Like, tell me I have to plank for thirty seconds (but really, don't you dare); and the only way I push through is watching the clock BECAUSE I KNOW the exact millisecond I can drop down (and I will collapse not a moment later . . . if not a touch earlier). But tell me to plank, with no end in sight? LOL. ROFL. SMH. NTY.*

I have so many questions, but here's the top two:

1. **Why would Joshua omit the most motivating part?**
2. **How and why did the Israelites keep their mouths shut?** These were fighting men READY TO GO, but all they're charged to do is take a power walk around the block? Excuse me, *what*?

Don't forget who we're talking about here, though: Joshua, for one, learned the hard way that not everyone can be trusted with all the details. If there's a chance they're going to waver in faith, which in turn could influence *others* to waver in faith, nah. Hard pass.

Not only that, but these men and women were the children raised in the wilderness because of their parents' skepticism. For much of their lives, they had a front-row seat to see for themselves the consequences of distrusting God, and worse yet, they had to hang tight in no-man's-land until every single one of that generation died off. (Can you even imagine being the last one standing? Like "no rush, Aunt Judy, but hundreds of thousands of us are just *kinda* waiting on you . . . but TAKE YOUR TIME. Live, laugh, love!")

These Israelites were a different breed than the ones before. They had their own issues, for sure, but their parents' disobedience would not be theirs. No matter the height of the walls or the size of their giants, they weren't interested in prolonging their wilderness stay and understood better than most the importance of believing their God was greater.

You may not have been raised by Christian parents, and if that's your story, you know the ripple effect of living in a home without a single mention of God. Now because of it, you're determined to raise your kids

---

* Answer Key: LOL=laugh out loud, ROFL=rolling on the floor laughing, SMH=shaking my head, NTY=no thank you. Challenge: Test these out in a text to a Gen Zer, and see what happens.

differently. You've invited your Lord into every room, conversation, and relationship—and as for you and your house, it's going to stay that way.

Or maybe your parents did love God, but you grew up watching them prioritize their careers or ambitions first and foremost. Now? It's time that habit is left behind in the wilderness. You've resolved to center your life not around checking emails or answering phone calls, but around Christ and Christ alone. You don't need to bring the wasteland with you any longer.

Girlfriend, ROUND OF APPLAUSE because we vividly see here how the choices we make affect more than just our own lives—they impact the trajectory of generations ahead. For sure, we are in *no way* better than those who have gone before us; we all fall short of God's perfect standard (Romans 3:23), and we're dealing with our own sin. Did someone say the age of anxiety? But just as we can learn from the wisdom of our parents—along with their consequences—may our kids also learn both from *our* wisdom and the consequences we've received, so they too can keep marching forward in the faith.

Oops, the Israelites actually are marching now! Better catch up before we're left in the dust. "'Do not shout; do not even talk,' Joshua commanded. 'Not a single word from any of you until I tell you to shout. Then shout!'" (Joshua 6:10).

One lap around Jericho: DONE. We hungrily turn to Joshua, clenching our swords and spears. Does he give the command to shout? Is it time to race inside the walls?

Nope. He simply directs everyone to return back to camp . . . talk about a buzzkill. At least we got our steps in for the day, though, you know?

Next morning, same drill. Some of the priests pick up the Ark of the Covenant of the Lord and march forward, while others blow their horns. The rest of us hoof it in front and back. SURELY today is the day! Lord knows I need the exercise, but what's the point of all this *walking*?

What's the point of all this budgeting and saving?

What's the point of inviting my friend to church when she's already declined . . . *multiple times*?

What's the point of praying the same request when it's doing absolutely nothing?

What's the point of picking up all the toys when my kids dump them out SECONDS LATER? (TBH, this last one I'm not sure we'll ever understand on this side of eternity.)

All in all, what's the point of these seemingly monotonous, mundane, dare I say unprofitable acts of obedience?

Well, just throwing it out there—but what if these challenges are testing our faith, producing endurance in our spirit, and molding us into the image of Christ—so that down the road, we "will be perfect and complete, needing nothing" (James 1:4)? I'm just guessing! But if we're called not just to talk the talk but walk the walk—could this be one of those times?

Or possibly, like me, you've put wayyyyy too much stock in yourself. You'd love to tear down the walls single-handedly, and if you *just so happen to* swipe all the credit, bask in the applause, and build up your own reputation and brand, THEN SO BE IT. But maybe, just maybe, God sees our hearts and is more interested in teaching us that "the LORD will fight for [us], and [we] have only to be silent" (Exodus 14:14, ESV) than seeing what we can carry out in our own strength and charisma. Again, just another guess! Hard to claim the fame when our mouths are closed though.

Or lastly, God has a track record of asking His people to do things that seem absolutely ridiculous *at the time* and senseless *in our own eyes*. Ask a poor widow on the verge of bankruptcy to borrow as many empty jars as she could and pour her last bottle of olive oil into every last one (2 Kings 4)? Well, we'll find the oil keeps dripping, the jars keep coming, and there's enough to sell, pay off debts, and then keep for leftovers to live off of! Or tell fishermen—who spent their entire career learning the local waters and finding the best hot spots, but had a bad day and came up empty-handed—just try to throw their nets on the other side of the boat and see what happens (John 21)? You know, because seven feet of water makes a huge difference? We may find out like the disciples that faithfully obeying seemingly foolish asks from the Lord Almighty results in a net full of fish so heavy we can't haul it all back in.

Maybe it's time we learned more about the God we serve and the limitless power at His disposal. Not only are His ways not like ours (Isaiah 55:8-9)—they're higher and better—but also we sometimes fail to remember that His ways are *supernatural*, which means "everything is possible for one who believes" (Mark 9:23, NIV)! That includes that poor widow, those profitless fishermen, the whole army of Israelite men sent out to take a nature walk around the Jericho block—*and* you and me, girlfriend!

For there is no one like our God. "None can do what you do!" (Psalm 86:8). Do we believe that? Live like that?

Maybe not now, but after the hike around our own walls, *we just might.*

Speaking of which, the Israelites just finished their second trip around the block, and what does Joshua do? SHOUT? CHARGE? MOVE FORWARD IN THE PROMISE OF THE LORD? Nope. Just another "Head back to camp, y'all, and try to catch some beauty sleep!"

Third day? Same.

Fourth day? No different.

FIFTH DAY? *I'm sorry, but can I at least chat with Suzy about the blisters on my heel or giggle about the priest who squeaked off-key from the rest of the band? I MEAN, IT WAS FUNNY. I was crying from holding it in! I don't feel like it's asking too much to just* whisper *among ourselves?*

Nope. Again, just like a preschool teacher, Joshua motions for us to zip our lips and throw away the key—and that's that. Back to the tents we go.

It would be easy to get frustrated after day four. I don't blame anyone wanting to throw in the towel after day five. After the sixth? I'D BE DOWN FOR A CHANGE OF SCENERY TOO.

When the majority of my friends had already married off, I was FED UP celebrating birthday after birthday still single. When I prayed for a misdiagnosis or outright healing, but God still allowed my battle against cancer? I was tempted to cave in to disappointment and discouragement. When the doctor couldn't find our baby's heartbeat and we saw a motionless ultrasound, I fought against hopelessness as I was wheeled into surgery. And when I later held a colicky baby—day after day, refusing to be comforted, soothed, or quieted—I was more than ready to move to different surroundings. I was exhausted from all the laps and frustrated by the end of the day when I was right back to where I started. My prayers echoed, "Ready when you are, God!"

Maybe you're there too?

Here's the HOW we learn from Joshua's story: **The march isn't forever.** God knows how our walls are coming down (and those giants along with them), and our participation—putting one foot in front of the other—is *part of the plan*. He still asks us to keep going on day three, to not give up on day four, to keep the faith on day five, and to persevere in trust on day six. Will we do that? Because what God has for us is FOR US, and nothing—not a seemingly unconquerable city, supposedly impassable walls, or reportedly towering giants—can stop His plans or thwart His purposes.

> What God has for us is FOR US, and nothing can stop His plans or thwart His purposes.

P.S. Jericho is already ours, but **it'll take obedience all the way to day seven to seize it** (Joshua 6:15-16, 20). Will you choose to last? Cling to faith until the end? If so, don't blink. Because in an instant, just as you push off to take another small step of obedience, breakthrough will come. While you're doing the same thing you've been doing for days and days and days, God will move. And all of a sudden, without warning or even a moment's notice, those insurmountable walls will come tumbling down, and the city will be *yours for the taking*.

Move forward, girlfriend. It may look like an unfought battle is ahead, but to the Lord, *it's already a done deal*. In Christ, victory is yours, so don't short-circuit what God has for you—keep marching on in faith.

FEAR:

"What if God's promises don't line up with my reality?"

THE HOW: Remember the march isn't forever. God knows how your walls are coming down, but He still requires faith and obedience. No matter what stands before you today, you can believe in God's promises that haven't happened yet as if they already have—solely because He said they would.[4]

WHAT'S THE FIRST STEP TO TAKE WHEN I HIT A WALL? Seek the Lord's instruction. The Bible is relevant to all areas of life, and the more you learn His promises and the names He's given you, the more you can stand strong in the wait, through the monotony, and while stuck on the outside.

JOSHUA KNEW THE WHOLE SCHEDULE OF EVENTS. WHAT DO I DO WHEN I'M UNSURE WHEN AND WHAT THE LORD HAS FOR ME? You fol-low the example of the rest of the Israelites. Instead of grumbling about His timing, getting annoyed over the execution of the plan, and feeling impatient with the seemingly fruitless hoops you have to jump through in the meantime, keep marching forward in full faith—not focusing on what you want to happen, but on God's hand and prevailing promises.

HOW DO I KNOW WHICH DETAILS TO SHARE WITH OTHERS AND WHICH TO KEEP TO MYSELF? Have you been able to trust these individuals with information in the past—or have they allowed fear or doubt to dictate their response and influence? If so, learn from that. Above all, ask our generous God for discernment. You can be sure that when you ask for wisdom, "he will give it to you" generously, without finding fault (James 1:5).

WHAT IF I DON'T SEE ANY PROGRESS? You may not. It's not as if the Israelites saw a layer of brick chip off after each lap around Jericho. No, they woke up and carried out the same act of obedience, day in and day out for six days, prepared for more if need be. Although day seven was when the walls crashed down, it started out like all the days before it. We cannot anticipate God's timing because His ways are not like ours—but we *can* choose to be faithful even when the walls are still standing. Then, "if you walk every lap like it's your last, one day, you will be right. . . . Don't stop on six."[5]

Chapter 11

WHY THEM AND NOT ME?
WHY ME AND NOT THEM?

The Early Church

(like, the very first Christians ever)

I hate to bring it up, but remember that big prayer you once prayed for with *full faith* and *so much hope*, but . . . it didn't get answered the way you wanted?

Agh, I know. I tried to block it from my memory too.

Maybe you also prayed for healing and clean scans, but you were still diagnosed with cancer (HOLLA). Or your marriage was on the rocks, and as much as you fought to save it, it still ended in divorce. Or to this day, you're continually praying for a baby, but Clearblue keeps telling you, "Not pregnant" and it feels like a personal vendetta. Why didn't God answer our prayers? DID WE DO IT WRONG?

Let me take a stab in the dark here. Besides this, if you were to list all the prayers God has answered and all the gifts He's lavished into your life, there would be TOO MANY to name, right?

For starters, He saved you from the punishment of your sins and gave you an eternal home in heaven. From there, maybe your mind instantly went to that friend God brought into your world when you needed it most or that godly man He ushered in when you wondered if there were any left. (P.S. If you haven't met him yet, he might just be at home feeding his fainting goats. #talkingfromexperience) Or maybe God brought in the exact amount to pay off that one bill when you were strapped for cash, protected you in a literal storm that destroyed a row of houses on your block, or gave you wonderful in-laws who are amazing grandparents to your kids.

You've prayed. He's answered. And you're *grateful* for it all, 100 percent, no hesitation.

I feel you. But if we're being honest with each other, that one prayer *that shall remain unnamed* did something to both of us. That lone plot twist chipped away at our confidence, and now, in its wake, there are times it's caused a bit of hesitancy in the back of our minds. *If He allowed* that *to happen, who's to say He won't allow* this *to happen?* or *What if He doesn't answer this prayer either?*

Without further ado, let's flip over to the New Testament and step into Acts 12. Here we have two guys with very similar circumstances. Take James:

- ☑ One of the 12 disciples
- ☑ One of the three in Jesus' inner circle Talk about being in the in-crowd.
- ☑ A leader of the early church
- ☑ Arrested
- ☑ Killed by King Herod

Waa, waa, waa . . . That last one's a downer, *for sure*. The worst part though? King Herod's approval rating skyrocketed with the people after he murdered James. You read that right—James's *own people* were so against Jesus and the gospel that they were thrilled when James died by sword, and they loved King Herod all the more for carrying out the order. Sidebar: Seems obvious but if ever we feel a *tickle of joy* over someone's oppression, suffering, or misery, *maybe* our heart is in the wrong place?

Here we watch on as King Herod's chest puffs out in pride, and he realizes what he has to do to gain more followers on Instagram—persecute more Christians. So who does he set his sights on next?

You got it! In walks the second guy, chained up and surrounded by guards—our man Peter:

- ☑ One of the 12 disciples
- ☑ One of the three in Jesus' inner circle
- ☑ A leader of the early church
- ☑ Arrested
- ☐ Killed by King Herod

Just like Michael Scott screamed when Toby returned to the office, *"NOOOOOOOOOOOOOOOOOOOOO."*

I know, my stress level just climbed through the roof too. The Bible really lathers on the suspense sometimes. But aren't we glad? When we find ourselves on the edge of our own cliff-hangers, we don't have to jump off in panic or stumble down in despair. We can find sure footing in God's peace by simply remembering we're in good company—for uncertainties and page-turners have always marked the lives of believers.

The early church is no exception. On the night of Peter's arrest, our brothers and sisters get together, and it's impossible for them to talk about anything else. "WHAT'S GOING TO HAPPEN?" they all wonder. As we sit on the edge of our seats too, it's tempting to whip out our complete modern-day New Testament and point to the end of the story to put everyone's mind to rest. A little peek won't hurt anybody! But the first believers had no such luxury. Instead, we watch as no answer comes, and they're forced to wait it out because the Passover festival has just begun.

Excuse me, what? HOW ARE WE SUPPOSED TO PUT ON OUR PARTY HATS AND CELEBRATE IN A TIME LIKE THIS? How are we expected to sit around the table, stuff our face with unleavened carbs, and give thanks to Christ for saving us from death *when it feels like we're facing certain death*—Peter today, maybe us tomorrow?

How are we supposed to work with a positive attitude when it feels like life back home is crumbling? How are we supposed to make lunch for the kids when we can barely muster enough energy to get up from the couch? How am I supposed to walk into my annual oncology appointments with peaceful confidence when these are the same people who told me bad news before?

Ultimately, how are we supposed to live life to the full when life seems only half-full (or half-empty, for my fellow pessim—er, realists)?

> We trust in, focus on, and celebrate this same God who will save the lives of His children.

We follow the example of the early church: Just as God saved the Israelites, who marked their doorposts with the blood of a spotless lamb, we trust in, focus on, and celebrate this same God who will save the lives of His children, who are marked by the blood of the Lamb. No detail of today can change that reality, so with a shift in focus, let's give a toast to our God, who still saves and liberates His people.

At the end of this eight-day festival, we finally get to the 24-hour countdown to when Peter's scheduled to face a public trial. Look closely at these first-century Christians, though. Knowing what we know of James, it would be totally understandable if some doubt was floating around, right? Like if God didn't spare James, sorry, Pete—but who's to say He'll save *you*?

I mean, why would He save one and not the other? Why would He give a baby to that family, but not ours? Why would He heal that person's body, but not mine? Why would He restore their marriage, but not ours?

But even in the question marks, we don't see any sign of these early

Christians giving up. Instead of letting their past disappointments curb their prayers or lower their expectations, they pray FERVENTLY (Acts 12:5).

Swing over to Peter, and things don't look great. King Herod was *set* on an execution, and it appears he pulled out all the stops to make sure it would happen. Not only was Pete fastened with two chains between two soldiers, but did I mention he was placed under the surveillance of four squads of four soldiers who stood guard at the prison gate? Yeah, there were layers upon layers of security, and it looked airtight.

But even when the clock is running out, the worst-case is right around the corner, and everything is working against us, we serve a God who is not limited by our time, fretting over the impossibilities at hand, nor restricted by any human effort. So we shouldn't be surprised when this very evening, a light beams into the prison cell and an angel shakes the apostle awake. "Quick! Get up!" (12:7).

What's that we hear? Chains that were locked onto his wrists fall off, *clanging* to the ground.

"Get dressed, put on your sandals and your coat, and follow me," the angel orders (see Acts 12:8). Apparently, this isn't the time for questions, and for once, Peter just does as he's told. He follows the angel out of the cell, past the first guard post, beyond the second, and just as they get to the iron gate that leads into the city, *creeeak*. The gate swings open on its own, and soon "they were out on the street, free as the breeze" (12:10, MSG). Like a full-detail security escort, this angel continues to usher the way down the street, and when the coast is clear, Peter finds himself alone.

As a free man.

WHAT JUST HAPPENED? James was just as loved by God, chosen to face similar circumstances, shackled in Herod's prison too . . . yet his story ended with brutal martyrdom. Why did God allow that ending, yet about the same time, command His angel to bring about a different ending for Peter?

Ultimately, *Why them and not me? Why me and not them?*

Were you expecting an answer? Yikes, I AM SO SORRY. As much

as I wish I could flip through God's playbook that details the depth of His riches and wisdom and knowledge, the truth is "such knowledge is too wonderful for me, too great for me to understand!" (Psalm 139:6). I mean, you should be scared if I *pretended to know*, for "how impossible it is for us to understand his decisions and his ways!" (Romans 11:33). Even when Job challenged the Lord on His reasoning, um . . . well, let's just say God had some words to say right back—*for multiple chapters* (Job 38–41). And I'm not about to get tangled up in that same dialogue that started with "Who is this that questions my wisdom with such ignorant words? Brace yourself like a man, because I have some questions for you, and you must answer them" (Job 38:2-3).

Nervous laugh. Times like this I'm SO GRATEFUL TO BE A WOMAN.

Here's the deal: While we don't always know how God's going to answer or why He allows certain things but not others, that isn't the point of this story.

The priority of this chapter I want to give attention to: Unlike the early church, some of us have allowed our past to impact our faith. That supposed "unanswered" prayer, as much as we hate to admit it, left us questioning God and doubting His goodness, and now our prayers aren't always marked by fervency like the early church's. Rather, they're cold and vague, maybe even angry or nonexistent.

Further down the spiral, once we hear or know someone else's story, it's all too easy to take on *their* experience as if it'll no doubt also happen to *us*. "I know someone who tried this in their career. MAJOR FAIL—so now I'm scared it's just going to be another embarrassing flop for me, too." Or "I remember when my friend was constantly fighting with her husband, and now they're getting a divorce . . . what if this is the day my husband breaks off our marriage too?" Or "I know someone who had the same symptoms I do, but it was stage 4 cancer and they died two months later . . . I feel like that's going to happen to me!" Do I look close to the end? DON'T ANSWER THAT.

And just like that, we take on someone else's story that was never meant to be ours and find ourselves rehearsing a farewell speech to our kids in the shower one night when it wasn't stage 4 cancer, BUT IBS, PEOPLE. Take it from me—WHAT.A.WASTE.OF.TIME.

The point: Your story may not look like your sister's, mom's, or best friend's story, and *that's to be expected.* It may not look like the majority *or* the minority—God is not restricted to statistics or expected to follow what's been done in the past—and that should be *a given.*

No one's autobiography is the same; that's the cool thing about our creative God. You can ask someone about their life story, and every single person will tell you a different one—because God didn't copy and paste with anyone. God is doing a new thing—in you and in them. So

> God is doing a new thing—in you and in them.

then what in the world are we doing dwelling on a stranger's story on Facebook instead of God's story, the Bible, and the promises He gives us?

When we stop looking at others, fixating and obsessing over their lives, and keep our eyes fixed on the race set before *us,* that's when we can find some contentment, some hope, some peace in ours. The same Author who wrote these Bible stories is your Author too. His pen strokes are still just as good. His storyline is just as creative. And His commitment to good endings is *sure.* "I have told you these things, so that in me you may have peace. In this world you will have trouble." (It's absolute, it's promised.) "But take heart!" (How?!) "I have overcome the world" (Bingo!) (John 16:33, NIV).

P.S. This is the HOW to choose faith over fear that we can learn from the early church: **The Author of your life has purposely marked out a unique path just for you. Don't get off-course by tripping over someone else's story or looking over your shoulder at past obstacles. Stay in your lane, eyes ahead, soul full of faith, and trust how your God has mapped out the road ahead—because with Him at the helm?** *It's gonna be good.*

Wait a second, but HOW DO I STAY IN MY LANE? Whenever you start fixating on the circumstances of those around you, bounce your eyes back onto God, remembering who He is. Everything in heaven and on earth is His (Colossians 1:16). With man, many things are impossible, but with God, all things are possible (Matthew 19:26). "[He] is able to do immeasurably more than all we ask or imagine" (Ephesians 3:20, NIV). *Deep breath in.*

Don't you already feel your hope quotient rising? Me too.

When we switch gears and bring our focus back to the Lord, the apostle Paul's prayer comes to life in a whole new way. "I pray you will understand the INCREDIBLE GREATNESS of God's power for us WHO BELIEVE HIM" (see Ephesians 1:19). **Key: For those who** *believe Him.* His power is *for you*, girlfriend—but it matters if you recognize that.

So don't give up. Keep asking, knocking, having confidence in the God who can still make the sun stand still. He's doing a new thing, He still has a good plan for your life, and just like with Peter, He longs to set you free.

It's time to get our hopes up. (Oh, and breathe out. SORRY, I FORGOT.)

FEAR:

"Why them and not me? Why me and not them?"

THE HOW: The Author of your life is doing a new thing—in you and in the lives of those around you. Instead of looking at others' stories, fix your eyes on who God is and the race He's marked out for *you*.

HOW CAN I PRAY WITH FAITH THAT SOMETHING WILL HAPPEN WHEN MY TRACK RECORD (OR THAT THING THAT HAPPENED TO SOMEONE ELSE) REMINDS ME IT MAY NOT HAPPEN? Just because God did or did not do something yesterday doesn't mean He will or will not today— He is not stuck in a particular pattern, nor does He only answer prayers one way. Rather, He is a creative God who offers you a clean slate, a new beginning, and fresh hope every day. Pray with full faith in your God who is *able*—grounding your confidence in Him, not in your own desires and plans.

HOW WILL I KNOW WHEN TO STOP SEEKING AND KNOCKING? Is the battle done? The battle wasn't nearly over with the Canaanites when the Israelites forfeited the Promised Land by giving up on God, His power, and His promise. So while you're in the battle? Pray with the Psalmist, "As for me, I will always have hope" (Psalm 71:14, NIV). If once God makes His answer clear and it doesn't pan out how you wished it would, submit that disappointment to the sovereign God and continue to move forward in faith—knowing someday you will see and understand. For now (when the war is still being waged) as well as in the meantime (when you don't understand why), trust that *He* sees and understands and is still bringing purpose out of your hard circumstances.

RUMOR HAS IT PETER ENDED UP DYING BY CRUCIFIXION UPSIDE DOWN. WHAT IF GOD SAVES ME TODAY BUT ALLOWS TRAGEDY TO OCCUR TOMORROW? Skim down toward the end of Acts 12: "Meanwhile, the word of God continued to spread, and there were many new believers" (verse 24). God's ways are not aimless nor futile. If God put more time on the clock for Peter, it's because He had a *purpose*—and this verse alone shows that God had plans to send out His ambassador to preach the gospel to more people and spread the Good News to anyone who would listen. If your life is submitted to Christ, you can rest assured that God will fulfill His purpose for you too (Psalm 57:2) and nothing is wasted in the hands of a God who makes every moment count.

Chapter 12

WHAT ABOUT WHEN THE WORST-CASE HAPPENS?

Martha

You had faith. You believed in God. You knew His power.

You claimed the promises of His Word and waited expectantly for Him to show up.

You were so confident He would do it.

But then . . . He didn't. And maybe He still hasn't.

What do we do when we've held on in faith, only to be disappointed, and the opposite of what we wanted happened? When a loved one passes away despite how much we prepared for a full recovery? That chronic illness is still an everyday burden no matter how much we've prayed for healing? A special relationship fell apart, infertility feels never-ending, or we're *still* swiping through Tinder looking for Mr. Right (at this point, even Mr. Mostly Right)—all the while, God has yet to make an appearance?

One step further—what about when our worst fear *actually happens*? When the rug is pulled out from under us, and we stumble backward confused, shocked, surprised, and disappointed—in our God, in the seemingly "unanswered" prayer, and in (what we feel is) His bad timing and lack of protection?

I'm sorry, forgive me if I'm lacking faith—**BUT WHAT THEN?** I'm so glad you asked.

Although she appears to be a Debbie Downer, sometimes even a buzzkill or party pooper whenever she enters the spotlight in the New Testament, let me introduce to you the *most relatable* woman in the entire Bible IMO (which, I guess, with a degree in marketing instead of a master's in theology may say very little . . . BUT YOU'VE ALREADY INVESTED $17.99 IN THIS BOOK, SO SORRY).

Anyway.

Have you met my girl Martha? In very much the same tone as Buddy the Elf overhearing someone mention Santa, Martha has every right to shout "I KNOW HIM" whenever anyone name-drops Jesus. Because she *does* know Him—more than just going to the same church, waving across the street, or having a conversation in passing. Martha *intimately knows* Jesus as a personal friend, as do her sister Mary and brother Lazarus. Not only did she open her home to Jesus having Him over for dinner, but she spoke openly with Him, and we see in John 11:5 that Jesus loved this little family very much.

But jump into the scene of John 11, and we don't see these three hosting a dinner party or kicking back for a family movie night. Rather, Lazarus is sick, the prognosis is bleak, and things seem to be getting worse by the hour.

So what does Martha do? Well, if you were close friends with the Son of God and felt like family with the One who calmed storms, made the blind see, and healed the lepers? Yeah, you'd probably call for Him too.

Better yet, she sends the message, "Lord, *your dear friend* is very sick"

(11:3, emphasis added). No need to even mention his name, guys! Just "Your best friend isn't feeling well!" will do, and Jesus will know *exactly* who you're talking about. "Lazarus, hold on, buddy. *Jesus is coming.*"

But minutes went by. Hours passed. And with no word, no sign, no Jesus, no healing, we look over at Lazarus as he takes his last breath and his body lies still.

What happened?

Why didn't He come?

Jesus . . . where you at?

Let's go find out. Past the Jordan River, having just left the area of Judea, we find Jesus. He's not scrambling to pack His suitcase nor lining up camel arrangements to catch the last ride over. Wait a second—He doesn't even show any *hint* of being in a hurry, and it certainly doesn't look like He's leaving anytime soon.

And He wasn't.

Rather, He receives the "Lord, your dear friend is very sick" message with a nod and turns back to His disciples, explaining, "Lazarus's sickness will not end in death. No, it happened for the glory of God so that the Son of God will receive glory from this" (11:4). Then He proceeds to drink His glass of water like NBD.

Hold up, though. I'm confused, because we just saw Lazarus and homeboy was OUT COLD. I don't mean to be morbid, but his body was pale and stiff, lungs no longer breathing, and funeral arrangements were already starting. Um, does somebody wanna tell Jesus it, in fact, *did* end in death? Nose goes.

"So although Jesus loved Martha, Mary, and Lazarus, he stayed where he was for the next two days" (11:5). TWO FULL DAYS? When my grandpa had a cardiac arrest and my sweet grandma was waiting for the helicopter to get to their home, every minute mattered. Every second that passed by was precious, and we all prayed it wasn't too late. But after 30 minutes without oxygen, in the end, it was. He had passed away, and as with Lazarus, the funeral shortly followed.

So, excuse me, but Jesus—who, by the way, *created* our bodies and placed the short time stamp of mere minutes on our lungs' ability to go without oxygen—heard the news and knowingly stayed *although He loved them*? What kind of love is that? Couldn't He have given the word, as He did with the centurion in Matthew 8, so when the messengers were running to report the news to the sisters, Lazarus could've been healed along the way? If death could have been avoided altogether and Jesus' beloved friends could've been spared some heartache, then why wouldn't He do that?

This is where some of us are at, and we have to answer this question—otherwise, our fear of prospective bad news will forever cripple us. The possibility **or reality** of tragedy will derail us. The troubles and trials we're promised to face in this world will not make sense, and we'll shake our heads along with Martha, drowning in our grief and shocked that our God didn't come through for us.

But just because it looks like the end . . . Just because the damage seems irreversible . . . Just because everyone else has given up . . . Just because no one has ever seen a comeback after a situation like this . . . *does not mean* the story is over, death holds the final say, or it's time to give up.

You'll see what I mean.

"Finally, [Jesus] said to his disciples, 'Let's go back to Judea. . . . Our friend Lazarus has fallen asleep, but now I will go and wake him up" (John 11:7, 11). **Didn't you tell Him? WE DID NOSE GOES.**

> Just because it looks like the end *does not mean* the story is over.

Guys! I didn't want to be the bearer of bad news, but Lazarus isn't just resting his eyes, okay? He's not taking a catnap, catching a few z's after church, or nodding off during a commercial break. No, at this point, Lazarus's body has already been wrapped tight in graveclothes, buried in his tomb for four days, and y'all, the stench was B-A-D. As a former NCAAA DIII athlete (**you** know, just a *couple* steps down from Misty May-Treanor), I have enough experience in the locker room (AKA the ultimate incubator of bad BO) to know I *would not* be interested in rolling aside Lazarus's tombstone simply to double-check his pulse. It's a closed case at this point, *right?*

But maybe our situation doesn't appear to be what it is either. Maybe what looks like death, smells like death, has been declared as death is not actually the final demise for us either.

Growing up, whenever I was freaking out—which was approximately 24-7, I know this full well—my dad would always say, "Don't worry about it—it's not fatal." While that was helpful in not sweating the small stuff, when I later faced cancer and walked into scans, it was like, "WELL, WHAT IF THIS *IS* FATAL?"

But let's look at the Bible. When God's people died, Scripture often describes them as being asleep. Like here in John 11:26, it was important for Jesus to emphasize that everyone who believes in Him will actually never die. Our bodies will one day breathe their last breath on earth, but we'll be more alive than ever in the presence of our Savior and in our heavenly home. So whether we're fearing the death of a relationship or the literal death of a family member, we as Christians can declare, "Even this is not fatal because we know the Lord over all—death included."

The disciples had a hard time wrapping their brains around this too, so Jesus "told them plainly, 'Lazarus is dead. And for your sakes, I'm glad I wasn't there, for now you will really believe. Come, let's go see him'" (11:14-15). Hold it right there. I'm sorry, but did we hear that right? Jesus is *glad* He wasn't there in time to save Lazarus? (P.S. Someday you'll be glad too. It may not be tomorrow or even in this lifetime, but the day we understand God's timing in carrying out His purposes, we too will be pleased. It's up to us if we'll believe this or not, trust His character or not, in the meantime.)

As we pan back over to the sisters and their entire dressed-in-black entourage catching word Jesus is coming, we hold our breath as Martha marches out to meet Him. Possibly with hands on her hips, tears in her eyes, finger wagging and head shaking, we hear the first words burst out of her mouth the second she sees Him. "Lord, if only you had been here"—you know, *LIKE I ASKED*—"my brother would not have died" (11:21).

Notice the change. When once Martha confidently nicknamed Lazarus "the friend you loved," we now see her pull it back to "my brother." In other words, *I don't trust how you feel about us anymore.*

Are you saying the same thing to Jesus today? "Lord, if you would've come LIKE I ASKED? Like I clearly and specifically and continuously prayed for? Then _____ wouldn't have happened."

Or maybe you're responding more like Mary, who stayed back, not that interested in what Jesus had to say right about now. You'd rather be with the people who actually came in time, showed their face in your moment of need, and consoled you in your loss instead.

When it feels like God has failed you, what you didn't want was the very thing you got, and you're sinking in your loss, where do you go? Do you still turn to God in prayer? Lay out all your feelings and thoughts and show your empty hands? Do you still go to church, not giving up meeting together like some are in the habit of doing (Hebrews 10:25)? Or have you, like Mary, found consolation elsewhere—*and sure, I may speak to Jesus later, but not now . . . not with all of this going on . . .*

Personally, I like a spicy, forward Martha, who doesn't seem to have a filter with Jesus. As Proverbs 8:17 affirms, "Those who seek me find me" (NIV) and Jeremiah 29:13 echoes, "If you look for me wholeheartedly, you will find me." Martha reminds us that our God is Immanuel— God with us—so when we make the choice to seek Him out, no holds barred—*we will find Him.*

Watch on as Jesus sees her emotion, feels her grief, hears her out, and tells her, "Your brother will rise again" (John 11:23). This same God who reassured His beloved friend then is the same God who wants to reassure you, His beloved, that He is *still* in control, He will *still* restore, and His plans to flip this are *still* good.

Here's what's so admirable about Martha—she does find reassurance in this. She's all, "Yes, he will rise when everyone else rises, at the last day" (11:24). But if we're being honest, sometimes that's not the truth we want to hear. Yes, we believe Jesus ultimately overcomes, and we know eternity in heaven will someday be perfect . . . *but we wanted this. Here on earth. NOW.*

Pressed to make an ultimatum, we'd choose the blessings here on earth—a biological baby, fulfilling marriage, optimum health, and world peace—over crowns in heaven, because we're still going to *be* in heaven, right? *I don't need to be at the head of the table, I just want what I want* today. But Jesus was able to endure the Cross in this world because of the joy set before Him—His eyes were fixed on the ultimate prize, the joy awaiting Him in the future (Hebrews 12:2).

Do we live for the joy awaiting us too or for the joy we want now? As **extremely** hard as it may be, part of following Jesus looks like putting our eternity into focus through the help of the Holy Spirit, "so we don't look at the troubles we can see now; rather, we fix our gaze on things that cannot be seen. For the things we see now will soon be gone, but the things we cannot see will last forever" (2 Corinthians 4:18).

It's only with this eternal perspective, that in the midst of our trials and unmet expectations, we still do not lose heart (2 Corinthians 4:16)—because even when our circumstances look bad and the trajectory looks worse, we don't live and grieve like those who have no hope (1 Thessalonians 4:13). With all our stock in Jesus, we remember that our citizenship is in heaven (Philippians 3:20) and truly, "there are better things ahead than any we leave behind" (C. S. Lewis).[1]

Instead of the perspective "Life is short—better enjoy it!," the only way to choose faith over fear, hope over grief, joy over sorrow is to reorient our outlook: "Eternity is long—better prepare for it!"

Don't get me wrong—Jesus still heals on this earth. God desires to build unity and harmony in our marriages. He says children are a blessing and a reward. And hands-down, He knows how to give good gifts. We *very well* may see the things we want come to fruition in our lives, but I'm simply asking: Are we putting our stock in this world or in the one to come? Living for Jesus first and foremost or living for ourselves?

How we answer that brings us back to either the voice of fear or the Voice of Truth. Our answer will either cause our hands to cramp because we're clenching SO TIGHTLY to what we want here on earth, or it'll usher God's peace back into our soul as we go forward.

As Proverbs 3:5-6 puts it, "Trust in the LORD with all your heart and lean not on your own understanding; in all your ways submit to him, and he will make your paths straight" (NIV). Even when we don't understand, will we trust?

When Mary finally comes out to join her sister Martha and Jesus takes in the entire scene of the procession bawling and wailing over Lazarus, "a deep anger welled up within him, and he was deeply troubled" (John 11:33). Is Jesus mad because they're sad? Is He annoyed because there's a lack of faith here? Is He exasperated over how they're processing the situation?

No. A deep anger surged within Him because He didn't create us to experience death and its devastating repercussions. Did you know that? When God created human beings and the world, He created us to always *live*—with no sin or brokenness.

So, death? An interruption and end to life? As the Creator, this was not His original intent and not the best for His people, so to witness His beloved friends crumbling over their brother's death? It should not be so, and it *broke His heart.*

The same goes for you. He sees you crying over a negative pregnancy test. He sees you staying up at night, soaking your pillow with tears, heartbroken over your difficult marriage. He sees you bawling over a wayward child, a dream unfulfilled, a loved one passing, and guess what? He doesn't take it lightly either. He isn't calloused to your pain, annoyed by your tears, or indifferent to your heartache. No, God *cares.*

Just as grief-stricken—if not *more*—He looked on at Lazarus's tomb, "then Jesus wept" (11:35).

This is the glory of the gospel: Jesus saw us sinking in our sin and knocked down by the curveballs of life, and He heard our cries and knew we had *zero power* to save ourselves. Because He SO LOVED you, me, and this world, He entered into our pain, died the most painful death the human race has thought up, and willingly took our place so we could have hope once again.

But that's only half of the Good News. It doesn't stop there. Jesus rose again and obliterated death and sin altogether! He holds the final word—not *death*—and here's where we see the HOW behind Martha's story: While we are living in the middle of the worst-case scenario and redemption is nowhere in sight, **He weeps with you AND still has a plan.** Jesus sympathizes with our every weakness (Hebrews 4:15), *and* He's our sovereign God. Although Jesus cried with Mary and Martha, He still knew full well what He was going to do for Lazarus—**and He knows exactly what He's going to do with your situation too.**

When I was diagnosed with cancer, this is the truth that gave me the most peace. Because like Martha and Mary, a lot of family members cried with me, and I needed more than just an empathetic God who could add more tears to the puddles.

No, I needed to know I had a sovereign, powerful, redemptive God who still had a handle on my life—because while other people had no control over the effects of chemotherapy on my body, they couldn't stop the

> While we are living in the middle of the worst-case scenario, He weeps with you AND still has a plan.

hair loss, and they only offered consolation, I knew Someone who could do so much more. Jesus not only supports and upholds us with His presence and love and sympathy—He also offers resurrection power, and that's when faith arises. Hope for today blooms. And the peace that transcends *all* understanding guards our hearts and minds (Philippians 4:7).

The time has come. Jesus walks over to Lazarus's tomb and tells them, "Roll the stone aside" (John 11:39). Martha not only protests but also winces, "Uh, Lord . . . he's not gonna smell like a myrrh-eucalyptus blend anymore."

And maybe you're objecting to what God's asking you to do too. "Please don't ask me to do that, Lord. That doesn't make sense. That actually *reeks*, and I'm not sure if you realize, but . . . here's why it's not the best idea." You know, because we need to educate the Son of God as to why His commands won't work in our lives . . . LOL. And, well, can't He just make it easier, more pleasant, and, I don't know, LESS OFFENSIVE TO THE SENSES?

But His ways are not like ours—they're higher, they're always better, they're perfect.

Jesus replies to Martha, "Did I not tell you that if you believe, you will see the glory of God?" (11:40, NIV). Same thing He's asking us today too. As we question who God is, think through every what-if scenario, and determine which voice we will listen to, Jesus asks us in the midst, "Did I not tell you in my Word, over and over again, that if you believe in Me, *you will see* the glory of God?"

And although it's kind of a rhetorical question, it's also not. The answer is clearly yes, but *He wants to hear it from you.* He wants to see your faith— not just in your heart, but overflowing in word and deed as well.

Remember how we may not understand *why* in the moment, but someday we will? Well, did you know according to Jewish tradition, a person's soul remained with his or her dead body for three days, but after that, time was up and the soul departed?[2] Before, it was easy to assume that Jesus was cruel for choosing to hang back even though He could've saved Lazarus. But does it make sense now why Jesus intentionally stayed put for two days before He set out for Martha's house? What assumptions are you making about God based on how your circumstances have played out?

WHAT ABOUT WHEN THE WORST-CASE HAPPENS?

Now, four days later, when everyone is in agreement that yes, Lazarus is officially dead, there's no way of reviving him, and his soul is long gone? This is when Jesus comes onto the scene, and this is when we hear His voice boom, "Lazarus, come out!" (11:43).

Every head whips toward the tomb. No one dares to blink or breathe.

"The dead man came out, his hands and feet bound in graveclothes, his face wrapped in a headcloth. Jesus told them, 'Unwrap him and let him go!'" (11:44). Gasps fill the air, and not a single soul knows what to say or think or do.

Hmm, so maybe Jesus *did* have a plan all along . . . and maybe He does for your situation too.*

Since this is my ultimate favorite story and I cry like a baby whenever I read it, we get a bonus HOW this chapter: **While Martha already knew Jesus as Healer, it was time she knew Him as Resurrection, too.** And while you (hopefully) know Jesus as your Lord and Savior, you may not know Him yet as Friend, Healer, Protector, Redeemer, the Alpha and Omega, Beginning and End . . . and He may have stayed put a couple of days because it's time for you to know Him in that way.

No matter the reason, we see there is *always* a reason—and in case it wasn't crystal clear by now . . . P.S. It's gonna be good.

In the end, because of Jesus' finished work on the cross, it won't be long until we also hear His voice booming, calling out to *us* and *our loved ones*, "Lazarus, come out. Heidi, come out. Tyler, Oscar, Mabel, Hazel, Dottie, *come out.*" And then? We will forever be united with Him and our beloved friends and family of faith for all eternity.

In the meantime, though? Like Martha, go out to meet Jesus. Seek Him out, pray without giving up, learn more about who He is, and wait expectantly for His goodness and purposes to prevail.

Someday, we too will understand why and celebrate how He *never* disappointed us.

---

* He absolutely does.

"What about when the worst-case happens?"

THE HOW: Not only does Jesus weep with you, but He still has a plan and knows full well how He's going to redeem the situation. He may have stayed put longer than you wished, but it's not without purpose. Rather, if you seek Him out in your pain, heartache, and grief, you'll walk away with a more intimate knowledge of who your God is.

HOW DO WE RESPOND TO THE VOICES—INCLUDING OUR OWN—ASKING, "SHOULDN'T HE HAVE KEPT LAZARUS FROM DYING? SHOULDN'T HE HAVE BROUGHT WORLD PEACE BY NOW, CURED MY MOM'S CANCER, SENT ME THE MIRACULOUS SIGN I'M LOOKING FOR?" While Jesus was standing right next to Martha, assuring her that her brother would rise again, His voice isn't the only one in the mix. Remember Mary's comfort entourage, her friends, her tribe? They saw Jesus crying and asked skeptically, "This man healed a blind man. Couldn't he have kept Lazarus from dying?" (11:37). Martha had a choice—and you do too. Whose voice are you going to listen to? Onlookers, ill-willed or well-meaning alike, or the One who holds all power?

I'VE LAID IT ALL OUT BEFORE GOD IN PRAYER . . . NOW WHAT? After Martha told Jesus about the situation and made her feelings known, she waited on Him to respond. She wanted to hear what He had to say. We can be assured every time we pick up our Bible—His living and active Word—that we, too, will hear from Him. Read through the pages and wait on the Holy Spirit to help, comfort, convict, and direct.

HOW CAN I KNOW HE WILL FOR SURE COME THROUGH FOR ME? If we remember that Jesus endured the horrific Cross, conquered death, rose back to life, and is advocating in heaven for us today, well, then, how could we reasonably and logically and rationally ever believe He would abandon us now? Withhold from us now? Give up on us and allow evil to reign in our lives now? Surely, He will not. One day, when faith becomes sight, we will be so glad for every time we chose to believe Him and wait expectantly.

Chapter 13

WHAT IF IT'S TAKING FOREVER? WHAT IF IT NEVER HAPPENS?

Abraham and Sarah

W hat's that one thing you *constantly* dream about?
        No matter if you're scrolling on Instagram, talking with friends, or simply grocery shopping, it's lingering in the back of your mind. (Chips and queso=a given. What else, though? I BELIEVE FOR BOTH OF US WE'RE MORE THAN THAT.)

When people ask, "How are you?" we realize "Good" or "Fine" is the expected answer. But because of this *one thing*, we're tempted to take every bit of small talk to a whole new level. It does not matter if it's with the teenage cashier at Target, the local barista, or that older lady passing on the sidewalk who looks motherly and sympathetic; our emotions play no favorites. Catch us at the right time, and we will unload. amiright or AM.I.RIGHT?

It's no different with God, either. This is the first thing we think about when we bow our heads in prayer, and as quickly as we can speed ahead to the whole supplication part, it's the first thing we mention, begging God (yet again) for this to be the day He answers.

What's that thing for me?

Well, in the last three months, a sketchy mole appeared, my heart randomly palpitated, my stool was a different color, my period heavier, my breast lumpier, and WHY DO I HAVE A WHITE SPOT ON MY GUM AND WHAT'S THAT DOT FLOATING ACROSS MY LINE OF VISION? Back-to-back doctor appointments were made. Scans were done. And as much as I wish this were a rarity, it is not.

In the midst of this chaos, I heard a friend say, "I haven't seen a doctor in like . . . ten years." My jaw dropped. As someone who has MyChart bookmarked, that's my dream. I'd love to live a long span of time in total freedom without weird, unknown symptoms knocking at the door, threatening to steal my peace, robbing me of my life. Either that, or I'd also like the world's fastest metabolism, a million-dollar shopping spree at the Mall of America, to sleep in every day, be on texting basis with Lisa Harper, and if we're really talking, having our grown children and their families as next-door neighbors, all loving Jesus, living somewhere in the heart of the Bible Belt, freed from puffy parkas and Minnesota winters forevermore. I don't think that's asking too much?

Your turn: What's *your* dream?

Anything keeping it from becoming reality?

What are you on the verge of spilling whenever someone asks, "How's it going?"

Maybe you hoped your family would be complete by now, but it's taking longer than you anticipated to get pregnant.

You thought you'd be married by this point, but that bare ring finger on your left hand is like a walking billboard: Still single.

Or you dreamed of hitting a rank in your career, graduating with a certain degree, or starting your own business or ministry, yet the timing was never right and now you're knee-deep in a job taking you down a different course.

Have you met Sarai? We first make her acquaintance in Genesis 11:29-30 with this killer introduction: "The name of Abram's wife was Sarai. . . . But Sarai was unable to become pregnant and had no children."

TALK ABOUT AN OPENER. Nice to meet you, Sarai! Any hobbies? What do you do for a living? Cat or dog person?

Oh, your culture determines your rank and significance by the status of your uterus? My turn? Welp, okay: "Hi, I'm Heidi, wife to Tyler. Chemotherapy can cause infertility, so when we didn't get pregnant our first month of marriage, I cried for hours in the bathroom wondering if I too was barren—because you know, that's a perfectly acceptable amount of time to reach that conclusion. But we now have four children! Is this also where I mention we miscarried a baby? Just didn't know if that subtracted from my overall worth. Oh, and can we talk about the pros and cons of getting one's tubes tied?" TMI? Hard to know where to draw the line with this . . .

Before we move past these proper-yet-extremely-personal introductions, I want you to look back at Sarai. Like really look into her eyes. In Genesis 11:10-28, we get an entire rundown of Shem's family tree. Verses upon verses of fathers and births are listed, and then it all comes to a halt at the mention of Sarai's name and the condition of her lady part.

While, sure, there would be plenty of bullet points in Sarai's résumé under "work experience"—from grain processing to caring for animals— her most important contribution to their marriage *and* society would (someday) be childbearing. Without it, well . . . there was only shame and a supposed curse.

And this is where we catch up with Sarai. This girl, once so full of life, now walked around carrying this burden and facing this reality, and our stares are among the many she received each day. Furthermore, with no IUD yet on the market, Sarai's friends would've had strollers full of kids even five years down the road, and their jokes would've heavily revolved around potty training gone wrong and how many cups of coffee are you on? Not to mention cries for breastfeeding constantly interrupting girl talk midsentence.

Yet year after year, as her friends get pregnant, her nursery? Empty. Abram's and Sarai's 30s go by . . . nothing.

40s . . . no double lines.

50s?? Nada.

60s! For sure 60s! *biting my lip, shaking my head*

Okay, 70s! This is when God bursts through the silence, comes onto the scene, and makes it clear to Abram: "I will give this land to your descendants" (12:7). HE SAID *DESCENDANTS*. DICTIONARY.COM SAYS THAT MEANS "OFFSPRING" as in . . . *plural*! Icing on the cake: God later pulls Abram aside and says to him, "Look up into the sky and count the stars if you can. That's how many descendants you will have!" (15:5).

As we're gazing up at the night sky trying to calculate the constellations like jelly beans in a jar, we can't help but feel overwhelming relief for our friends. At this point, Abram and Sarai had possibly been married for *50 years—and five decades of waiting for any dream to be fulfilled is, well, five decades longer than any of us would prefer.*

Especially now, in this world of instant gratification—when we'd rather microwave than wait out the oven, go through the drive-through than walk into the store, stream a movie than go to an actual theater, and buy now with a card than later with cash—we want the baby THIS YEAR, the big house our parents got in their 50s in OUR 30s, and the explosion of our influence TODAY.

Ultimately, we want God's good plans NOW.

Thankfully, for Abe and Sarai, the wait is over, right? God actually spells it out in black-and-white: Children are coming. He gave them His word! So any day now, right?!

crickets

> Ultimately, we want God's good plans NOW.

Not so much. The year Abram blew out 86 candles on his birthday cake, they saw just about everyone else's pregnancy announcements hit their Facebook feed, but had yet to post their own.

Then when her period stopped and, in its place, hot flashes started, her hope for a child stopped along with it. Sarai was *over it*. "The LORD has prevented me from having children," she said (16:2), and with a click of her tongue and a shake of her head, she of course took her Egyptian slave Hagar to Abram, and he had sexual relations with her.

WAIT, WHAT?

Yeah, sorry—I didn't know how to segue into that. It *feels like* two mature, God-honoring adults would realize this is probably not the best course of action, doesn't it?

But I can hear their objections because we voice similar ones today: "EVERYONE'S DOING IT." Sarai's parents apparently weren't around to quip back the age-old "DOESN'T MEAN YOU HAVE TO" like ours did, but the general public sure let her know it was perfectly acceptable. Go ahead! Make your servant your surrogate and count their children as your own! So instead of waiting in faith, Sarai gave up on the dream and gave into culture's easier payment plan.

After all, God didn't mention anything about *Sarai* bearing children . . . right? Only that Abram would have descendants. So maybe God's waiting on *us* to provide an alternative plan? Maybe if we present Him with a smorgasbord of options, *then* He will move? I mean, everyone else floundering in this hopeless situation encourages the man to sleep with the female servants of the household. *MAYBE I'M JUST TOO TRADITIONAL. MAYBE THE PROBLEM IS ME. MAYBE GOD NEEDS MY HELP AND WANTS ME TO DO SOMETHING.*

So she looked the other way and hoped for the best. And they lived happily ever after!

LOL, not a chance. But we aren't all that surprised, are we?

When Abram *does* sleep with Hagar and she actually *does* get pregnant, the women get all catty, and it's awfully hard not to be like . . . "I coulda told you THAT. I mean, what'd you expect?"

Yet how many times do we take matters into our own hands when things aren't happening as fast as we'd like? How often do we reason with ourselves that we've got to do *something* or it's just never gonna happen? Have we really never wanted something so bad that we haven't in the least adapted our convictions, let it dull our spiritual fervor, or allowed it to override good judgment?

Or are we going to pretend Sarai and Abram are the lone sinners in this world? (You own up first, I'll be right behind . . .)

Flip over to the next page, and GOD CLEARS THE AIR AGAIN, emphasizing the promise He previously made: "I will make you the father of a multitude of nations!" (17:4). To seal the deal, God changes Abram's name to Abraham, which means exactly that—"father of many."

At this point, though, the aging couple still thinks Hagar's son Ishmael is the promised son God's been talking about all along. Yet this is when we hear God break some news that changes their lives forever. "Regarding Sarai, your wife—her name will no longer be Sarai. From now on her name will be Sarah. And I will bless *her* and give you a son *from her*! Yes, I will bless her richly, and she will become the mother of many nations. Kings of nations will be among her descendants" (17:15-16, emphasis added).

SAY WHAAAAAAAAAAT?

Abraham bows down in respect but laughs to himself in disbelief. "'How could I become a father at the age of 100?' he thought. 'And how can Sarah have a baby when she is ninety years old?'" (17:17) Ever been there? Sing about His faithfulness outwardly, but deep down inside doubt He will come through? Pray about your situation, but disbelieve your request will actually make an impact? Read the Bible, but hesitate to trust that some of God's promises are truly for *you*? We too have the choice to either succumb to what we can see or trust God with what we can't.[1]

Abraham tried to give God an out: "May Ishmael live under your special blessing!" (17:18), but God had already made Himself clear, and He emphasized yet again, "No—Sarah, your wife, will give birth to a son for you. You will name him Isaac, and I will confirm my covenant with him and his descendants as an everlasting covenant" (17:19).

Before we pop the confetti, overnight baby shower invitations, and get caught up in the brunch menu (always team donuts), take a closer look at Abraham's deep-set wrinkles and gray hair. Remember: Just a chapter ago, he became a father at age 86 with Ishmael. But today? Homeboy's 99.

You read that right. By the time this promised baby actually arrives, Abraham will hit **triple digits**. It took an entire century of life to see the birth of his son Isaac—which means "he laughs" (because at this point, let's be real—it's either that or cry)—and this is where we find the HOW to choose faith from these Bible heroes' story . . .

My only B+ in high school was in Geometry—I still have yet to express CF:FD in terms of three positive relatively prime integers in real life, but that is neither here nor there—but let's do a quick calculation to uncover the principle. *Deep breath*, here we go:

- Abraham is 10 years older than Sarah, so if they exchanged vows when she hit the customary age of 16, then he was 26 on their wedding day.
- Abraham was first promised descendants at age 75.
- He became a father for the first time at age 86.
- God promised a baby when he was 99.
- Abraham witnessed Sarah become a mother at the ripe age of 100.

When it's merely a flip of a page and a few chapters in between, it's easy for us to assume that Abraham and Sarah lived to see their prayers answered that minute, day, week, or even year. But these Bible heroes we admire did not get their blessing with just a snap of a finger or a zap of a microwave.

In Abraham's case—as well as Noah's, David's, Joseph's, and oh yeah, *basically every Bible hero known to man*—we see that God's timetable was not that predictable, and He had His people wait . . . for quite some time. These men and women had to hold on to hope for *years* and sometimes decades, but when God saw that the timing was right, He opened up the floodgates.

You may wish God moved faster (oh hey, me too), but here's some evidence we can't brush past—this baby they waited almost a century for? Isaac wasn't destined to simply fulfill all their parenting dreams, carry on the family name, or take over the family business when his pops retired. We tend to think that way only because we're shortsighted and can't see into the future (and *tend to* only think how it benefits us), but the God who knows all things and sees all things and works for the good of *all* those who have been called according to His purpose? He acts and moves with the end goal in mind.

While Isaac *could've* been born 75 years prior, you and I—living thousands of years later—have farsighted vision, the privilege of knowing what Abraham and Sarah simply did not. This boy was born exactly when he was supposed to be—at the right time to then marry Rachel, who would then birth Jacob (AKA Israel. Yeah, the OG), and his 12 sons would become the 12 tribes of Israel. Coming down this family tree, "when the right time came, God sent his Son" (Galatians 4:4).

HOLLA, THEIR WAIT SET UP THE PERFECT TIMING TO USHER IN THE ACTUAL MESSIAH'S BIRTH.

It's almost too much, isn't it? Like, I need a minute. #waterbreak

There's the HOW: Just because a few years have passed and seemingly nothing has changed in our lives does not mean the truth has changed. God is the same yesterday as He is today, so we need to fight for patience, be persistent in prayer, and stay full of hope—because He sees what we cannot, and someday we'll be able to look back on our own stories and see that *He always had a plan* and there was a reason and a purpose coming down the pipeline.

> Someday we'll be able to look back on our own stories and see that *He always had a plan*.

(Oh, and P.S. it's always gonna be good.) HAD TO.

Our times are in His hands, and trying to take them into ours only breeds frustration, anxiety, anger, and stress. So even when God's timing may not line up with ours 100 percent of the time *cough* or even half, the wait is promised to be worthwhile—because we know the God we serve, and He is good and faithful to the end.

No matter how long it takes, His promise remains: "The LORD will withhold *no good thing* from those who do what is right" (Psalm 84:11, emphasis added).

He's not holding out on you, girl. Do you see that now? He's merely setting the scene to do exceedingly more than all you could ever ask or imagine (Ephesians 3:20).

Our Times	His Times
Two years and no baby? *HELLO, BIOLOGICAL CLOCK TICKING.*	Abraham, you'll have a son . . . when you turn 100 (Genesis 21:5).
30 minutes in the oven? *NOBODY GOT TIME FOR THAT.* Throw it in the microwave *stat*.	David, you'll be king . . . but you'll have to wait about 15 years for the crown. You know, after the current king hunts you down in an attempt to take your life *MULTIPLE TIMES*. (2 Samuel 5:4).
15-minute wait in a drive-thru? *Is this a joke? WHAT'S WRONG WITH THESE PEOPLE?*	Your dream, Joseph? You'll see it come true, but not for 22 years. First, you'll be sold into slavery by your brothers, wrongfully accused of raping someone else's wife, and sentenced to serve a good amount of time behind bars (Genesis 42).
Kids, I told you once—*DO I NEED TO SAY IT AGAIN?*	Earth filled with violence, Noah? Start building an ark because a flood is coming to wipe everyone out . . . *quite possibly* a full *century* down the road. Let's be glad our calling isn't his . . . (Genesis 7–8).
I prayed last night; *NOTHING'S CHANGED. Has God forsaken His people? Abandoned us to the grave? Will He reject me FOREVER?*	Still a virgin, Mary? Not yet married? Perfect. You'll bear God's one and only Son (Luke 1–2).

FEAR:

"What if it's taking forever? What if it never happens?"

THE HOW: Someday we'll be privileged to look back on our own stories and see that *God always had a plan* and a purpose was coming. So fight for patience, be persistent in prayer, and stay full of hope—because our times are in His hands, and the wait is promised to be worth it.

HOW DO I KNOW IF I'M MOVING IN STEP WITH GOD OR WITH CULTURE OR MY OWN DESIRES? Take a close look at Abram and Sarai's concubine plan. You won't see them consulting God once on what He thinks about the matter. Sarai simply goes to Abram, and he agrees. Whenever you need wisdom, God says just ASK HIM FOR IT, and He'll give it "generously to all without finding fault" (James 1:5, NIV). You don't need to wonder what He wants you to do—you can ask Him directly and seek His will in His Word.

WHAT IF I DON'T WANT TO WAIT ON THE LORD? Where else are you going? It's easy to see why the Psalmist repeats, "Wait on the Lord," because really, what's the alternative? We're either walking toward Jesus or away; may we never be like those disciples who deserted Him, but instead repeat Simon Peter's words, "Lord, to whom would we go? You have the words that give eternal life" (John 6:68). As the Bread of Life who alone can satisfy, Jesus really is the only Way, and you and I can find that out the easy (or the hard) way.

HOW CAN I KNOW GOD IS ON THE MOVE WHEN NOTHING IS HAPPENING? Beyond Abraham and Sarah's story, take Saul. After the Lord declared, "This man is my chosen instrument to proclaim my name to the Gentiles and their kings and to the people of Israel" (Acts 9:15, NIV), he went on his first missionary journey—around a decade later. God still had a work to do in the meantime, and in the mundane, unrecorded moments, God is still on the move bringing about purpose in our lives too. It may not look like anything is moving the needle forward, but be encouraged by these Bible stories that even still, our God is actively carrying out His plan and making every moment count.

IF GOD PROMISED ABRAHAM WOULD BE THE FATHER OF MANY NATIONS, WHO ARE HIS DESCENDANTS TODAY? You and me, girlfriend! "The LORD counted him as righteous because of his faith" (Genesis 15:6), and now Abraham is the spiritual father of all those who have faith in Christ (Romans 4). Quite the legacy, amiright?

Chapter 14

WHAT IF MY TIME HAS PASSED?

Elizabeth

I saw a meme that said, "1980 and 2021 are as far apart as 1980 and 1939," and I was immediately unwell.

"Why? Did you eat too much dairy? HEIDI, YOU KNOW YOUR BODY CAN'T HANDLE LACTOSE."

No, actually. I've made the necessary substitutions, thank you (queso excluded for obvious reasons). But to your point, I felt old. I've had moments of warning before this—like when I asked my *seven-year-old* to troubleshoot our streaming problems *even after* I tried the foolproof "turn it off, turn it back on" method. Or when I needed to turn down the radio because I couldn't hear myself think. It doesn't help that the young'uns on TikTok are somehow *very innocently* asking, "What was it like living in the late 1900s? Did you have electricity?" Dagger to my heart.

Regardless of *your* actual age, what makes *you* feel old? When you're looking forward to checking the actual mailbox, getting new towels, or slipping into your own pair of house shoes because duh, #archsupport?

On the same note, what do you feel too old *to do*? Maybe too old to go back to school, change career paths, run a marathon, or get married? Drink coffee past 3 p.m., have another baby, or shop at Forever 21?

Before we fall into step with Elizabeth in Luke 1, you've got to know a few things about our girl. First of all, by almost all standards, Elizabeth was #blessed and would've proudly listed it in her Instagram bio—you know, after *"God first,"* but before *"And if not, He's still good."*

Not only was she a pastor's kid, a descendant from the priestly lineage of Aaron, but she was a pastor's wife, too. Yep, you read that right—she grew up never missing a Sunday (although technically, services were on Saturdays), basically lived in the Temple when her husband served (outer court to be exact), and wanted nothing more than to pass off the spiritual torch to her own kids.

Except . . . there weren't kids. Elizabeth and Zechariah tried for decades to start a family, but no matter how thoroughly she tracked her cycles, how healthy her diet was, or how long she lay in bed after you-know-what . . . for whatever reason, year after year, they stalled out in the TTC part of the journey.

"For *whatever reason*?" snarls Elizabeth's neighbors. "Nah, we can tell you the *exact* reason."

Rolling my eyes and looping my arm through yours, I move us along before they can babble any more of their nonsense. I don't have to tell you how infertility has *always* formed a dark cloud over women, but back in this moment of time, children were considered a sign of God's blessing and favor. Don't have them? Well, most assumed that said something about a person—you know, like their standing with God.

It was toxic. As if infertility wasn't heartbreaking enough already.

But what perpetuated the problem even more was how family, friends, acquaintances, and total strangers alike deemed themselves worthy to pass along God's supposed judgment. Women in Elizabeth's situation were met with raised eyebrows and disapproving stares—behind their backs *and* to their faces. There'd be an abundance of whispers about their "unfortunate state" among moms at playdates, plenty of gossip around the theories of what their secret sin could possibly be, and lots (and lots) of nosy questions invading their personal privacy. *Whose fault is it? Have you tried losing weight? What if you let go and let God?*

Women struggling with infertility today feel all the emotions around this hardship too, but there was an added layer of stress back in Bible times that we need to grapple with before stepping into Elizabeth's shoes.

In Jewish society, having a boy was *a must.* Not because these dads desperately wanted a mini to play catch with in the backyard—but beyond carrying on the family name, without those blue balloons and sports-themed nurseries, if anything were to happen to Zechariah, Elizabeth couldn't just apply at Walmart or open up an Etsy shop to make ends meet. Since women didn't work, these sons would be the ones to provide financially for their moms when their husbands passed. So worse than being lonely, Elizabeth was staring ahead at a real risk of someday being alone *and* desolate *and* starving *and* unprotected *and* broke *and* helpless. Living through the reality of today was hard enough, but the future didn't look much better either.

One last thing—the husbands in this predicament had a choice: Stay or divorce. A sensitive lot, those divorcés.

Their wives, of course, had no such option, but this gives us a clue into the kind of couple we're dealing with. This was not a union just built on formalities, and Elizabeth wasn't a nagging, wet blanket of a wife either. Rather, their marriage was clearly based on love and commitment, and she was the kind of girl you didn't want to let go. Even when Zechariah's peers would've chosen differently, he was here for the long haul *no matter what.*

And we love the guy for it.

To seal the deal, even in *God's eyes,* "Zechariah and Elizabeth were righteous . . . careful to obey all of the Lord's commandments and regulations" (Luke 1:6), and when God *Himself* puts your name in His book in such high regard? Well, ain't nothing better, folks.

Slip on your walking shoes, because today is a big day! We're gonna nosey our way into Elizabeth's house, but on our way, let's swing by Jerusalem and peek in on her husband. It'll be worth the detour.

Remember how I said she was married to a pastor? Out of the 24 divisions of priests (18,000–24,000 men total), they took turns being on duty in the Temple, and today, Zechariah's order was finally chosen. But mind you, they only had this honor two weeks out of every year! With just a handful of priests needed each day to carry out all the jobs and around a thousand guys to choose from *just in his group alone*, well, it was a hold-your-breath kind of moment. Not everyone made the cut. Pretty much like volleyball tryouts on steroids—it was an honor to make the team, sure, but you did NOT want to be stuck on the bench while your friends gloried in the limelight. You know, what with all the cute boys in the front row to impress!

And now we're no longer talking about Zechariah . . .

Back on track: Who gets the coveted job? To ward off any favoritism or politics that may be in play, they drew lots. The one role they all hoped to be picked for? To enter the Holy Place and burn the incense. And all the oily mamas throw up their hands with a "HERE FOR IT!"

But more than just diffusing oils, this was considered the highest act of mediation between God and man at the time. Many priests went their whole lives without burning this fragrant offering. But this time around, out of a box containing a score of names, someone pulled out a slip that read, "Zechariah," and no doubt Elizabeth's husband's eyes grew wide as his friends slapped him on the back in congratulations. Considered "very old" in Luke's flattering account, our guy was finally chosen for what he thought would be the highlight of his life.

Little did he know something *even better* was coming.

When the time comes to step into the dimly lit room of the Holy

Place, awe overtakes Zechariah as he leaves behind the rest of the priests and worshipers in the court outside. He knows full well this is a once-in-a-*lifetime* opportunity, the top achievement that could ever be listed on his résumé, the culminating moment of his entire career.

But as he steps forward to the altar to perform the sacred act . . . an angel appears, and OUR BOY ZECH IS SHOOK.

I don't blame him, either—I jump when *my husband* rounds the corner unannounced, and his presence in our home is *kind of* expected since, you know, he pays our mortgage and we share the same bed. I can't imagine if a towering celestial being suddenly appeared at my right hand when I was all alone in a dark room with hot coals underfoot.

> But the angel said, "Don't be afraid, Zechariah! God has
> heard your prayer. Your wife, Elizabeth, will give you a son,
> and you are to name him John. You will have great joy and
> gladness, and many will rejoice at his birth, for he will be
> great in the eyes of the Lord. He must never touch wine or
> other alcoholic drinks. He will be filled with the Holy Spirit,
> even before his birth. And he will turn many Israelites to the
> Lord their God. He will be a man with the spirit and power
> of Elijah. He will prepare the people for the coming of the
> Lord. He will turn the hearts of the fathers to their children,
> and he will cause those who are rebellious to accept the
> wisdom of the godly."
> LUKE 1:13-17

Um, OKAY. SOUNDS GOOD TO ME, MESSENGER OF THE LORD.

Right? I mean, Zechariah's waited *decades* for this. Prayed *around the clock* for this. Faced *public shame* and *continual grief* over this. And now not only is God going to answer his prayer, but an angel who stands in the very presence of God came specifically to our guy to deliver this message. Not to mention, very few members of the entire human race have actually experienced an encounter like this—but, oh, it also broke the *400-year silence* between God and His people too.

TALK ABOUT SO MANY THINGS GOING ON AT ONCE. Sometimes, I can't handle having my period while also struggling to put on my shoes, so I can relate. This kind of stuff is a lot for one person to handle.

But instead of gratitude or praise, we only see skepticism from Zechariah. "How can I be sure this will happen? I'm an old man now, and my wife is also well along in years" (1:18). Before we lunge at the guy to wring his neck, quick question: Have we ever asked the same?

God, how can I be sure you will come through for me?

It's been a closed door for years. How can I be certain you will make a way?

It's only resulted in struggle and disappointment. How can I know you'll redeem this situation?

Just as God's Word should've been enough for Zechariah then, the promises of God in the Bible should be enough for us today:

- He *will* come through, for He is faithful. "Understand, therefore, that the LORD your God is indeed God. He is the faithful God who keeps his covenant for a thousand generations and lavishes his unfailing love on those who love him and obey his commands" (Deuteronomy 7:9).
- Because He is the Way, He *will* lead us in the way. "Trust in the LORD with all your heart; do not depend on your own understanding. Seek his will in all you do, and he will show you which path to take" (Proverbs 3:5-6).
- Nothing is wasted in His hands; He *will* use it all. "And we know that God causes everything to work together for the good of those who love God and are called according to his purpose for them" (Romans 8:28).

Yet how often do we still doubt these promises? How many times do we give more weight to our circumstances than to the power of God? How regularly do we allow what we see to trump what we cannot yet see?

The plot thickens: This same angel, Gabriel, not only visited Zechariah, but Mary as well with *almost* identical news. Elizabeth and her virgin teenage cousin would both miraculously bear a son! (Emphasis on "almost" since, you know, one being the son of a human; the other the actual Son of God. #notexactlysemantics)

Although we hear the same response—*"How?"*—this identical question was spoken with *very different tones*. While Zechariah spat it out in disbelief, Mary was in awe and responded in faith: "I am the Lord's servant. May everything you have said about me come true" (Luke 1:38). Pretty impressive to nail the whole submission-to-God thing being 14ish years old and all . . .

See what this stark contrast teaches us? Sometimes the older we get, the more life we've lived, the more stories we hear, the more letdowns we've experienced? If we're not careful, they can plant seeds of doubt rooted so deep that even when an angel appears or the Word of God is spoken, we still can't receive it.

[Insert your impossible situation here.] Will you respond like Zechariah or Mary— with disbelief or belief? No matter what you chose yesterday or even a second ago, it's up to you, right this very moment, whether or not you'll trust in the God of the impossible.

> It's up to you, right this very moment, whether or not you'll trust in the God of the impossible.

Speaking of, I heard a knock all the way over at Elizabeth's house. Before we slip in the back door and greet a certain special guest, let me quickly bring you up to speed: Because of Zechariah's choice, Gabriel dished out the consequence of Zechariah being unable to speak until the child is born. (As someone who's never won "See Who Can Be Quiet the Longest," I can't even imagine.) But when they finally saw those double pink lines, Elizabeth declared what they both felt,

"How kind the Lord is! He has taken away my disgrace of having no children" (1:25).

This was always His plan, by the way. It's still His plan for His people today. We may not be able to see any possible way for God to take away our shame of _____, but this truth remains: "You, O LORD, are a shield around me; you are my glory, the one who holds my head high" (Psalm 3:3). Our God is still the Lifter of our chin, and He has every plan to wipe away those tears and restore every lost thing. Like Elizabeth, though, we *gotta* keep holding on.

Knock, knock. Okay, ONCE WAS ENOUGH!!! (I guess she is only a teenager.)

Mary barges right in. "Hi, Elizabeth!"

"At the sound of Mary's greeting, Elizabeth's child leaped within her, and Elizabeth was filled with the Holy Spirit. Elizabeth gave a glad cry and exclaimed to Mary, 'God has blessed you above all women, and your child is blessed'" (Luke 1:41-42).

Pause. We as women know the comparison trap is *so real*. When we come across someone living out OUR DREAM, it can produce a wave of envy, rivalry, and resentment. So I wouldn't blame Elizabeth one bit if she looked on at her *much younger* relative—who, mind-you, got a positive pregnancy test WITHOUT EVEN TRYING—with just a snippet of disdain. No marriage, no man, no tears, no heartache; this baby just *fell into her lap* (er, womb)?! Was gifted to her without challenge? Girlfriend isn't even old enough to legally drive a camel, but she gets what Liz has sorely wanted without all the baggage or effort.

MUST BE NICE.

And while it was a cool surprise for Elizabeth six months ago to find out they'd have the honor of bearing and raising the one who would fulfill an Old Testament prophecy and was chosen to prepare the way for the Messiah Himself? Who would have the same spirit and power as Elijah? Who would turn many Israelites to the Lord their God? Well, that *felt* like the highest privilege and source of pride . . . until this adolescent comes along and gets to raise THE ACTUAL SON OF THE LIVING GOD.

Putting ourselves in Elizabeth's shoes is all too easy, isn't it? *How do I rate? Always second to* you *apparently. A lesser call on* my life, *I guess.*

But look at our girl's face. Hear Elizabeth's "glad cry." Soak in this moment as she gushes out nothing but a blessing, "Why am I so honored, that the mother of my Lord should visit me?" (1:43).

Since "what you say flows from what is in your heart" (6:45) and "whatever is in your heart determines what you say" (Matthew 12:34), well then, we can confidently bob our heads in agreement: This girl's THE REAL DEAL. There's no ounce of jealousy or hint of resentment in this sacred visit—just two women in pure joy, celebrating the gifts their good God has given them, breaking out in song, and speaking blessing over blessing over one another.

Isn't this the type of women we want to be too?

HOW, THOUGH? Elizabeth shows us the actual HOW to move forward in faith when we're wondering if our time has passed: God shows no favoritism (Romans 2:11) and no matter if we're 14 or 60 or anywhere in between, **a life yielded to God is always a life that can be used by God.**

Moses was 80 when God called him to rescue His people from Egyptian slavery; Abraham was 75 when God asked him to move to a new land to start over; and Sarah became the "mother of many nations" like God had promised at age 90. This truth is emphasized from the beginning of the Bible to the end—age is never a deterrent for God—so why in the world would we entertain the lie that we ran out of time even though we're still living? That our mission is over even though Jesus has not yet called us home? That our supposed limitation of older age, less energy, or lack of opportunity could ever limit our God and His purposes for our lives?

There's a reason Proverbs 16:31 says "Gray hair is a crown of glory." What our culture and personal doubt seem to be forgetting is that the more years we live equal the more experiences we have, and there's a wisdom that's forged after you've lived through the turning of seasons, a perspective that's only uncovered after you've taken a few laps around the sun.

But the second part of that proverb is the key to it all: "It is gained by living a godly life." We can keep adding candles to our birthday cakes, accrue more wrinkles, and notice an increase of age spots and skin tags—*and still be foolish* if we miss that last piece.

> But the godly will flourish like palm trees
>> and grow strong like the cedars of Lebanon.
> For they are transplanted to the LORD's own house.
>> They flourish in the courts of our God.
> Even in old age they will still produce fruit;
>> they will remain vital and green.
> They will declare, "The LORD is just!
>> He is my rock!
> There is no evil in him!"

PSALM 92:12-15

God never put an age limit on the promises of the righteous, and I don't think it's wise we begin to do so either. With the Lord at the helm of our lives, once-in-a-lifetime experiences are always a possibility. Elizabeth not only knew this; she lived it and still praised her good God after living through decades of unanswered prayer and unfulfilled dreams.

> God never put an age limit on the promises of the righteous.

Because she did, our girl lived to see the day when it all made sense to her and the timing of it clicked. Now, *clearly*—just like with Abraham and Sarah—God wasn't late in delivering this baby to their home. He didn't go all those years ignoring their prayers and turning His back on them—for just a decade earlier, Mary was a toddler herself and in no position to be a mother. Since their son was hand-selected to prepare the way for Jesus' coming, well, John the

Baptist *simply couldn't have come sooner*—because Jesus' time to enter the world hadn't yet come.

God, of course, knew this all along. He knew that if Zechariah and Elizabeth would just remain faithful and trust in His timing, their son *would* come . . . but they'd have to give up their plans and trust in His.

Will we do the same today? Things may not be happening as fast as we'd like. Your biological clock is ticking. Opportunities are getting more and more scarce.

Don't fret. God is never late, He knows His timeline, and He still wants to use your life in supernatural, Kingdom-building ways . . . **but your trust and faith are required**, no matter your age. He wants to hear *you* too declare, "The Lord is just! He is my Rock! There is no evil in Him!"

So what do you say? Will you, like Elizabeth, be confident that an even better plan than yours is unfolding?

All of heaven is hoping you say yes. (Oh, and P.S. I am too. #xoxo)

FEAR:

"What if my time has passed?"

THE HOW: God shows no favoritism. A life yielded to God—no matter if you're 14 or 60 or anywhere in between—is always a life that can be used by God.

HOW CAN I GENUINELY BE JOYFUL FOR OTHERS INSTEAD OF RESENT-FUL? Just because Mary didn't struggle with infertility for decades doesn't mean she avoided all adversity and challenges. Try explaining to your fiancé how you, a virgin, are pregnant with none other than the Son of God. Not exactly the most believable story. Can we blame Joseph for being set to divorce her? And just because he eventually came to terms with it via another angelic visit doesn't mean the rest of the town did. Gossip, judgment, and strained relationships may very well have been an everyday reality for this teen. Fast-forward to when Mary witnessed her Son brutally crucified on a cross, and I wouldn't consider that a moment to be coveted. Case in point, no one's life is perfect or free from pain— their struggle just isn't the same as yours. When you remember everyone has their hard fights, long nights, and ugly cries—while also times of happiness, answered prayer, and mountaintop experiences—you can "be happy with those who are happy, and weep with those who weep" (Romans 12:15).

WHY HASN'T MY DREAM COME TRUE YET? The stories of Sarah and Elizabeth, as well as Hannah (1 Samuel 1), demonstrate that just because something hasn't happened yet doesn't mean it never will. Craig Groeschel puts it this way: "God's delays are not necessarily God's denials."[1] Each of these women could've had every reasonable and logical reason to give up—but something kept them holding on. That something was the promises and hope of God. Maybe your dream is still coming; maybe something even better is down the road. Either way, you can declare, "As for me, I will always have hope" (Psalm 71:14, NIV) because you know who is still in control—and He has good plans for you.

WHAT ABOUT WHEN OTHERS DON'T SEE MY AGE AS A POSITIVE TRAIT? Then they're stupid. LOL, just kidding (although there's a grain of truth in every joke). But truly, don't live for the approval of men, but God—and when you realize age has never been a limitation or hindrance to Him and His purposes? Then you can keep your chin up in spite of any negativity by listening first and foremost to *Him* and the value He sees in your station of life. Straighten your crown, girlfriend! **You still have much fruit to bear.**

Chapter 15

WHAT DO I DO WHEN GOD FEELS SILENT?

Esther

How do you pass the time when something dark looms overhead? When your spouse's deployment is around the corner, and the assignment is risky? When every day is a battle against postpartum depression and anxiety, with no evacuation notice? When you're waiting to have that hard conversation with your teenage kids? Or when you finally get pregnant, but it's considered high-risk and all the variables have your nerves constantly on edge?

There was a total of three weeks between that initial symptomatic appointment with my doctor and meeting with an oncologist to discuss next steps. While waiting on blood test results, sitting in the hospital lobby for the biopsy, and constantly feeling this lump poking out of my neck, the clock kept ticking—which meant I had to keep living.

So I spent time with family.

Went to work per usual.

And tried not to crumble every time someone asked, "How's it going, Heidi?" IT'S GOING, OKAY, PEOPLE?

But more than anything, I prayed. I knew who my God was. I was well aware of all that He could do, so I pleaded for His healing hand to move and hoped for this to be another grand display of His power. I mean, ISN'T THAT HOW BIBLE STORIES WORK? You go to Jesus, have the faith, and hear in return, "Daughter, your faith has made you well. Go in peace. Your suffering is over" (Mark 5:34). All I needed Him to do was give the word, and I was ready to move forward in the all clear. Any day now, God!

But . . . a different sort of day came. I got the results. The diagnosis was clear. And it was not the good news I had been expecting or praying for. Now, with this big disease overshadowing my life, chemotherapy and radiation imminent, and the trajectory of my entire future in question, the only question that dominated my thoughts was . . .

What do I do now?

As I lifted my eyes to the heavens, tears a constant stream down my face, desperate for an answer, it felt like I was only met with dead air. So I repeat: What do we do in these moments when God seems silent, His hand feels untraceable, and we're standing face-to-face with an obstacle He's not removing?

Look no further than Esther. When we step into the beginning of her story in the Bible, she not only has some dark days ahead (currently unbeknownst to her), but also has survived quite a few in her past as well. For one thing, her current zip code falls in Persian territory, away from her homeland of Judah, in exile under captivity. Making a home away from home is hard enough, but add the death of her mother and father on top of the whole ordeal? Cue "How Can You Mend a Broken Heart" by Al Green.*

THE BEST IS YET TO COME THOUGH, RIGHT?

Well, yes—but first, Esther's taken from her guardian, Mordecai, and

---

* If somehow unfamiliar with this tear-jerking classic, YOU HAVE NOT LIVED. (Just kidding.) But actually very seriously, let this be today's homework assignment—add it to your playlist. In the meantime, tell Siri to play "Tell Your Heart to Beat Again" by Danny Gokey . . . maybe that's more your speed.

forced to compete in a beauty contest thrown by King Xerxes. Speaking of, here—I grabbed us tickets. I don't want to gossip . . . but rumor has it—

DON'T LOOK AT ME LIKE THAT. Technically, this is all recorded in the book of Esther in the Bible, so it's not *actually gossip*, okay? It's all *true*.

. . . Do you want to know or not?

grabs your hands and excitedly sits on the couch to spill the beans Okay, so there was this huge banquet King Xerxes threw for all his officials and ministers. I don't want to name-drop, but there were certain princes and nobles of Persia and Media in attendance. . . AGH, I WOULD'VE GIVEN ANYTHING TO BE ON THAT INVITE LIST. Can you imagine the dresses? How much they cost? Do you think there were doubles? I didn't see "who wore it better" in my feed, though . . . but I'm sure a meme is coming.

Oh, right—FOCUS. Well, King Xerxes pulled out all the stops. For 180 days, everyone paraded around his empire and admired all "the pomp and splendor of his majesty" (Esther 1:4). After this whole six-month charade, he opened up the garden courtyard of his summerhouse to everyone living in Susa for a weeklong party. SO FUN, RIGHT?

But in the middle of this huge, elaborate, well-attended party, when everyone was reclining on these silver and gold couches, and the drinks were flowing, with waiters at every elbow ready to refill, the king called for Queen Vashti. Except . . . *cheeks blushing* . . . from what one rabbinical tradition says—and this is just hearsay; don't quote me on it—when he ordered her to appear wearing her royal crown, well . . . he meant *only her royal crown*, if you catch my drift.

I KNOW, RIGHT? HOW EMBARRASSING. I quick change in my closet so my own kids don't barge in and see me wearing only a smile! Can you imagine hundreds of eyes staring at you in the buck? And while, yes, Queen Vashti has every right to be confident in her own skin (girlfriend is downright BEAUTIFUL), she has her decency, too. So she put her foot down! She refused to be a pawn in his game and an object for those pigs to drool over, so she said nope. Sorry. "Maybe come talk to me *after* your hangover." That's real-life advice right there.

But . . . it was not well received. Everyone who's anyone was there, mind you, so with their eyes gawking and their authority threatened, these men got all nervous like, "Women everywhere will begin to despise their husbands after they hear what Queen Vashti has done, and before this day ends, all these wives will rise up, and *they'll* start treating *their husbands* (*cough* . . . *us*) the same way. There will be no end to their contempt and anger" (see Esther 1:17-18). Essentially, the original "hell hath no fury like a woman scorned."

Long story longer, Queen Vashti got booted from the palace and forever banished from the presence of King Xerxes (after that stunt he pulled though, I'm not sure she was *that* devastated)—and now *flashing tickets like a fan* WE HAVE FRONT-ROW SEATS to Miss Persia as he selects his next queen to replace her. They've already gone through 12 months of prescribed beauty treatments and only get *one chance* in front of the king, *so it's gotta be good.*

I know, I know, this kind of stuff is always rigged anyway, and it's lame to google any spoilers ahead of time . . . BUT I caught wind of some chitchat that the chief eunuch already singled a girl out, assigned her seven maids, lavished her with a special menu, and moved her into the best room in the harem. I CAN HARDLY HANDLE THE SUSPENSE!

As we rush into the king's palace, though, our excitement is quickly replaced with deep-set disappointment. What we *thought* was going to be an entertaining cocktail hour ahead turned into "There will be no rose ceremony tonight. The king has already made up his mind; he knows who is going home." YOU WOULD DO THAT, ABC—er, King Xerxes . . .

Turns out the final rose belongs to our girl Esther, and just when we think this story ties up in a neat little bow with a "happily ever after," the unthinkable happens.

King Xerxes promotes a guy named Haman to be his second-in-command, and while everyone else honors him, kneeling and bowing down before his presence just as the king commands, Haman looks back to see one lone man standing: Mordecai. And oh, the OUTRAGE. You would have thought he just folded an entire basket of laundry, and NO ONE PAID HOMAGE. I mean, *that* we could understand! But no, Mordecai was just a Jew who believed only the Lord Almighty deserved that kind of worship, so there he stood. And man, the *audacity* of that man's faith made Haman's blood boil.

So what does the most powerful, high-ranking official in the government do when his pride is wounded? Well, annihilate a whole race, of course! Because how silly and wasteful would it be to just confront and converse with *one man*! "Let's wipe out his entire nationality—that'll teach him a thing or two! Show him who's boss!" Proverbs 16:18 in the making, y'all: "Pride goes before destruction, and haughtiness before a fall." I'M CALLING IT.

As we skim through Haman's royal decree, sealed with the king's very own signet ring, our eyes land on the singular, startling order: "All Jews—young and old, including women and children—must be killed, slaughtered, and annihilated on a single day. This was scheduled to happen on March 7 of the next year" (Esther 3:13).

Oh, okay—saved the date! Just another year until our imminent demise, our scheduled murder. Thanks for the heads-up! Got it marked down on our calendars!

WAIT—EXCUSE ME, WHAT?

Mordecai will have *none of this*. He went out on the town in just burlap and ashes—a little bold, yes. Not the fashion statement most of us would envision, but back in Esther's day, this outfit of black goat's hair signified heartfelt sorrow, desolation, and ruin. Sprinkle on some ashes, and this was next level, only used in times of national disaster.[1]

Where was he headed? The palace, and "when Queen Esther's maids and eunuchs came and told her about Mordecai, she was deeply distressed. She sent clothing to him to replace the burlap" (4:4).

LOL. Sometimes, Ty walks down the stairs wearing something (kind of) absolutely hideous, trying to bring back middle school vibes or resurrect a shirt he found in the back of his closet. After a few hard blinks and a moment of silence, I do what every respectable woman does. I pick something else out (anything else, really), giving him the benefit of the doubt that this unsightly fashion faux pas must've been made under some sort of duress. "Here, honey. Try this instead . . ."

Our soul sister Esther takes one look at her cousin and does the same. He refuses.

Ty has never been so bold.

She pushes back. "What's your problem?" Mordecai unloads to her attendant and "told him the whole story, including the exact amount of money Haman had promised to pay into the royal treasury for the destruction of the Jews" (4:7). As he hands over a copy of the decree, Mordecai slips in a P.S. himself, but . . . his isn't cute or all that funny. "Don't think for a moment that because you're in the palace you will escape when all other Jews are killed. If you keep quiet at a time like this, deliverance and relief for the Jews will arise from some other place, but you and your relatives will die" (4:13-14).

Subtle.

Esther, though, has a whole laundry list of reasons why she cannot and should not get involved. For starters, everyone knows the fate of every person who approaches the king without an invite: *Death.* Oh, and one other thing. "It's been 30 days since he's asked for me, Mordy. (In other words, there's a new girl on the block. I'm thinkin' I'm old news by now.) So sorry, pal—but the timing's off." *insert cute emoji with girl shrugging her shoulders, palms up in the air*

Mordecai lathers it on some more. "Who knows if perhaps you were made queen for just such a time as this?" (4:14).

Can we slap the guy across the face, or would that taint the integrity of the Scriptures? Like, I'm sorry, but DIDN'T YOU JUST HEAR WHAT SHE SAID? Stop it with the guilt trip, bud. Easy for *you* to say what she should do—on the *outside* of the gates. Don't you think, as the queen, Esther probably knows the situation just *a tad* better?

The problem: We sometimes fantasize about our callings being glamorous (or at the very least, likable)! We daydream about having a growing Instagram platform with nothing but viral posts and zero haters, or a successful business with little overhead and ever-increasing profits. Or maybe we visualize a certain degree that'll set us up perfectly for that next promotion or being a stay-at-home mom who's constantly bombarded with unending kisses, hugs, and words of gratitude.

But what if our calling isn't all roses? What if it's actually less about our dreams and desires and more about serving the Lord where He's planted us? Our world is so focused on following our hearts and building our own kingdoms, but what if the call is actually to follow *Jesus* and build *His Kingdom*?

> What if our calling is less about our dreams and desires and more about serving the Lord where He's planted us?

Esther may have fantasized about being queen, reclining on Pottery Barn couches, popping figs, and being waited on hand and foot—but what if her calling wasn't necessarily and ultimately to *be* the queen, but to be used by God to save His people *as* the queen? Mordecai wasn't grilling her out of jealousy, annoyance, or some other evil intent. As her loving adoptive dad, he gave her the third degree in hopes of reframing her perspective, and . . . maybe . . . this is the question someone needs to ask us today too.

"I know you don't want to put your life on the line, but what if you were made queen FOR such a time as this?"

I know you don't want to go to the doctor's office *again*.

I know you don't want to move.

I know you're sick of the snail's pace of the adoption and foster care process.

I know your husband's deployment came at a bad time.

I know you're fed up with being single.

I know this job loss has not *at all* been rewarding.

I know being passed over for that promotion hurt.

I know this surgery was not what you hoped for.

I know your in-laws are far from easy to live with.

But *who knows*? What if you were put in that position for such a time as this?

A den of lions and a flaming furnace wouldn't have ranked high if we were given the choice of how to be used by God. Being crucified certainly wouldn't have made the cut, and from Esther's response, putting her life on the line when she could've remained in the cushy royal life instead? Not a coveted calling either.

Something about that last part of Mordecai's words clicked with Esther, though, and while she still couldn't see anything positive or reassuring about the situation, she responded, "Go and gather together all the Jews of Susa and fast for me. Do not eat or drink for three days, night or day. My maids and I will do the same. And then, though it is against the law, I will go in to see the king. If I must die, I must die" (4:16). WOW, okay, anyone else still back at "MUST I, THOUGH?"

Trying to catch up with Esther's quick submission, I'm sure with a whole nation seeking the Lord together, something miraculous, encouraging, breathtaking, and unmistakably extraordinary happens, right? Well . . . flip over to the next chapter, and there is *no sign* or recorded proof of God's answer in response to Esther's total surrender. We only see her moving forward in obedience to her previous conviction.

And maybe after you've prayed, nothing supernatural happened either. There wasn't writing on the wall (Daniel 5), a wet fleece on your doormat (Judges 6), or a dream during the night that was obviously sent from God (Genesis 37)— but there was still that unwanted path ahead, the conviction to remain faithful even in this time of testing, and the trustworthy Word of

> We must keep taking steps of faith, believing He alone controls the final outcome.

God, which promises He will never leave us nor forsake us, even when His presence isn't evident to us.

What are we to do? Esther shows us we simply must keep taking steps of faith, trusting God will somehow meet us along the way, believing He alone controls the final outcome.

Here's the highlight reel of what happens next:

1. "When [the king] saw Queen Esther standing there in the inner court, he welcomed her and held out the gold scepter to her" (Esther 5:2). Phew, the king responded in the only way that would spare her life! Girlfriend can officially check in "safe" on Facebook.

2. Esther doesn't come right out and blow Haman's cover—even though she *could've*, since the king was at the ready to grant her every request, "even if it is half the kingdom!" (5:3). Timing is everything, though, and when you've submitted to the Lord in prayer, He is faithful to lead you on.

3. Esther hosts a dinner for both King Xerxes *and* Haman. Seems questionable, right? Like why invite the enemy to the table? It could've easily turned sour—what if the king ended up believing *him* over *her*? But when the favor of God rests on you, it doesn't matter who's in the room or what devious plans are schemed against you. The Lord's plans prevail, and His protection over His own is fierce.

4. Even at this dinner, Esther doesn't let the cat out of the bag, but invites the king and Haman to yet *another* feast. Single ladies, are you picking up what she's dropping down? "The way to a man's

heart is through his stomach" might just be biblical *and* strategic! #allyoukneadislove

5. If we would've polled the Jews, asking when they'd like to see their murder decree abolished, they would've all said in unison, "NOW." The sooner the better! But Esther puts off the conversation . . . *why?* What looked like buying time was actually waiting on the Lord, and someday, we'll understand like Esther how God's delays are not arbitrary or cruel. He has perfect strategy, and His timing is impeccable.

FINALLY, here's where we get to the good part: The night before the last banquet, while Esther is busy preparing the food, decor, and seating arrangements for her dinner, Haman pounds the final nail in his backyard gallows, bent on killing Mordecai in the morning. No thanks on *that* landscaping inspo . . . Kind of ruins the aesthetic IMO—a pergola might've been more cozy? Better for entertaining, more inviting for guests? At the same time, we pan over to the king, who's having trouble sleeping.

What's the best remedy when counting sheep, installing blackout blinds, and drinking a warm glass of milk still doesn't do the trick? Read. And while I prefer something *light*, possibly some sort of beach read or mystery novel, our man Xerxes tells his attendant to dust off the book containing the history of his reign. Nothing like a good *Chronicles of Me.*

Just as morning comes and Xerxes is about to halt the narration and dive into the to-dos of the day, his attendant reads a part he's unfamiliar with. "Wait a second, two guys tried to kill me? A guy named Mordecai saved the day? How was he rewarded?" (see Esther 6:1-3).

Turns out . . . he hadn't been. (Which, P.S. Mordecai could've been frustrated that this good deed had gone unnoticed. When we clean the house, put out a fire at work, or serve above and beyond at church, and *no one* seems to care? It can be tempting to get annoyed. But the Bible assures us that God sees the good deeds we do and will reward every last one, someday, in His timing.)

Fun for Mordecai: His repayment comes today.

At that very moment, Haman *just so happens* (#nocoincidences-withGod) to arrive in the outer courts of the palace *to specifically unveil his plan* to impale Mordecai on a pole. Yet what happens instead? He's met with a thankful king feeling indebted to the very guy he wants to kill off. Haman's not only ordered to dress Mordecai straightaway in the king's royal robes, but he's also forced to take the reins and personally lead his opposer on horseback throughout the city square shouting at the top of his lungs, "This is what the king does for someone he wishes to honor!" (6:11).

Now that's justice *served.*

Oh, but God's not done. After this grand parade, the king's eunuchs whisk Haman off to the meal Esther's prepared, and when the king asks about her request once again, affirming yet another time how willing he is to hand over anything, even half his kingdom, Esther's discernment kicks in, giving her the green light to lay it all out there: "I ask that my life and the lives of my people will be spared. For my people and I have been sold to those who would kill, slaughter, and annihilate us" (7:3-4).

I imagine the king spitting out his wine as he explodes, "Who? Where is he? This is monstrous!" (7:5, MSG).

All eyes turn to Haman as his face flushes red and he slinks down in his seat. "'An enemy. An adversary. This evil Haman,' said Esther" (7:6, MSG). *Cue the B-roll gasps.*

It's almost too good from here on out.

After Haman is ushered away and executed on the very pole he had built, this story ends with a happily ever after as the king reverses the decree, the Jews are saved and empowered, Esther continues to reign as queen *plus* steps up into a government adviser role, and Mordecai is promoted to prime minister, ranking second only to King Xerxes.

Do you see it now? God is never mentioned in the book of Esther (yeah, like not even *once*), and we may see very little evidence of His presence in any given moment of the story . . . until we get to the end. Now, looking back, we can trace God's hand through the unfolding of events: A beauty contest, the insomnia of a man, and a scared queen who didn't like the pressure she was facing included.

It's still the same today, too. Here's the parallel, the HOW to choose faith when God seems silent: While you may not see what God's doing in your life, that doesn't mean He's not working. Someday, we *will* see—but as with Esther, stepping into God's plans will require us to stay faithful to our convictions and obedient to His Word. When the time is right, you'll see how God was lining up things all along to bring about good in your life and glory to His name.

Make no mistake: You were born for such a time as this. And in case I failed to mention, P.S. it's gonna be good.

FEAR:

"What do I do when God feels silent?"

THE HOW: While you may not obviously see God at work today, that doesn't mean He's not in action behind the scenes. Someday, you *will* see—but girl, you gotta stay faithful in the meantime. Saturate every situation in prayer, keep taking those steps of obedience, and God will meet you along the way.

HOW DO I KNOW WHAT TO DO IF GOD REMAINS QUIET? For one, you have something Esther did not have—the complete, written Word of God, which not only is living and active, but is your guide to righteous living. Therefore, God is never completely silent—you can hold 66 books of His words in the palm of your hand. Second, God gave us the church—brothers and sisters in Christ—for a reason: To exhort and build one another up (1 Thessalonians 4:18, 5:11; Hebrews 10:25). God used Mordecai to give His direction to Esther, and He may be using your Christian friends, family, or mentors to do the same. Like Esther, listen and then bring it to God in prayer. He will direct you through the Bible, His people, and discernment given by the Holy Spirit.

BUT WHAT IF I DIE? Like Esther declares, "If I must die, I must die." We put too much stock in the things of this world, and as Paul Azinger remembered, "We're not in the land of the living going to the land of the dying. We're in the land of the dying trying to get to the land of the living."[2] The truth is this world is fading away (1 John 2:17), creation itself is in bondage to decay (Romans 8:21), and our bodies are wasting away (2 Corinthians 4:16). So why are we surprised and trying to work against this reality? When we realize every day of our lives is already recorded in God's book (Psalm 139:16) and nothing can change our expiration date, then we can focus on maximizing the days we've actually been given and living a life that matters. As Mordecai said, if we don't follow God where He leads, He will still make it happen but with someone else. Don't pass up the opportunity to be used in powerful ways by the Lord Almighty—**you'll never regret it**.

Chapter 16

WHAT ABOUT WHEN GOD LETS BAD THINGS HAPPEN?

Joseph

Sometimes, I open my DMs and read, "We're obsessed with cats too" or "I pulled a muscle while sleeping JUST LIKE YOU SAID would happen the day I turned 30" or "your kids playing with the Nativity set in May is the best thing on the internet right now." *Last one may have just been my mom . . .*

But most other times, I get messages that say, "I'm struggling with infertility and wondering when God's gonna show up" or "My friends ask how I can believe in a God who allowed this trial to happen" or "The doctor gave me bad news. I know God is good . . . but I'm really having a hard time seeing it today."

I snort-laugh with the first batch (getting a side cramp while reaching for toilet paper has a way of bonding thirtysomethings forever), but the whole reason I show up is for the second group. Clearer than I'd like, I can still easily picture myself sitting across from the oncologist. It doesn't take much to remember his voice running through the never-ending list of short-term and long-term side effects from treatment. And I'll never forget that trifecta feeling—heart racing, blood draining from my face, spirit hopeless—frozen in that chair but clamoring for any way out on the inside.

Every day, I realize someone else is sitting in that same seat. They've just been sucker punched in the gut by bad news today. They're blindsided by some tragedy this very moment. They're looking for God, desperate for His help, and wondering when (or if) it'll ever come—and they need reassurance. Like *NOW*.

So then how do I respond to these types of messages? What kind of answer or encouragement could I possibly give in situations that feel so far gone?

I'm glad you asked. Genesis 37 is the place to start.

Here we watch as a dad, who *clearly* adores his son, holds out a "just because" gift to Joseph: A custom-made robe that would make even Barefoot Dreams jealous. As this 17-year-old turns around to try it on and slips his arms through the sleeves, we see his dad just beaming. Such a precious father-son moment! WHERE'S THE CAMERA? GET IT ON VIDEO. SOMEONE, UNLOCK THE SCREEN. WHAT'S THE SIX-DIGIT PASSCODE?

While Joseph had a good thing at home, beautiful gifts, and a hopeful future, he also had a set of half-brothers who hated.his.*guts*—and not exactly for no reason either. While Jo paraded around in high-end apparel, they were looking down at their hand-me-downs and the best finds at garage sales. As they glance over at their father, who's gushing with pride and simply cannot conceal his favoritism, they look back at each other like, "When's the last time he ever looked at *you* like that? Oh, NEVER? Same . . ." It got to the point where their jealousy raged and "they couldn't say a kind word" to Joseph (37:4).

Have you ever slipped a fun treat to your kid but said, "*Shhh*, keep it to yourself!"? What do they do? Well, like every good sibling . . . they strut directly into whatever room their brothers and sisters are in, fanning their evidence of favor in the air for all to see and gleefully rubbing it in their hungry (now tear-stained) faces. (Or is this just us raising complete sugar hounds? Note: Ty, take Oreos off the grocery list.)

Joseph seems to do just that. He adds fuel to the fire by sharing his dreams out loud: "Someday, I think I'll be your king, and *you'll* bow down to *me*." I'm picturing my niece in high school dropping that bomb with absolute seriousness, and I can see how things got divisive. *Check yo'self before you wreck yourself. *lots of snaps**

Confident ol' Jo still had some growing up to do. But the last straw came when his dad sent him off to micromanage his brothers' work. What did these brothers do when they saw Joseph traipsing onto the scene and the sibling rivalry reached its breaking point?

Well, sell him into slavery, of course! They *were* planning to kill Joseph, but without shows like *NCIS*, *CSI*, or *Criminal Minds*, it seemed too risky. How would they cover it up? As the next best option to full-fledged murder—and one that would actually make them a profit—they sold him to a group of traders (*and we think our families are dysfunctional*). With nothing more than a good riddance, off their little bro goes, forcibly carried hundreds of miles away to who knows where.

Seems like a real low, right? Not only has Joseph been taken away from his beloved dad and cherished home, but now he's unjustly enslaved, subjected to whatever his master asks him to do every hour of every day.

Where's God now?

It's mighty tempting, isn't it? To look at our current set of circumstances and doubt God's goodness and presence because of it?

Because if He were actually real, loving, and in control, He would've stepped in by now, right?

But it's a dangerous thing to jump to conclusions before we hear the whole story.

So let's do that first. Turns out Joseph is purchased by Potiphar, Pharaoh's captain of the guard, and instead of being whipped, starved, or forced to clean toilets, Jo is treated *good*. I'm talking put in charge of this guy's entire household—given complete administrative responsibility over everything Potiphar owned and full access to anything he wanted on the property. "The LORD was with Joseph, so he succeeded in everything he did as he served in the home of his Egyptian master. . . . With Joseph there, he didn't worry about a thing—except what kind of food to eat!" (39:2, 6).

Now that's my kind of stress—steak or buffalo chicken? Waffles or pancakes? Oatmeal chocolate chip cookies OR JUST REGULAR CHOCOLATE CHIP?! Someone please decide before my blood pressure rises.

Yeah. I could get used to that.

However, just when it seems like Joseph doesn't have it so bad after all, Potiphar's wife starts making some demands—and I don't mean having him flag down an Uber for her hair appointments or schedule out her manicures in advance. Girlfriend is *thirsty* and, well, has other things on her mind: "Come and sleep with me" (39:7).

Yikes, that's pretty forward. Take it up with HR, Jo! File under sexual harassment!

Oh shoot, Joseph, *you're* HR too? "No one here has more authority than I do. [My master] has held back nothing from me except you, because you are his wife. How could I do such a wicked thing? It would be a great sin against God" (39:9). Looks + integrity + faith = HOW IS THIS GUY STILL SINGLE, LADIES?

Potiphar's wife must've thought the same, the chase making him all the more irresistible. Just like HBO would've scripted it, she grabs his cloak at the height of her lust and commands, "Come on, sleep with me!" (39:12).

But our hero tears himself away, leaving her and his coat in the dust, and runs out of the house. (Fun fact: It's still up for debate whether he was wearing a loincloth underneath or straight-up went commando . . . so it's very possible he may have raced outside while flashing every observer along the way. Now that's literally fleeing temptation. #roundofapplause)

We're dealing with a smart lady, though. She looks down at the evidence in her hands, and in the heat of rejection, devises a plan. As she screams for any and all servants to come, this undercover temptress has one thing on her mind—*This guy's gonna wish he would've* never *turned me down.* With one false accusation—"He came into my room to rape me" (39:14)—we watch it snowball downhill from there.

Joseph's finding new clothes and rebounding from his marathon of a streak as Potiphar's footsteps pound right toward him. In the guy's fury, all Potiphar can think is, *HOW DARE HE TAKE ADVANTAGE OF MY WIFE,* and the next thing we know, Joseph's thrown into prison. The cell door slams shut, and Potiphar whirls around in complete rage, never looking back at his faithful servant ever again.

Sad. Another low, right? Seems like evil is winning . . . *yet again.*

First, the boy's sold into slavery, which, IMO, seems like more than enough tragedy for one lifetime. But now we look on as he's serving time for something *he didn't even do.* We're not talking a quick sentence, either. He was behind bars long enough to gain favor in the warden's eyes, be put in charge of all the other prisoners, and cross paths with Pharaoh's personal attendants, who were also incarcerated for what's recorded as "quite some time" (40:4).

So . . . where's the justice? Why would God allow this? And for so long? How could any good *possibly* come from that forsaken place?

Didn't the story say, "The LORD was with Joseph, giving him success in *everything* he did"? (39:3, emphasis added). But, like . . . *how?* I'm sorry, but I'm not seeing a lot of success here?

Oops, LOL. WE ALMOST DID IT AGAIN! Made some hasty assumptions right in the middle of his story (and maybe in the middle of ours, too) without yet having the full picture.

Back to gathering more info.

Being locked up in jail seemed like another real low for Joseph, "but the LORD was with Joseph in the prison and showed him his faithful love. And the LORD made Joseph a favorite with the prison warden" (39:21). *We see it again!* The Lord was not only with him in that cold cell, but also showed Joseph His faithful love—you know, while he was still locked up, wrongfully accused, far from his family, with dreams unfulfilled.

> How could any good *possibly* come from that forsaken place?

Seems like a backward way to showcase love, doesn't it? God could've demonstrated His love via a jailbreak—or, better yet, what if Potiphar's wife's testimony fell through for all to see? That would've made sense to me! A miracle, some vindication—yeah, I would consider *those* clear expressions of love!

Simply putting Joseph on good terms with the head jailer seems . . . *nice* . . . but not necessarily the best plan A we could drum up, right? Especially knowing God can literally do anything—like break those shackles, bend those bars, and send an angel to escort prisoners into freedom.

But God allowed this in Joseph's life—just like He allows cancer, hurricanes, and a shortage of Chick-fil-A sauce at my closest location. WHY THE AGONY?

If we concede God hasn't *forgotten* about Joseph, it's not like He's doling out the miracles we know He *could* do—in Joseph's life and maybe ours too—so at the very least, we can surmise He's withholding good things, right?

And there we go again, acting as if we know better and could write a better script than the Lord Almighty. LOL, and that's just in *Joseph's* life. I'll spare you the stacks of journals detailing my own plans. But let's just say I've got *a few* ideas of how I want things to go down in my life too. Maybe you can relate?

Here's what we simply cannot understand right here in this moment, but will obviously see in the next chapter: Because Joseph ends up managing the whole internal operations of this penitentiary, he's placed in charge of Pharaoh's very own chief cup-bearer and baker, who both *just so happened* to have puzzling dreams one night.

Joseph replied, "Go ahead and tell me your dreams" (40:8).

As they dished out all the juicy details, he turns to the cup-bearer, "In three days, you'll be hired back." He had bad news for the baker, though: "But you'll be impaled on a pole and birds will come and peck away at your flesh" (see Genesis 40:12-19). Joseph's brothers would agree—he's always had a way with words, hasn't he?

Turns out Pharaoh's birthday came three days later, and it all unfolded *exactly* as Joseph predicted. Instead of charging for these dream consultations, he simply asks the cup-bearer, "Do me a favor when things go well for you. Mention me to Pharaoh, so he might let me out of this place" (40:14).

FINALLY, THEN, this seemed like his big break! The cup-bearer would pass along his name, and sayonara! No need to pull a Shawshank Redemption and chip away at the walls with a mere rock hammer. By way of the Pharaoh, Joseph would be a free man back on the road to his hometown of Hebron in no time. Dad, here I come! Only a matter of minutes now . . .

Unfortunately, "Pharaoh's chief cup-bearer, however, forgot all about Joseph, never giving him another thought" (40:23). Waa, waa, waa. This man of God saw a glimmer of hope, but then has to endure yet another couple of years in prison . . . for what? And why? *And for real, let's get an ETA here—SIRI, HOW MUCH LONGER?*

What a sad way to close out that chapter—and maybe this chapter of *your* life isn't looking too hot either. You had faith; your symptoms didn't get better. You worked with integrity; someone else got the credit. You offered God what you had; He didn't multiply it. Like Joseph, you've hit a real low. You've been struggling against the same fear, doubt, worry, problem, or set of complications *for years*, and you're wondering, *Why aren't things working out for me? Why does evil seem to be winning? How much longer do I have to put up with this, and when do I get to see the silver lining?*

By the time Joseph was 30 years old, Pharaoh starts having nightmares, and when no one could ease his mind, word finally got back to the king that there's a jailbird who could help a brother out. "Pharaoh sent for Joseph at once, and he was quickly brought from the prison" (41:14).

Never give up hope; your circumstances can change in a mere moment too.

Clean-shaven and finally freed from his prison clothes, Joseph leans in as Pharaoh wastes no time diving into the details—something about fat cows and shriveled grain. Semantics. Without skipping a beat,

> Never give up hope; your circumstances can change in a mere moment.

Joseph interprets: There will be seven years of great prosperity throughout Egypt, but seven years of famine will come on its heels. Oh, and spoiler: It'll be so severe that it'll destroy the entire land. #dropitlikeitshot

Before Pharaoh even has time to lift his jaw off the floor, our guy jumps into next steps as if he's been preparing for this strategy meeting for months. "Therefore, Pharaoh should find an intelligent and wise man and put him in charge of the entire land of Egypt" (41:33).

Pharaoh drumming his fingers Now, whoever could *that* be?

Cough, cough, elbow jab, elbow jab.

"He'll collect a fifth of all the crops during the good years and guard it in the storehouses. That way, there will be enough food to go around during those seven years of famine. Otherwise, again, all of Egypt will be destroyed . . . *your choice.*"

Pharaoh turns to his advisers. "Can we find anyone else like this man so obviously filled with the spirit of God?" (41:38).

(OKAY, SO MAYBE GOD *WAS* OBVIOUSLY WITH JOSEPH.)

No other candidates? Okay, Jo—here's the signet ring off Pharaoh's very own finger. Now, go! Dress only in the finest linen, and your escort from here on out will be the limo—er, chariot—ride reserved only for the second-in-command—because *that is now what you are.* Lastly, "no one will lift a hand or foot in the entire land of Egypt without your approval" (41:44).

In the words of Michael Scott, "Okay, it's happening. Everybody, stay calm. EVERYBODY STAY CALM!" (Tried to minimize *The Office* quotes, but who am I kidding? Nothing is more relevant.)

This isn't even the best part, though! Fast-forward past those seven years of plenty as predicted, and Joseph's dad and brothers find themselves in a tough spot when the famine hits. "Go down [to Egypt], and buy enough grain to keep us alive. Otherwise we'll die" (42:2).

The very next thing we see is all 10 of the brothers bowing before Joseph with their faces to the ground—*not even aware this bigwig is their own flesh and blood they casted off years ago.* I'm tempted to reach over and check Jo's pulse; pretty sure, with the intensity and emotional crescendo of this moment, it's skyrocketing past 100 beats per minute. But to preserve the integrity of Scripture, I'll restrain myself. Let's just be clear, though: Boy is a *wreck* right about now.

He instinctively puts up the tough-guy facade first: "'Where are you from?' he demanded. . . . 'You are spies! You have come to see how vulnerable our land has become. . . . I swear by the life of Pharaoh that you will never leave Egypt unless your youngest brother comes here!'" (42:7, 9, 15). Then of course, he throws them in prison a few days just to teach them a thing or two. You know, brotherly love–type stuff.

After they serve their time, he shifts gears from bad cop to good cop: "I am a God-fearing man. If you do as I say, you will live. . . . Choose one of your brothers to remain in prison. The rest of you may go home with grain for your starving families. But you must bring your youngest brother back to me" (42:18-20).

It takes some convincing and a desperation for food once again, but by the time they actually do come back and Joseph sets his eyes on his one and only full-blood-related brother for the first time *in decades*, he has to run out of the room. Instant waterworks. Cue the ugly cry. No longer pent up, Jo is feeling ALL THE FEELS, and I can't blame the guy! You find out your dad is still alive. You overhear your brothers admit among each other they're sorry for what they did. And you're reunited with the only other person who carries the genes of your mom, who passed away long ago.

Oh, and their whole future hangs in the balance, and you get to decide how it's all going to play out. Dish out revenge or lavish with grace?! THE SUSPENSE IS KILLING ME.

"Joseph could stand it no longer" either (45:1). He orders his attendants out of the room, blows his own cover, unmasks his true identity, and weeps "so loudly the Egyptians could hear him" (45:2).

Our eyes bounce back and forth between the brothers and Joseph. What will they say? Who's going to make the next move? And most importantly, IS THERE GOING TO BE A GROUP HUG?

"Please, come closer," he tells them. "I am Joseph, your brother, whom you sold into slavery in Egypt." (Here we go! LAY IT ON 'EM, JO). "But don't be upset, and don't be angry with yourselves for selling me to this place." (Wait, what?) "It was God who sent me here, not you!" (But we saw them rip off your robe, throw you into a cistern, and pocket 20 shekels of silver in exchange for your enslavement . . . ?) "And He is the One who made me an adviser to Pharaoh—the manager of his entire palace and the governor of all Egypt" (see Genesis 45:4-5, 8).

Um . . . okay, that was unexpected.

His brothers thought so too, but before we speed up and join the egg toss at their family reunion, it's worth asking ourselves, "How are we interpreting the events *in our own lives*?" For Joseph, *Did they sell me or did God send me?*[1] Maybe for us, *Did he break up with me or did God end that relationship? Did the deal fall through or did God close that door?*

Being sold into slavery could make a man awfully bitter, but look at Joseph. Do we see any *hint* of such a thing illustrated on his face? Nope. Nada. Our hero is a *free man*—not just in status, but more importantly, in his soul—and how he interprets the ups and downs of life has much to do with it.

"God paid a high price for you, so don't be enslaved by the world" (1 Corinthians 7:23). Our souls were made to be free, and the Lord has made a Way—but you're the one who decides who's your master. The world and its obsessions? Your trials and fears? Or the sovereign God?

After Joseph's father comes to visit and the whole family decides to pack their suitcases and move close by, years later, Joseph again affirms, "You intended to harm me, but God intended it all for good. He brought me to this position so I could save the lives of many people" (Genesis 50:20).

And there you have it, folks—the HOW behind this Bible hero's story, the truth we can hold on to as we're riding up and down on the roller coaster of life: **Don't put a period where God intends a semicolon.** Our story is still unfolding and the course ahead is still becoming clear, so instead of jumping to conclusions at every tight turn, steep slope, and upside-down inversion, let's wait expectantly and faithfully instead.

Because P.S. (You saw it coming . . .) *It's gonna be good.* When we put every bad thing in the hands of a redemptive God, we have every reason to believe there is a purpose coming and a plan in the works. Today, we may not see, and I get that.

Someday, though, like Joseph, **we will.**

FEAR:

"What about when God lets bad things happen?"

THE HOW: Don't put a period where God intends a semicolon. We can hang on in the middle of our stories, knowing the end has already been written, God's goodness is inevitable, and there's a purpose and a plan—even here, even still.

WHAT ABOUT IN THE LOWS, WHEN THERE'S NO END OR REDEMPTION IN SIGHT? Sit in the middle of Joseph's story a little bit longer and push the ending out of your mind. Imagine how little hope he had when he was first enslaved, walking the distance to who knows where, with all his future plans dashed. Even later in his story, it would've been awfully hard to be optimistic standing wrongly accused behind bars, and the person he *thought* was his lifeline to hightail it outta there completely forgot about him. Yet do we read that Joseph wavered in faith? Do we see any evidence of him fixating on his circumstances and losing hope? No. Rather, we see the assurance that the Lord was with him and still gave him success everywhere he went. Even in your own lows, God's presence is still near and His plans for your life will prevail. *Doesn't matter if you can see it; you can still believe it.*

IF JOSEPH'S DEDUCTION IS TRUE THAT HIS BROTHERS DIDN'T SEND HIM AWAY, BUT IT WAS ULTIMATELY GOD HIMSELF WHO WAS RESPONSIBLE, HOW CAN I KNOW WHETHER GOD OR THE ENEMY IS BEHIND MY TRIAL? No matter who caused it, you can know with absolute certainty that God will always purpose it for good. All the details may not make sense today, but you'll see God's hands all over it in the end.

IF GOD IS LOVING, WHY DID HE ALLOW THIS? You and I don't get to choose how God showcases His faithful love. His ways are higher than ours, and as much as we'd like Him to swipe the prison key and free us *today*, if we're still here facing what we're facing, God must still be bringing purpose out of it. Perry Noble puts it this way: "When things are over our head, they're still under His feet. . . . He really is in control when things seem to be the most out of control. . . . He's actually shaping us for something greater than we could ever imagine."[2] Maybe God isn't punishing you or putting you off, but preparing you—so never give up on your Lord redeeming your story. He alone holds the final word—and He's already promised good.

Chapter 17

WHAT ABOUT WHEN EVERYTHING GOES UP IN FLAMES?

Shadrach, Meshach, and Abednego

The fire was hot on their faces, but even still, they weren't *nearly* as red as King Nebuchadnezzar—not because he's a redhead and that's just the permanent reality of our complexion. His face was filled with fury and "distorted with rage" (Daniel 3:19).

"Fire up the furnace seven times hotter than usual!" he bellowed.

While soldiers scramble over to crank it up a few notches, we look back to where the commotion originally started—with three young men, standing tall near the front of the ceremony, refusing to bow down to a 90-foot gold statue.

That's when the strongest soldiers in Nebuchadnezzar's army marched onto the scene, surrounded these handsome men with their resolute faces, and forcibly pushed them to the ground, wrapping ropes around their hands and feet.

Their orders were clear: Bind them up and throw them into the furnace.

That escalated quickly.

As they inch closer to the flames, smoke billowing, thousands of onlookers stand beside us as we all hold our breath. Is this how the story ends?! I mean, how did things go sideways so fast? These boys were the ones handpicked by the king's very own chief of staff, trained to be the top officials in Babylon, and out of all the other advisers and men in the land, the king found *no one* could match their wisdom and judgment. In terms of career achievements, fame, and riches, they were livin' on a mountain high! Snagged these big breaks! Life was going their way!

Until now.

Maybe you know the feeling. Your kids hit a fun stage. Your symptoms were almost nonexistent. You were climbing the ranks at work, felt super close to your friends, and your marriage was *so good* that you felt bad for all those people who kept complaining about how much work it is. #blessed

But after a heated conversation, a change of policy, a wayward decision, a bite of who knows what, or just inevitable growing pains, you could smell it . . . a faint hint of something burning.

Let's rewind a bit.

Remember our pal Daniel? When King Nebuchadnezzar infiltrated his hometown and took over Judah, he sought out the best boys from the best families and had them loaded up like cargo to be taken back to Babylon as captives. Daniel was amid the cream of the crop—and so were his friends Shadrach, Meshach, and Abednego.

In the king's eyes, they were now property of Babylon, and he lavished them with the finest food, introduced them to the wisest men in the land, invested time and resources into their education, and entrusted them to supervise much of his kingdom.

Up until this moment, the ROI was high. They continued to prove themselves as trustworthy, and the ripple effect of their leadership was nothing but positive. Sure, they refused to eat some of the food served, but in the end, it benefited everyone involved! They came out stronger and proved their diet was in fact the way to go, so the menu changed across the board for all captives—er, mentees—from that point forward. Since their wisdom had only *helped* the king, *improved* his training program, and *advanced* the country's overall strength, well then, no problems here. Nothing but a "Thank you for your feedback" email and a whoooooole lotta staff appreciation gifts.

Homeboys had it made. They were raised to the highest positions—even higher than the natives of Babylon, the Chaldeans—and carried influence and power wherever they went. (Not to mention, they ate like high school kids loading up their trays in the à la carte line with their parents' money.) No limits, unending benefits, and the world's applause.

LIFE AS A CAPTIVE DOESN'T SEEM SO BAD, DOES IT?

Yet here's where things get dicey. The king came with an agenda. He wasn't out just to build up his own little kingdom; his eyes were set on ruling a world empire. In the chapter just before this, however, Nebuchadnezzar had a dream that Daniel interpreted for him (Daniel 2). "Your kingdom is solid, Neb, like gold. But inferior ones will rise after yours comes to an end, and like a statue made with a blend of iron and clay feet, the final blow to send it all crashing down is a mixed group of people that will never unite."

Nebuchadnezzar was all show—"Thanks for the heads-up, brother . . ."—but tell a king his legacy won't last, and he'll do everything in his power to see that you're *dead wrong*—even if that dream was sent and confirmed by God Almighty Himself.

So we flip the page to Daniel 3 and immediately sniff out what's all going down. Daniel, you mentioned a statue with *iron-ceramic* feet? GUESS AGAIN. As the curtain pulls back and we take in this *pure-gold* statue, we realize the king may have missed the point and taken the dream a *little too* literally . . .

King Nebuchadnezzar still has something else up his sleeve. As Daniel, Shadrach, Meshach, and Abednego refresh their inboxes, a red-exclamation, high-priority email lands at the top. As members of the elite—high-ranking officers, governors, advisers, treasurers, judges, magistrates, and provincial officials included—they were formally invited to the dedication of this statue.

Oh, and the party was starting . . . NOW.

"Then a herald shouted out, 'People of all races and nations and languages, listen to the king's command! When you hear the sound of the horn, flute, zither, lyre, harp, pipes, and other musical instruments, bow to the ground to worship King Nebuchadnezzar's gold statue'" (3:4-5).

Wow, King Neb really pulled out all the stops and contracted a full-blown orchestra for this ribbon-cutting ceremony! Except . . . take a closer look at the invite list and swing back over to the instruments recruited. This was not just the A-list, and it wasn't a random group of musicians, either.

Wait a second, what did Daniel interpret as the weakness of the final kingdom again? Something about a mixed group of people who can never unite? What did the king in turn fixate on, hoping to strengthen, in order to prolong his reign and glory?

The feet.

The division.

MAYBE if every instrument from around the world was represented in this worship service? Every person would feel comfortable bowing down, creating one religion, one object of worship, one allegiance! A fortified kingdom so united and strong would be safeguarded against any threat of collapse or destruction, and just maybe, King Neb could alter the course of its demise altogether!

BRILLIANT, WOULDN'T YOU SAY?

So here in attendance we have virtually all who live in Babylon being welcomed to participate. Inclusion for all! No need to divide on anything—your beliefs and customs are all accepted here! Is there anything better than unity? Who would fight against that? I mean, don't we all want *that*?

Sounds good, doesn't it? It's the exact message our world is blaring on a megaphone today too—no need to draw a line and categorize anything as right or wrong! After all, what's true for you may not be true for me. So let's just slap a "coexist" sticker on our bumpers, speak your truth (just not *the* truth), and huddle up in a group hug!

Or *I guess* you could disagree and be a discriminatory, sexist, homophobic, intolerant bigot . . . *your choice. You know, as if those are your only two options . . .*

Important: God's always called us to unity *with other believers*, but He's never called us to unity *with the world*. Quite the contrary. No matter our differences or opinions, we can and should all band together as one under Jesus and the gospel. But believers have *always* been called to be set apart, not to conform to the behavior and customs of this world (Romans 12:2), and to be in the world but not of the world (John 17:14).

Oh, and a bit of a bummer: The world will hate us because of this (John 15:19). In Shadrach, Meshach, and Abednego's case, this hostility was projected through the king's order: "Anyone who refuses to obey will immediately be thrown into a blazing furnace" (Daniel 3:6).

Before anyone has time to process, the music begins. Our eyes bounce back and forth between the statue ominously towering over us and the furnace radiating heat into the crowd like a sauna.

Bow or burn.[1]

Whether they're scared, indifferent, enthusiastic, or just not wanting to rock the boat, everyone from the political powerhouses to the regular folk do as they're told. "All the people . . . bowed to the ground and worshiped the gold statue" (3:7).

All the people, that is, except for three.

The music cuts off, the ceremony halts, and all eyes turn to the last ones standing: Shadrach, Meshach, and Abednego. *Daniel seems to be MIA. As ruler over the entire province of Babylon, some* speculate he was out of office, traveling on the king's business.[2] If I didn't love the guy, I'd have my suspicions—but isn't it nice that God spares us from some battles we may be completely unaware of at the time? I KNOW. HE'S SO GOOD TO US.

With all eyes watching and his reputation on the line, the king offers them a second chance, jerking his head toward the heated consequence and wrapping up his threat with—little did he know—the worst thing he could have possibly said to persuade them otherwise: "And then what god will be able to rescue you from my power?" (3:15).

OH NO, HE DIDN'T. *snapping fingers*

(But really, yes. Yes, he did.)

Lean in close, because you're not gonna want to miss what comes next. "O Nebuchadnezzar, we do not need to defend ourselves before you. If we are thrown into the blazing furnace, the God whom we serve is able to save us. He will rescue us from your power, Your Majesty. But even if he doesn't, we want to make it clear to you, Your Majesty, that we will never serve your gods or worship the gold statue you have set up" (3:16-18).

BOOM, MIC DROPPED.

Remember: These guys were in the king's inner circle just moments ago, rubbing elbows and chest-bumping like buddies, until their beliefs no longer matched his. Now it was clear that Shadrach, Meshach, and Abednego's convictions didn't sync with the king's . . . and it offended him. Their refusal to fit the mold or follow in line lit the match, and their decision not to bow down to what they knew was wrong made it all go up in flames.

Our faith may at times be approved by the world. They like our whole "love others" policy, and they give out gold stars when our dollars go toward feeding the poor and freeing slaves from sex trafficking. Thanks for creating positive change in the world, Christians!

But then . . . we refuse to bow down to gender confusion in our kids as if it's an acceptable new norm. We call a baby in the womb an actual human life. We aren't interested in having drag queens lead our toddlers' story time, and the cheering stops. The high fives halt. As our faith stands in direct opposition to the expectations set by the world and we refuse to budge in what we *know to be wrong*, just like Shadrach, Meshach, and Abednego, we better get ready to take the heat.

This is where we come full circle to where we left off at the very beginning of the chapter. Speed past the king's contorted face (not your best look, Neb), the steam coming out of his ears (I'm all about the fiery analogies this chapter), and the whole tying-them-up part (Ironic how the person championing "tolerance" is actually acting very intolerant? #soundskindafamiliar). As these ripped militiamen in their bursting muscle tees (just guessing) fling the three young men into the fire, we hear screaming and wailing.

Except it's not coming from inside the furnace.

The cries are coming from these soldiers on the *outside*. They did their job: "Shadrach, Meshach, and Abednego, securely tied, fell into the roaring flames" (3:23)—but not a single one of these guards ended up surviving. And man, if those guys stationed outside in the *open air* couldn't live, then *NO WAY* could those boys chained up inside the flames make it out alive.

Right?

Suddenly the king jumps up in alarm! Not out of concern for his own men, of course—something else was amiss. As Nebuchadnezzar leans in, *1, 2, 3 . . . 4??* He pulls his advisers over in amazement. "Didn't we only throw three men in? Look, there's a fourth! Unbound! Walking around in the fire unharmed! And the fourth looks like *a god!*" (see Daniel 3:24-25).

INTERESTING.

Remember when these three men were facing the fire? They declared, "The God whom we serve is able to save us. He will rescue us from your power" (3:17). I don't know about you, but I grew up hearing the emphasis placed on the second part: "But even if he doesn't . . . we will never serve your gods" (3:18)—AS IF THAT'S THE PART WE STRUGGLE WITH.

I'd make the case though, if we're being honest, we may pray for deliverance—but it seems it's become our default to expect God won't show up. We add "but even if He doesn't" or "not my will, but Yours" as if we're purely being submissive like Jesus. But in our hearts, I'm not sure we're saying this out of strong faith, but maybe more so, creeping doubt. Instead of truly relinquishing control like our Savior did and being open to the possibility of something different from what we're so desperately praying for, we drop caveats in a way that curbs our prayers, curbs our faith, curbs our disappointment proactively. As if we need to give God an out if He doesn't come through to rescue us.

Ultimately, in these moments, we aren't submitting to God as much as we're submitting to our circumstances. Rolling over and playing dead without a fight, without persistence, without hope . . . without *faith*.

So then when He *does* deliver?! We're amazed! Our eyes bug out in astonished surprise! We're speechless because *we weren't expecting that* . . . right?

I still get sick to my stomach when I think of one particular morning when I woke up to hear our two-year-old daughter Hazel gagging. I thought she was just throwing up, and Ty, who was standing behind her over the toilet holding her hair back, thought so too.

Until she kept gagging. And nothing was coming out.

Ty fished in her mouth and felt something far too deep. I tried myself, could barely feel the top of whatever it was, and cried, "Jesus, HELP US."

While Ty ran downstairs to call 911, I did every CPR method I knew how—performing chest thrusts, twisting her upside down and using the heel of my hand to do back blows, trying to swipe it out with my finger. Still nothing. Minutes were going by, she was starting to look more faint, and the gasping was terrifying.

At the complete end of my rope, with absolutely nothing left I could do, I held her in my lap and heard myself say, "In the name of Jesus, come out."

Nothing.

This time more firm, "In the name of JESUS, COME OUT."

Clunk. There was a little plastic teddy bear sitting on our bathroom floor.

I wish I could tell you I expected this, but I skipped over that expectation part. I kicked off my prayer much like Shadrach, Meshach, and Abednego, knowing Jesus was able. But I left out the middle part of that declaration—convinced "He will"—and jumped straight to "but even if He doesn't," waiting primarily for the ambulance to arrive to save us. But Hazel stands as testament today that God's Almighty hand still can and does save—do we believe He will?

Notice that **Shadrach, Meshach, and Abednego weren't the ones amazed by their deliverance. That was their expectation. It was the king whose jaw dropped.**

When we're facing the fires of life, and the flames are hot around our marriages, our finances, our doctor appointments—and we can't see the light of day through the smoke—does our faith resemble the confidence radiating from these three faith-filled men?

Or do we look more like the pagan king?

Do we cherry-pick "Our God is able to save"—skip the middle part—"but even if He doesn't, I still won't waver?" Or do we hold unswervingly to the full declaration: "Our God is able to save, AND HE WILL. But even if He doesn't in this instant, I still won't waver"?

The middle portion of that profession changes the entire story. Do we actually know "His incomparably great power for us who believe. That power is the same as the mighty strength he exerted when he raised Christ from the dead and seated him at his right hand in the heavenly realms, far above all rule and authority, power and dominion, and every name that is invoked, not only in the present age but also in the one to come" (Ephesians 1:19-21, NIV)? If we do, it'll change the trajectory of our entire story too.

Psst, bonus (and maybe the whole point?): Those watching will notice too. They'll be amazed. And, like the king, they may have no other choice than to believe in the one true God who is *so obviously* real and who *so obviously* loves His people.

But it takes faith, and notice: We cannot afford to wait until *after* the fire to make our decision. We can't wait to speak up, to hold unshakably to the truth, and to declare the power of God *after* the rescue, good news, and answered prayer—because look closely: Three men came in, and three men came out.

It was only in the fire when the king could see Jesus.

> We cannot afford to wait until *after* the fire to make our decision.

The same is true in our own lives. Plenty of us have seen cancer destroy someone's future. We know how infertility steals someone's hope, and how stress at work, a broken marriage, or a chronic disease has turned many people into bitter cynics—*so why would we be any different?*

Well, girls, we are different because we are people who know God and trust He will do just as He said:

- We aren't abandoned or forsaken—He is with us wherever we go (Deuteronomy 31:8).
- When we are weak, He is strong on our behalf (2 Corinthians 12:10).
- No matter how the plot twists, we know He will use it *all* for our good and His glory (Romans 8:28).

When everything goes up in flames, remember that your Savior is with you in the fire, breaking any chains meant to tie you up, and He will make Himself known IN THE HEAT OF IT ALL. When you decide to put Him on display, the God you serve is certainly able to save you . . .

. . . and He will.

"Nebuchadnezzar . . . shouted: 'Shadrach, Meshach, and Abednego, servants of the Most High God, come out! Come here!' [They] stepped out of the fire. Then the high officers, officials, governors, and advisers crowded around them and saw that the fire had not touched them. Not a hair on their heads was singed, and their clothing was not scorched. They didn't even smell of smoke!" (Daniel 3:26-27).

Things may be heating up in your life—those custody battles are relentless, the divorce is tearing you apart, the depression is taking its toll, and the state of our nation has got you all stressed out. *Girlfriend . . . I hear ya.*

But here's the truth of the redemptive power of our God: He breaks the chains of bitterness and comparison. Jesus holds all authority to untie every negative thought pattern, protect our kids, and bring purpose out of pain. With Him on our side, knowing "he will order his angels to protect you wherever you go" (Psalm 91:11), we don't merely survive the fire—we're able to walk around unharmed, unbound, *free* amidst the fire.

Even when we hoped things wouldn't have gone this far, believed those flames wouldn't even touch us, and waited on the Lord to spare us from this fire, our hope can still remain even when we're thrown into the fiery furnace. Because we know that although we walk through the valley of the shadow of death, this is not where we stay; this is not our home. Our God will lead us *through* the valley, and not even the likes of cancer, financial ruin, or abuse can burn what the Lord is faithful to protect—our very souls.

Fire is deadly, for sure.

It's life-threatening, no doubt about it.

But just as real as those flames burning wild are His promises, and these three men held on to the reassurance that God would indeed deliver them from captivity and restore them as a nation once again (Jeremiah 24:4-7).

Our hope is even greater than that, and it's permanent—our Savior has delivered us from the penalty of sin, so now if we believe in Him, we overcome this world and can look forward to the day when we'll be restored in His glorious freedom forever (Romans 8:21). Until then, let's remember these words from the book of Isaiah: "Do not be afraid, for I have ransomed you. I have called you by name; you are mine. When you go through deep waters, I will be with you. When you go through rivers of difficulty, you will not drown. When you walk through the fire of oppression, you will not be burned up; the flames will not consume you. For I am the LORD, your God, the Holy One of Israel, your Savior" (43:1-3).

Spoiler: Shadrach, Meshach, and Abednego were promoted immediately after this furnace episode to positions even higher than the ones they held before. But what they walked away with was way better than a mere earthly promotion with better benefits and a higher contribution to their 401(k).

These men weren't just tested in Nebuchadnezzar's fire—they were refined by the Refiner Himself in the furnace of suffering (Isaiah 48:10), and like Job, they came out as pure as gold (Job 23:10). Our faithfulness in the fire can have the exact same results: "These trials will show that your faith is genuine. It is being tested as fire tests and purifies gold—though your faith is far more precious than mere gold. So when your faith remains strong through many trials, it will bring you much praise and glory and honor on the day when Jesus Christ is revealed to the whole world" (1 Peter 1:7).

> People are crowding around, watching your every move, and what you're putting on display matters.

In fact, our God hopes it does.

So when it all goes up in flames, *stay faithful, girlfriend*. People are crowding around, watching your every move, and what you're putting on display matters—your fear or your God. Your worries or His promises. Your weakness or His strength.

P.S. You'll never regret choosing the latter. Let your faith shine bright like a diamond, and the likes of King Nebuchadnezzar will live to answer their own question—from "Who can possibly save you from this?" to "There is no other god who can rescue like this!" (Daniel 3:29).

Bottom line: You have *every reason* to believe your God will deliver.

FEAR:

"What about when everything goes up in flames?"

THE HOW: Although fire tests, it can also purify. Remain strong. God will rise up to defend you, and you'll receive "much praise and glory and honor on the day when Jesus Christ is revealed to the whole world" (1 Peter 1:7).

HOW DID IT ALL GO DOWNHILL SO FAST? People are fickle. If your beliefs line up with their agenda, they'll cheer you on as your number one fan! But the moment your convictions threaten their plans or sense of acceptance, they'll turn on you *real* fast. They did it with these three men; they did it with Jesus, too. On Palm Sunday, the crowd was gushing over Him as the Messiah, laying down their coats and waving palm branches to declare His kingship and saving power! But when they realized He had no intention of overthrowing the government and rising up as their political leader, this same crowd that cried out, "Hosanna!" shouted, "Crucify Him!" later that very week. When God doesn't answer our prayers how we want, it's mighty tempting to stop worshiping Him too and allow our disappointments to pull us away from Him. But like our three heroes in this chapter, may our worship never be contingent on circumstances, but steadfast.

HOW DO WE KNOW WHAT TO STAND UP FOR IN THIS WORLD? While the king threatened, "Worship or die," Shadrach, Meshach, and Abednego knew the truth: Worship *and* die.[3] How? They knew Scripture and truly believed God's commands set us free, and the Lord had specifically commanded His people not to make idols of any kind (Exodus 20:4). The more you get to know Jesus—the Word who became flesh and dwelled among us—and heed the leading of the Holy Spirit—the Spirit of truth—the stronger your convictions and knowledge will become as well. Your steps will be sure, and you'll have the words to say the moment you need them (Luke 12:12).

WHAT IF MY TRIAL DOESN'T END WITH A PROMOTION LIKE SHADRACH, MESHACH, AND ABEDNEGO'S? WHAT IF THE FLAMES WIN AND IT GOES BADLY? We don't see Shadrach, Meshach, and Abednego's motivation founded in the promotion (for all we know, they didn't even consider that as a possibility), but their primary concern was remaining faithful to God. Craig Groeschel puts it this way: "Outcome is God's responsibility; obedience is yours."[4] Focus on what matters—seeking first the Kingdom of God and His righteousness (Matthew 6:33)—and everything else will fall into place. Also, when these men were being bound with rope, they could've looked at each other and determined, "Well, boys, this is it! It's been a good run." Likewise, when they were thrown into the furnace, it would've been reasonable to assume that was the end of their story. Yet both instances were merely a setup for what God wanted to do in the *middle* of their story. So even when the flames blaze all around you, don't be too quick to slap on the season finale title—God holds the final word, and no fire of hardship—literal or figurative—can ever derail His good purposes for your life.

Chapter 18

WHERE'S GOD?

Elisha

Ever been blindsided by bad news?

One day, you're talking with your dad on the phone; the next, he's in the hospital and no visitors are allowed.

One week, it's same old, same old at work; yet the very next Monday, HR calls you into their office informing you your position's been cut.

One year, you're celebrating an anniversary—in your marriage, at church, or in remission—but flip over the calendar and you've signed divorce papers, your church doors have closed, or a routine scan reveals your worst nightmare has come true.

I think that's why I seem to check my body for lumps every time I'm washing off in the shower, scratching my neck, or itching a mosquito bite. (They're ruthless in MN . . . you should come visit!) A lone bump was the only symptom I had when I received the cancer diagnosis, and if I could avoid being sucker punched in the gut by some terrible news that came out of NOWHERE again, well then, compulsive self-examinations and WebMD saved to my Safari favorites is just the way it's gonna be.

I know Ty's rolling his eyes—are you, too? I hope so, because this is clearly noooooooo way to live and certainly not a posture of resting in Christ's freedom and abundant life.

But . . . I have a suspicion I'm not the only one who's had the rug pulled out from under me. I don't mean to put you on the spot, but if you were blindsided by your parents' divorce, your struggle against infertility, or your spouse's addiction, there's some self-preservation going on, isn't there? We've been hurt once; shame on them. BUT BUSHWHACKED FROM BEHIND *AGAIN*? Shame on US. We will do *everything* in our willpower not to be fooled and assaulted in such a surprise ambush once again . . . even if that means living anxiously, biting our nails over things completely out of our control, and wasting hours worrying over something that actually *and statistically, probably* may not ever happen again.

Have you met Elisha? If you haven't, you're not alone—at the beginning of 1 Kings chapter 19, the current prophet Elijah hadn't yet crossed paths with him either.

In fact, Elijah felt like the last person on the literal face of the earth who still loved God—and he was *over it* (1 Kings 19:10). If you're the only Christian in your circle, the only person in your workplace who has faith, or the only mom in your friend group sending your kids to public school over private or homeschooling, you may have echoed the same prayer: "GOD, I'M THE ONLY ONE LEFT."

(Guess what? In Elijah's case, there were actually 7,000 people left who were faithful to God—Elisha included. Maybe there are other Christians at your kids' school or someone in another department who loves Jesus like you do? And maybe God has a plan to cross your paths with them sometime down the road? Don't @ me! I'M ONLY SUGGESTING.)

But being a prophet was not for the faint of heart—especially when it involved confronting an evil king, challenging 850 false prophets to a spiritual showdown, then fleeing a death warrant . . . all in a matter of days (1 Kings 18–19).

Cue Elisha. Elijah's ready to peace out of the craziness, and without needing a two-weeks' notice, God points him toward his replacement. When the time comes to pass off the baton to his young protégé, Elijah asks what he can put in his will for the boy. Not interested in the heirloom china or Grandpa's vinyl records, Elisha has the gall to say, "Please let me inherit a double share of your spirit and become your successor" (2 Kings 2:9). All directors, supervisors, and CEOs are not surprised. Nothing like a college grad fresh on the job, letting her superior know she's set her sights on *their* job, and plans to someday take over the entire company and maybe (doubtlessly) the entire world. We are the millennials. Hear us roar.

JK, Elijah was actually like a father to Elisha, so after spending years as his apprentice, this request wasn't by any means greedy. It was a compliment to Elijah's faithful service, and it showcased Elisha's zeal for the Lord and his excitement about doing His work! So *slap on the back* you want it, you got it!

By the time we get to 2 Kings 6, where we're going to park it for the remainder of this chapter, this apprentice has already gone on to heal the waters of Jericho (2 Kings 2:19-21), cursed a group of boys who called him "baldy" (to which they were then mauled by bears and met with sudden death because of it #fileunderthingsnottosay-tobaldmen—2:23-25), multiplied a widow's pantry and saved her life (4:1-7), and oh yeah, prayed for someone's son to be resurrected from the dead and witnessed it happen (4:32-37). Did I mention Elisha also salvaged a poisonous pot of soup (4:38-41), multiplied 20 barley loaves to feed 100 men (with some left over—4:42-44), and cured a man of leprosy in his spare time (5:13-14)?

I would say Elijah's star student got *exactly* what he asked for.

But even this man of God couldn't avoid the ambushes of life.

One night, Elisha went to bed in peace; the next morning, his servant got up early and went outside to do . . . what men do when they go outside. I won't pretend to know. Instead of getting the chance to check on the sprinkler system or inspect the driveway for cracks though, he's met with enemy troops, horses, and chariots surrounding the city.

NOT EXACTLY A SIGHT FOR SORE EYES.

He sprints back inside in his skivvies, and in complete helplessness, shakes Elisha awake shrieking, "What will we do now?" (6:15).

Maybe you're asking the same thing today too. Because of _____, you're caught off guard, facing a battle much bigger than yourself, and with no plan of attack, clear next steps, or resources at your disposal, you're panicking. "WHAT DO I DO NOW?"

It's easy to wonder next, *Where are you, God?* I get it! It can be down-right *H-A-R-D* to see God when that unexpected bill comes in the mail and you're already feeling financial strain, you wake up to a period when you were hoping for a baby, or you're talking with your kid who wants nothing to do with the church or God.

Where's God's protection? Where's His help? Where are His miracles?

If we only focus on this part of the story, we'd be clueless—and if you only focus on today's circumstances, you may be too. But if we rewind to the first part of 2 Kings 6, we see that God: (1) Not only knew all about the enemy's plans of attack, but (2) He also tipped off Elisha and (3) sent him to warn the king of Israel with the details. The fact that Aram's surprise attacks kept getting spoiled in this way frustrated the king of Aram *so much* that "he called his officers together and demanded, 'Which of you is the traitor? Who has been informing the king of Israel of my plans?'" (6:11). One of his men replied, "It's not us. . . . Elisha, the prophet in Israel, tells the king of Israel even the words you speak in the privacy of your bedroom!" (6:12).

LOL, remember growing up when we used to be paranoid someone was eavesdropping on the landline upstairs when we were on the phone downstairs? You know, because we wanted to analyze everyone's AIM away messages in peace with our girlfriends? Not much different today; we're freaked when Google ads pick up on our conversations. But this? It's just next level. Turns out the CIA doesn't need to bug a room; they just need God, y'all.

God has always been aware of the enemy's attacks well before any are put into action, and sometimes—like we see with the Israelite troops in

2 Kings 6—He gives warning and we stand prepared when they come marching. Other times, however, He allows us to stay put in Dothan like Elisha, giving the enemy time to circle around us, *for a reason*. It's *never* out of cruelty or some sick pleasure—even though the situation may appear to be certain death.

No matter what you're facing, what you're up against, what's working against you, perhaps God has His own plan of attack and is on the brink of showcasing His power through *you, too*.

> Perhaps God has His own plan of attack and is on the brink of showcasing His power through *you*.

Wait, don't miss this! Take your eyes off the shaking servant and narrow in on Elisha. Instead of giving into panic or crumbling into despair, this guy hasn't even flinched or budged *an inch*. Rather, completely calm and totally collected, he reassures his servant blowing in a bag, "Don't be afraid! For there are more on our side than on theirs!" (6:16).

Are you scratching your head too? Looking out the window over his shoulder, we can count along with his servant, and sure, we may not be good at math (IT WAS ONE B+) but 1, 2 vs. . . . 1, 2, 3, 4 . . . yeah, how'd you get to that, Eli?

Elisha doesn't even dignify that with a response. He just waves his hand. "O LORD, open his eyes and let him see!" (6:17). And that's when his servant looks up and sees an entire hillside around Elisha filled with horses and chariots of fire.

SAY WHAAAAAAAAT.

We have SO MUCH to debrief, and these men offer us little opportunity to do so—but I'm calling an audible. Let's pump the breaks and PAUSE quick. To be clear: God's angel armies were surrounding Elisha and his servant as they slept peacefully the night before, *and* they were still there when their enemy camped out on the nearby hillside just as the rooster crowed. Circumstances *looked* worse the next morning, but spiritually speaking, the circumstances remained the same.

Elisha could see this whole picture, but his servant could not.

What do *we* see today? Only our physical circumstances with our dilated pupils? Because those thousands of soldiers fully trained to wipe out the entire town by nightfall were what Elisha's servant saw. Elisha wasn't oblivious—he saw this too, *but he also saw so much more.*

You may feel lonely, in a dark spot, your mind consumed with doubts and heart filled with fear—but whenever that's the case, remember you're only looking at the shields and swords of the Syrian soldiers. However, God calls His people to "set [our] minds on things above, not on earthly things" (Colossians 3:2, NIV), which includes recognizing the full reality of our situation—physically *and spiritually.* Just like Elisha, not only does "the angel of the LORD [encamp] around those who fear him, and delivers them" (Psalm 34:7, ESV), but "he will order his angels to protect you wherever you go" (91:11).

This is the confidence God wants not just for Elijah but for all of His people to realize and live in. Not to give into panic or succumb to the enemy of today, but declare, "Though a mighty army surrounds me, my heart will not be afraid. Even if I am attacked, I will remain confident" (27:3).

But confident HOW? When attack is imminent and THE ENEMY IS STANDING OUTSIDE MY WINDOW?

Swing back to the scene. Notice how God didn't remove Elisha's enemy, and the angel army didn't slaughter the Syrians, either—both could've easily been done, and let's be real, that's what we would've PREFERRED. God instead illuminated His presence and showed Elisha and his servant all the help they had in the spiritual realm—and that backing was all they needed.[1]

Is it for us, too?

"As the Aramean army advanced toward him, Elisha prayed, 'O LORD, please make them blind.' So the LORD struck them with blindness as Elisha had asked. Then Elisha went out [to] them" (2 Kings 6:18-19).

Interesting request. Instinct tells me I would've made a run for it out back—like in the *opposite* direction of the enemy. But Elisha asks God to cover their eyes, and like a bunch of toddlers playing peekaboo, as he walks straight toward them, maybe they won't notice . . . ? LOL. **I guess no prayer is ever too foolish to ask the Lord Almighty!**

Put yourself in the shoes of Elisha's servant for a quick sec, though. If you heard, "I'm going to head out unarmed, meet up with that whole hillside of trained enemy warriors face-to-face, and ask God to make them all blind so they won't know it's me—you know, the one person they set out to find," how would you respond? Maybe stare with narrowed eyes like *YOU CRAZY*? Give an awkward laugh and avoid eye contact? **#blessedarethepeacemakers** Or try to talk him out of it? "For sure God *can* do that, Eli . . . but how about we keep thinking? I mean, we're bound to come up with something better!"

But striking all the men blind in response to the prayer of His faithful, beloved prophet was no big deal for God, and I reallyyyyyyyyyyy wish we'd bury this truth deep down in our own souls too. Because our God sits enthroned above the circle of the earth with limitless, unending resources at His disposal, all things—even the impossible—are indeed possible. So, no matter how big our problem is to US, it is never too big for HIM.

Furthermore, do you realize who you are to this King? **Lemme tell you!** You are His beloved daughter (1 John 3:1), His most prized possession (James 1:18), and the apple of His eye (Psalm 17:8). You are the one He chose and loved before He made the world (Ephesians 1:4). You are the one He saw when He sent His Son to this earth to die a painful death and take the penalty for your sin. You are the one He adopted into His family with *great pleasure* (Ephesians 1:5), so He could have a relationship with you forevermore.

Do you *really think* He'd leave you helpless and unprotected now?

Can you *truly believe* He doesn't care and isn't going to do a-n-y-t-h-i-n-g with what you're facing?

Girl, please. Satan is a trickster, but these lies especially are just pathetic. All evidence points to a God who loves us, is able to do immeasurably more than all we ask or imagine, and *will* work everything for our good.

But again, it all goes back to our vision—what are we fixating on? Obsessing over? Looking at and allowing to consume us?

Our problems or our God?

How we answer that determines whether we cower inside in fear or march out deliberately, headfirst into the danger without restraint, and praying big asks like Elisha, knowing *for certain* our God is going to come through for us in His almighty, unique way.

Turns out this whole blind-them strategy worked. Like a game of Follow the Leader, Elisha himself marshaled his enemies over to the town of Samaria, right into the hands of the waiting Israelite army, and these armed men *just followed*, completely oblivious and totally compliant. Only God, y'all. Now the tables were turned and once *they* were the ones surrounded, "Elisha prayed, 'O Lord, now open their eyes and let them see'" (2 Kings 6:20). When God did, these men weren't slaughtered or held as prisoners—instead, Elisha threw his enemies a big feast and sent them home.

IS THIS REAL LIFE? Yep. Elisha met evil with good, paid them back with a blessing instead of retaliation, and the men who sat at his table that day no doubt encountered the kindness and power of the living God instead of any deserved wrath.

I'M NOT CRYING; YOU'RE CRYING.

> The only factor that matters is *God*, who alone holds the final word.

All odds may be against you, and things may not look great. I've so been there. But even when your demise may look probable, remember . . . so did Elisha's defeat in the face of these Aramean soldiers. The only factor that matters, though, is *God*, who alone holds the final word, and we have the privilege and powerful position to look up to the heavens knowing **He's got our back.** What a friend we have in Christ!

P.S. God and His angel armies are still on guard and circling around you today. So lift your chin in the midst of any adversity, confident His backing will see you through, and get the popcorn, girlfriend—because you won't want to miss how He shows up.

O Lord, open our eyes and help us see.

FEAR:

"Where's God?"

THE HOW: Whether or not you *see evidence* of it, God's presence surrounds you today. So when you're tempted to panic, hear Elisha's reassurance, "Do not be afraid! There are more on our side than on theirs!" Then set your mind on things above, not on earthly things, recognizing the full reality of your situation—physically *and spiritually*.

IF GOD WAS PROTECTING ME, WHY DID HE ALLOW THIS BAD THING TO HAPPEN? Think of all the good that came out of Elisha's situation that never would have happened if it was avoided altogether—Elisha's servant's faith grew tenfold, the Aramean army witnessed God's power and kindness with their own eyes, and after this incident, "the Aramean raiders stayed away from the land of Israel" (2 Kings 6:23). We may not always see why, but in the hands of God, purpose is bound to come.

WHAT CAN I DO TO BUILD MY FAITH TO RESEMBLE ELISHA'S? Notice who Elisha spent his time with before all this happened—Elijah, the renowned prophet of God. Elisha watched this man pray, serve, call for miracles, and lead God's people back to their Lord. Very similarly, look at the position of Elisha's servant. He's doing the same—living his life day in and day out next to a godly man whose faith is rubbing off on him. The company you surround yourself with matters. We should eat with sinners, yes, but we need to do life with other believers.

HOW DO I KNOW WHAT TO PRAY FOR? IF I WERE ELISHA, I'D PRAY GOD WOULD TAKE CARE OF MY ENEMIES WHILE I WAITED INSIDE, WATCHING OUT THE WINDOW. Oh, girl, you and me both. But again, it's really less on us than we think it is: "The Holy Spirit helps us in our weakness. For example, we don't know what God wants us to pray for. But the Holy Spirit prays for us with groanings that cannot be expressed in words" (Romans 8:26). After we pray, *"Open our eyes and let us see,"* let's wait patiently, allow the Holy Spirit to pray for us, and trust Jesus is "sitting in the place of honor at God's right hand, pleading for us" (8:34). God may not lead us to pray for our co-workers to be made blind—and that's okay! (On their behalf, feel the need to emphasize: MORE THAN OKAY, LOL.) He is doing a new thing in our stories, so eyes up, girl! You and me are gonna see it.

Chapter 19

HOW DO I CHOOSE FAITH WHEN I DON'T FEEL IT?

David

Girlfriend, you're two CHAPTERS away from finishing this book, and I gotta shoot straight with you. I've strategically waited to break the news until this moment, but I think you're ready . . .

We can immerse ourselves in every Bible story of every Bible hero, gather the facts, realize who our God is and what He calls us to do, and gain the intel to walk down the same pathway in faith all day long—just like we've been doing. But if we don't implement these next two HOWs, at the end of the day, don't be surprised if we're still being shot left and right from the enemy's attacks and floundering in doubt, fear, hopelessness, and grief.

COME AGAIN?

I know. We were on a roll, but I PROMISE I'm not pulling a bait and switch on you. You're still on track! Every HOW you learned on all the miles of dirt path we've already covered are 100 percent absolutely *essential*—fundamental to building a firm foundation in Christ, yes, and also living a life marked by faith.

For instance, if we didn't learn about our roaring lion of an enemy who's been on the prowl since the very beginning, hoping to devour our faith, peace, and relationship with God? Then we'd likely fall into the same trap Eve did, wrongly assume God is holding out on us, and take a bite out of a poisonous apple that God never intended us to feast on.

Or if we didn't understand that it's less about us and more about Him, then like Gideon, we'd waste even more time fixated on our own shortcomings and lack of resources to carry out God's work. Instead of stepping into the assignment He has for us, we'd be the ones minimizing our days, still hiding out, threshing wheat inside when it's *meant* to be done outside.

If we didn't grasp God's promise to work *all* things for our good, then unlike Esther, we'd feel like God has deserted us when tragedy strikes.

If we didn't realize that life is a roller coaster, but—as with Joseph—God is with us in every high and every low, bringing about a purpose that someday we *will* see? Then we'd fail to be faithful in the loop-de-loops and give up well before our stories were even intended to be over.

And if we didn't remember the call to put Jesus on display in the fire, if we didn't have the eyes to see all the help we have in the spiritual realm, and if we didn't rise up in our convictions when culture tries to indoctrinate us otherwise, then we'd miss mighty opportunities to showcase our Savior to a world that desperately needs saving.

Ultimately, we'd miss the very reason we're here on earth.

We'd miss the resurrecting power available to us.

We'd miss God, and we'd miss out on becoming the person He made us to be.

You already know this, though, right? My guess is, like me, you realized it along the way. Those times when your knees buckled in fear, your spirit grew dim if the odds didn't look great, and your doubts in the valley became so loud and all-consuming? Well, certain Bible heroes spoke *specifically to that struggle*, and when you followed behind their footsteps in chapters past, you realized where you may have misstepped as you faced similar crossroads or how God's redirecting you back on the path He's been beckoning you to take all along.

So you're changing courses.

No longer do you want to live a life of defeat. Days consumed by fear and dread. Hours marked by defeat instead of victory. You're done praying weak prayers, and you're over having weak faith. You want to make this short life count, you want to see the miracles of heaven come to earth, and ultimately, *you want to make your Father proud.*

I hear you. I get you. And that's why I can't emphasize this enough: These last two chapters will either make it or break it. If all the previous HOWs are one big gift from the God who has great things for you, then this chapter is like the wrapping paper keeping it bundled up—and the last principle is the bow that ties it all together. Put these last two HOWs into practice, and you'll see the difference between being hearers and doers of the Word, following Christ or following our own emotions and desires, and standing when the rains come or being washed away by the flood.

Do we need to do a few jumping jacks first to get hyped up, or are you RARIN' TO GO, sleeves rolled up and all ready to dive in? Recently postpartum, I'll remain firmly planted with two feet on the ground. #iykyk But believe you me, I'M READY IF YOU ARE.

Good. **fist bump** Let's do this.

Have you ever talked yourself out of something? You wanted to try something new, pursue a dream, tackle a big goal, do the right thing, or say something to someone?

But . . . it just wasn't the right time. The funds or connections weren't there. You didn't know that person well enough. As much as you went back and forth—*should I or shouldn't I?*—at the end of the day, you let it go. Your reasoning seemed valid and logical then, but there's something in the back of your mind now that still makes you wonder—*What if?*

What would've happened if I said yes to that proposal? Remained in that relationship? Sold everything for that business opportunity? Switched to that major? Moved instead of stayed? Or stayed instead of moved?

You fill in the blank: How different would things be if _____?

Let's apply this train of thought to our spiritual lives: What would've happened if I prayed and waited on God instead of acting impulsively and impatiently? What if all these years, I would've remained convinced of God's good plans instead of doubting His goodness? How would the state of my emotions, home life, and marriage be different if I kept my eyes on God instead of the size of my giants? What if I cared more about God's glory than my to-do list and self-imposed deadlines? What if I waited expectantly to see God move instead of hiring a concubine to sleep with my husband?

LOL. Sorry, Sarah. #hadto But with all this in mind, we're ready to meet David.

Yeah, yeah, already know the guy. He's the kid with a slingshot. The teenager who took down the giant Goliath. That king over Israel, the man after God's own heart. Old news, already acquainted. What else you got for me?

OKAY, BIBLE SCHOLAR, THEN WHY DON'T YOU GO TEACH SUNDAY SCHOOL ALREADY?

Just kidding. (Although I'm sure kids' ministry IS looking for help . . . like this very Sunday, so you really should consider. #onceinkidsministryalwaysinkidsministry)

But back to it: I KNOW! David's kind of a big deal, and you don't even have to be a Christian to know his biography. His story has been around the block a few times. But if we want to be women after God's own heart, *it only makes sense* we peek into his diary, scrutinize his innermost thoughts, and comb through every confession, cry, praise, and plea to see what we can uncover.

GASP, stick our nose inside his very own diary? Isn't that a little, like . . . intrusive and a violation of someone's privacy? Well, for one, that's never stopped me before, but two, it's in the Bible. So *technically* it's public knowledge and proprietary to God. Also, David's been dead for 3,000-plus years (so I really don't think he cares anymore to be honest).

If you will, like a little sister who knows no boundaries, let's turn to Psalm 22 and get a peek inside big brother's head:

"My God, my God, why have you abandoned me? Why are you so far away when I groan for help?" (verse 1).

I knew it was going to be juicy. Did I mention he's dramatic? This entry is no outlier, either. David gives Shakespeare a run for his money, my personal favorite being: "I am worn out from my groaning. All night long I flood my bed with weeping and drench my couch with tears" (Psalm 6:6, NIV). Nothing like moving the cry fest to the living room because of the flood damage you did in the bedroom—only to drown the furniture there, too. Been there, done that, right? Or "My heart pounds in my chest. The terror of death assaults me. Fear and trembling overwhelm me, and I can't stop shaking" (55:4-5). Yeeeep, stress hormones'll do that for ya. Homeboy knew anxiety before 2020 knew anxiety.

Back to Dear Diary: "Everyone who sees me mocks me. They sneer and shake their heads, saying, 'Is this the one who relies on the LORD? Then let the LORD save him! If the LORD loves him so much, let the LORD rescue him!'" (22:7-8).

Maybe you're being teased about this same thing: Your co-workers, family, or supposed friends just don't get your faith or your God, so when bad times come, they roll their eyes with the same jab. "Where is this God of yours? I thought He would help you? You said He's mighty to save, but where's His rescue?"

That's not the only place we get an earful of it. These doubts aren't just vocalized out loud by other people or this world; we hear them inwardly, too. When it all comes crashing down, our prayers don't get answered how or when we hoped, and things continue to spiral out of control, we catch wind of our very own thoughts turning against us: "Where are you, God?"

He said *no weapons formed against me shall prosper (Isaiah 54:17), but . . . they sure look like they're prospering to me!*

I know God said He'd give me a way out of every temptation (1 Corinthians 10:13), but is there a trapdoor around here, or what am I missing? No LED exit signs in sight from my vantage point.

And yeah, Psalm 84:11 promises He's not withholding any good thing from me, but—isn't a godly spouse or children a good thing? Wouldn't starting a ministry be something He wants? Isn't climbing out of debt a God-honoring pursuit? Then, I'm sorry, but why isn't He allowing it? Giving it? Blessing it?

Brace yourself: "Have you realized that most of your unhappiness in life is due to the fact that you are LISTENING to yourself instead of TALKING to yourself?"[1]

I know, I wasn't too sure how to ease into that, but *hear me out*: So far with David, his journal entries look A WHOLE LOT MORE LIKE OUR THOUGHTS than the Lord's Prayer in Matthew 6, right? Like when stuff hits the fan and we're sitting in a pool of our own waterworks, our knee-jerk reaction isn't necessarily, "O Father in heaven, hallowed be Thy name . . ." is it?

Well, maybe for you it is. But for *me*, it's more like, "O Lord, how long will you forget me? Forever? Restore the sparkle to my eyes, OR I WILL DIE" (see Psalm 13:1, 3) or "I am on the verge of collapse. Come quickly to help me, O Lord my Savior" (see Psalm 38:17, 22) or "Slap all my enemies in the face!" (see Psalm 3:7) and "Don't let them get away with their wickedness; in your anger, O God, *bring them down*" (see Psalm 56:7), and—oh yeah—"may they be like snails that dissolve into slime" (see Psalm 58:8). Try that for trash talk.

Now *that* I can resonate with. David's diary isn't too far off from my own.

But in David's laments, after he lays it *all out* (and I mean, ALL OUT) before God, withholding no thought, feeling, or vindicative hit list, something startling always happens. As we're snooping—er, flipping our way into his writings and comparing psalm after psalm under the microscope, we see it time and time again—a certain unexpected pattern emerging, making a trend across the board.

In the beginning, David gives ear to his trials, fears, enemies, and past—to the point where he doesn't just have bloodshot eyes, but his bones are out of joint (Is now a bad time to mention chiropractic care?), his tongue sticks to the roof of his mouth (I can relate . . . nothing worse than crackers without water), and he feels God has laid him in the dust and left him for dead (re: Did I mention he was dramatic?).

But then David makes a pivotal shift: "I will proclaim your name to my brothers and sisters. I will praise you among your assembled people" (Psalm 22:22).

Hold up, did David get hit with amnesia or COVID fog? Just earlier, he wrote, "Why are You so far from helping me? . . . O my God, I call out by day, but You do not answer" (22:1-2, AMP), and he was the guy on the run from the king and his men, who, oh yeah, HAD A DEATH WARRANT OUT FOR HIS ARREST. So all the essays about being discouraged? Upset? Feeling a little bit heartbroken and abandoned by God? Seems understandable . . . In light of *his circumstances*, it made sense why David was sad!

But in light of *his God*? That's when it all changed: "I will praise you in the great assembly. I will fulfill my vows in the presence of those who worship you" (22:25).

In other entries, it's like the Psalmist waffles, has a moment of weakness, and swings back for a second to remind God about his grief and the oppression of his enemies. But then we read it again, just like in David's psalms, he moved from pleading and protesting, to praising and preaching to himself: "Why, my soul, are you downcast? Why so disturbed within me? Put your hope in God, for I will yet praise him, my Savior and my God" (42:5, NIV).

Interesting, isn't it? David and other writers of the Psalms spent a whole lot of time listening to themselves, and if it's true that 80 percent of our thoughts are negative and 95 percent of them are repeated like research claims,[2] then we are spending a lot of time listening to ourselves too. What's that negative thought *you* keep replaying over and over again in your mind? You've rehashed it with God a thousand times in prayer. Try as you may, you can't seem to give it up and keep swinging back over to it.

Question: **Is it time for us to also make the shift—from *listening* to ourselves to *talking* to ourselves?**

Instead of entertaining every single thought in the name of processing, what if we took every thought captive (2 Corinthians 10:5)? Declared His truth over our trials? Chose to proclaim His praise in the midst of our trouble?

This is the HOW that must be coupled with *every* truth we've learned along the way. This is the pathway not just to knowing the truth, but living it out too. This is the HOW to choose faith over fear, doubt, discouragement, and our own negative thoughts that we can and *must* glean from David's diary and incorporate into every single one of our own journal entries as well: **We need to recognize when it's time to stop listening to ourselves and high time to start preaching to ourselves.**

> We need to recognize when it's time to stop listening to ourselves and high time to start preaching to ourselves.

Don't get me wrong: God wants you to go to Him with every concern, trouble, and request. He welcomes you in His presence every second of every hour of every day, thanks to Christ, who made a way and is the Way. And Jesus brought it home: "Whoever comes to me I will *never* drive away" (John 6:37, NIV, emphasis added). So please, go boldly to the throne of our gracious God, and like David, lay it ALLLLLL out there. God knows every thought anyway!

But too many of us just stop there. We've closed our PowerPoint presentation of prayer requests with an "in Jesus' name, amen," and then the next day, we go back and repeat. Same requests, same plea, same prayer—duplicated until it's either answered or, in our eyes, unanswered. Then we give up, let it plant a seed of doubt in our minds, and move on jaded as if God didn't give us His best.

But we're short-circuiting our prayers when we do that. We're crippling our faith when that's all there is. And we're putting God in a box, as if we could limit His response and options, and living with clenched fists over THIS IS HOW IT SHOULD BE DONE, frustrated when our will (*cough,* with no concern for His) isn't done.

Essentially, we're missing what marked the very prayers of David, the man after God's own heart.

When we're spiraling in a downward cycle, our thoughts are plunging deeper into "woe is me," and we've rehashed our fears, trials, and requests before God, we can't wait until He answers our prayers before praising Him. We can't sit around waiting for the doctor or news stations to finally give us good news before finding peace. We can't even wait for another Christian or our church to lift us up. When the battle is raging NOW, we have a choice to make.

Plummet or pivot. Protest or preach. Panic or praise.

Before we even say "amen," we can start a shift in our own souls by reminding ourselves of the things God has for us. Like His power over sin (Romans 6:14), His peace that transcends all understanding (Philippians 4:7), and His hope that never puts us to shame (Romans 5:5).

> Plummet or pivot. Protest or preach. Panic or praise.

What does this look like?

The Psalmist shows us: "I will praise [Him] more and more"

(Psalm 71:14). When we're done talking to God about our problems, it's time to talk to our souls about God.

"Lord, my heart is heavy with recent headlines . . . but my hope is in YOU, who still sits on the throne and is always keeping watch over our lives."

"Father, I wanted this baby, this pregnancy, this positive test, but I trust in YOU to work all of this, even this, for my good according to your purpose. I'm going to live today with this confidence in mind."

"Jesus, they're just getting sicker and sicker. I keep bringing them to you, knowing you can heal, and I'm asking if you're willing? I put my hope in YOU, my Savior and my God."

Ultimately, "this is what's on my mind, God. Now, mind, this is what's in God's Word." Then as we live out our day, dive into work, navigate through hard conversations with our kids, open up to our friends, and scroll past the latest doomsday story in our feed, we carry forth the same declarations, "My hope is in HIM. I will praise HIM. I trust in HIM." When we start to waver, we return to God in prayer until we've confessed it all yet again—and then face the world with the same proclamation, "He is my faithful Savior and forever my God." Repeat approximately 5.38Mx/day.*

This, my girl, is the difference between a Christian living in defeat and a Christ-follower seizing the abundant life.

P.S. You may not be *feeling it*, but praise God, His truth isn't dependent on our emotions, and our praise doesn't have to be subjected to them either.

Hear that? I think the timer went off. It's time to make the shift today—from prayer to praise to preaching the truth to our souls. Joy, peace, and hope are on the other side. You with me?

Make no mistake: **Your praise is the doorway to your freedom.**

---

* Not an official statistic; purely an uneducated guesstimate with zero research done.

FEAR:

"How do I choose faith when I don't feel it?"

THE HOW: Instead of listening to yourself, it's time to make the shift and start preaching to yourself who God is and what His promises are. "The truth will set you free" (John 8:32).

WHAT IF I DON'T KNOW WHERE TO START? The cool thing about being privy to David's journal is, it's actually not his private property. It's God's Word, His book, so He gives you full permission to not only peek around, but to savor every entry. You can start by echoing David's words as your own prayers and go from there!

HOW DO I KNOW WHAT TRUTH TO PREACH TO MY SOUL? Out of all the Bible characters we stalked in this book, which one left the biggest imprint in your mind? That may be because their struggle is also yours, and the truth, the principle, the HOW behind their story is the one God wants you to remember and claim today. Start there.

WHAT IF I'M NOT FEELING IT? From the sounds of it, David wasn't "feeling it" a lot of times either. Not sure he was in the mood to be thankful when he wanted his enemy's bones broken, and he couldn't have been riding high on endorphins when one of his sons raped his daughter and another son wanted him dead (2 Samuel). But too many of us are letting our emotions dictate our actions, and the opposite needs to be true. Follow God and His commands, and allow the Creator of your emotions to soothe, restore, redirect, and guide the tornado that is your heart. He knows what He's dealing with, He knows your thoughts, and He still asks you to *COME*.

Chapter 20

WHERE DO I GO FROM HERE?

The Disciples

"What do I do now? Where do I go from here?" A few hours of premarital counseling, and we're just expected to "figure it out"? You're sending me home *with* a newborn but *without* an owner's manual? You mean, this company onboards new hires with sink-or-swim training . . . *like, on purpose?*

And I made the decision to follow Jesus as my Lord and Savior, get a new Bible, and . . . ? That's it? WHAT ARE THE NEXT STEPS? Where's the clearly labeled road map—and does God's voice sound at all like Siri? Because I kinda like how "Hey Siri" is all that's needed to activate her help and get real-time answers. Oh, and she also shows me traffic conditions! Nothing worse than venturing out only to be delayed by an accident, closed road, or those guys in orange reflective vests frantically waving their hands to slow us down. Unrelated: Are speed limits more of a rule or *recommendation?*

Isn't this how much of life feels? We're looking ahead at the unknown, tomorrow is one big question mark, and as we're straining our eyes to gain some semblance of direction, we'd give just about anything for a blinking marquee arrow to randomly appear and show us the way.

But instead, someone cuts us off on the freeway and gives the bird. #PEOPLEAREDELIGHTFUL

The disciples get it. Before Jesus left, He gave them a *somewhat* alarming warning: "In a little while you won't see me anymore" (John 16:16).

I'm sorry, COME AGAIN?

These men gave up their *entire careers* to follow Jesus. The fishermen left their boats and nets behind, no turning back. Matthew forfeited his employment license as a tax collector. Simon switched his allegiance from a certain political platform to Christ alone. And when their fathers thought they'd take over the family business, they walked away.

This was it for them.

For years, they traveled beside Jesus and grew accustomed to life on the road—going from town to town, bouncing from crowd to crowd, taking in miracle after miracle.

They ate every meal together.

As a group, they got a room under one reservation every night.

Ultimately, they followed this Man day in and day out. But now . . . they couldn't? He was *leaving them*? And He expected them to do *what* in the meantime?

THEY PANICKED. "How long will you be gone? Why are you leaving? What's the exact timeline of *air quotes* 'a little while'? And really, Jesus, you're *kind of the main act*, so without you, I mean . . . do you really expect the show to still go on?

"This can't be true! We gave up everything for you! I thought we were building toward something? We'd see your Kingdom come to earth? Didn't you bust in to save us, reign victorious, and conquer all evil in the world? I THOUGHT WE'D OVERTHROW THE GOVERNMENT AND BE SITTING AT YOUR RIGHT HAND ON OUR OWN THRONES. I'm still up for it if you are!"

But listen close as Jesus leans in, fully aware of their questions and uneasiness. "I said in a little while you won't see me, but a little while after that you will see me again. I tell you the truth, you will weep and mourn over what is going to happen to me, but the world will rejoice. You will grieve, but your grief will suddenly turn to wonderful joy. . . . I have told you all this so that you may have peace in me. Here on earth you will have many trials and sorrows. But take heart, because I have overcome the world" (John 16:19-20, 33).

Are we good? Hands in? "Go Jesus" on three?

Or are you too scratching your head with an open mouth and squinted eyes like the disciples? It's not like He answered some of their questions and brushed past the others—I don't know if He answered *any*. I didn't hear His flight departure details, did you? Also, I'm not sure what we'll be weeping and mourning about, either (and, all due respect, but that whole "you will have many trials and sorrows" part seems avoidable too since, you know, HE'S THE ONE IN CONTROL).

The disciples felt very unsettled, and maybe you do too. That problem of yours without a solution? Those worries growing bigger by the day? That trial making you wonder, *HOW LONG WILL THIS LAST?*

Lean in. Hear Jesus' reassurance again: Take heart.

Like the disciples, while we don't know when, where, or how, we certainly know WHO and WHAT. Our Lord has already overcome, and even though sorrow may last for the night, joy will *always* come in the morning. He specifically told us all of this *so that* we can have peace in Him and know *no matter what* . . . it's gonna be good.

But Friday came, and that reassurance and peace they had in the moment quickly dissolved.

In fact, it was worse than they ever could've imagined.

Jesus was arrested and found guilty. A crown of thorns was crushed into His skull. Signet rings were pounded into His face, so He didn't even look human anymore. He was whipped, with broken glass digging into His skin, and then with every tug, sharp rocks tore His flesh apart. As if that weren't enough, the disciples watched as their Savior was forced to carry a cross, then stakes pounded through His wrists and feet, and finally, blood dripped in a pool down below.

As the soldiers and onlookers continued to curse, mock, and spit on Him, and as Jesus heaved His body up and down against the splintery wooden cross, this is when we hear Him say, "Father, forgive them. . . . It is finished" (Luke 23:34; John 19:30). With one last breath, His body went limp, and as much as Jesus' friends and family tried to hold it together, this was the final nail in the coffin. They crumbled at this point. When Jesus' body went down in that grave, their hopes and future died along with Him.

As the disciples scurried away from the crime scene and gathered in the upper room waiting for updates on their newsfeed, they were biting their nails, bloodshot eyes darting back and forth, and everyone was thinking the same thing: *We may very well be next.* I mean, if that's what they did to *Jesus*, it only makes sense that's what they had up their sleeve for *His followers* too, right?

How did things go *so* wrong *so* fast? Just the week before, this same crowd rolled out the red carpet and cheered Jesus and His followers along as they entered Jerusalem. Now, they all moshed together at that skull-shaped hill called Golgotha, yelling, "Crucify Him! Crucify Him! Crucify Him!"

What an unexpected plot twist.

Except . . . it was more than that.

This wasn't just a book they could put down, a movie they could turn off, or a post they could scroll past. No, this was their *life*. As much as they wished they could grow numb or detached, their hearts were broken in an unignorable way, and one blaring question remained: **Where are we supposed to go from here?**

One disciple's answer was to commit suicide. Peter quit the ministry and went back to fishing. And when we feel stuck and begin to question God's hand in our own disappointments, it's easy to go back to old habits, old thought patterns, and our old way of life too. It's easy to give up altogether.

But in those moments when your spouse wants to separate, and you think your marriage is on its last legs; your boss lets you go, and you're convinced your career is done for; your doctor delivers a devastating update, and you're tempted to throw in the towel, I hope you realize that while you may be living in the Saturdays of life and things couldn't *possibly* get any worse than they are now . . . **Sunday is still always coming for those who know Christ.**

How do we know? Well, quite simply, because He told us. **"For it is written."**

This is the HOW to glean from the disciples—what we can learn rightfully where they went wrong. Jesus had plainly talked about His death. He told them quite a few times that He would be killed, but "on the third day he [would] be raised from the dead"

> How do we know? Well, quite simply, because He told us.

(Matthew 17:23). Jesus even mentioned the whole "[they] will mock him and spit on him, flog him and kill him. Three days later he will rise" bit (Mark 10:34, NIV). I mean, that's *quite the detailed prediction.* You'd think if the disciples had *actually been listening,* instead of huddling behind closed doors and allowing fear to consume the atmosphere, they'd start the timer. Paper-chain countdown. *Alexa, set an alarm for 3 days!*

But instead of focusing on "it is written," they lasered in on their anxiety and awful circumstances. Instead of recalling Jesus' words and promises, they relived their worst-case scenarios. And instead of trusting Jesus would do just as He said, they questioned everything—their Savior included.

I know you wish things could be different. Your ultimate dream seems like a long shot, and you'd like to fast-forward past the hard parts of this season. If you're still living and breathing, though, there's time left on the clock, **and it's not over.** God isn't done. There's still opportunity for a comeback, because we serve a God who does the impossible and knows no limits.

Not even the grave.

But it'll require you to take your eyes off your circumstances and put them back on the Word of God. It'll necessitate you declaring "it is written" instead of succumbing to "but what if this happens?" It'll demand trust in Jesus, who said, "Didn't I tell you that you would see God's glory if you believe?" (John 11:40).

Because, truth be told, the truth has already been told—all 1,000-plus pages, organized in 66 books, recorded from the beginning to the end of time. It has all been written—but how much are we paying attention to it? Listening to it? Heeding it, saturating our days in it, *BELIEVING* it? "By his divine power, God has given us everything we need for living a godly life. We have received all of this by coming to know him, the one who called us to himself by means of his marvelous glory and excellence" (2 Peter 1:3). Do you hear all the absolutes? "Everything we need" . . . "all of this" . . . God has given us ample proof, power, and revelation in His Word.

But are we acting like the disciples, giving more weight to our circumstances and the reasons to fear we've invented in our minds than the very Word of God?

Sunday came around, and the disciples woke, hoping it was nothing more than a bad dream. But their eyes scanned the damage done, and reality confirmed their worst nightmare. Jesus was still gone.

Throughout this Sunday, as they hid behind closed doors and drew in deep breaths, the question remained, *Why did Jesus leave us with this mess?*

But as much as these disciples *thought* He had abandoned them and all hope was lost, this was far from reality. In fact, it only took **one second** for things to change, and **one moment** for them to realize otherwise.

"Peace be with you."

At the sound of His voice, our heads whip around to see Jesus standing right in front of us! He miraculously skipped past the locked door and stepped right into our fear, doubt, and hopelessness, literally declaring peace (John 20:19). Holding out His hands, showing us His wounds, He announced it one more time to dispel any leftover alarm: "Peace be with you" (20:21).

When things aren't looking great and we're lost in the Saturdays of life, we must know the same is true for us, too: Jesus is coming, and when He does, everything will change. He hasn't left us to deal with this mess on our own, and He would never leave us helpless or afraid. Rather, we too will find that He seeks us out in the shadows, breezes past doors we (or others) attempted to lock up, and meets us in the middle of our panic, trial, and short breaths. What seemed hopeless merely a moment ago will then be instantly redeemed and flipped for good—and understanding will finally come.

But Jesus can repeat "Peace be with you" a million times over . . . and it's still up to *you and me* to believe Him.

This lone statement is Jesus' offer each and every day as we face the unknown, since He Himself is our peace (Ephesians 2:14). When we don't know where to go from here, we can rest in His presence surrounding us. When we don't know what to do, we can pick up His Word and read His promises. And when we don't know the next step, we can trust He has already gone before us, making a way, and will faithfully lead us on.

"Peace be with you" is our permanent truth and endless reality.

But if you already walked out the door and moved on like Thomas or turned your back on Him like Judas, then you'll miss it. You won't be around when He shows up.

It's up to you. Belief, trust, faith? Or disbelief, doubt, fear? Either is yours for the taking.

Jesus lived out of His earthly suitcase for a little over a month after this reunion before He returned to the Father in heaven, but He was still set on leaving. It was important for Him to go—but He made it clear that the disciples wouldn't be alone. "No, I will not abandon you as orphans—I will come to you" (John 14:18). Not only is He coming back for us again, but in the meantime, God was sending the Advocate—the Holy Spirit, the third member of the Trinity, "who will never leave you" (14:16)—in Jesus' place.

Since we can't see this Spirit, we tend to think of Him as a "what" instead of a "Who" and a force instead of a Person.[1] While we *know* He's just as personable as Jesus in the flesh and we're *told* He's just as much

God as the Father . . . well, if given the option, it'd be REAL TOUGH to pass up Jesus walking right beside us and talking face-to-face, right? Even those of us who ranked 0 for "physical touch" on the love language scale (#itme), IF WE COULD HUG JESUS? Like reach out to hold His hand at any time? Shake Him awake when the storms of life are engulfing our boat? Ask Him to heal the cancer before it spreads and actually hear His response? Bring our kids and their spiked fever to His lap instead of racing off to urgent care? Run to Him in the kitchen when our in-laws make a surprise visit, and He multiples our empty pantry into bottomless rolls and a fish fry? Or simply ask Him, "What does this all mean?" when we don't understand?

I'd choose that a million times over.

So I get the disciples' unease. Quick imagine for a sec if this physical proximity to Jesus was your *norm* (because it was for them)! They experienced all of this interaction and closeness for *years*. Yet now they've just been told Jesus is going to peace out—like for the rest of their lifetimes—and send this unseen Spirit instead. This seems . . . like a step back, no? Wasn't this what we had with God the Father for the last, oh, I don't know, thousands of years? Unseen to the naked eye? Silent for the majority of the time—unless you were a prophet?

Nope. Not at all, actually. And Jesus knew the disciples wouldn't be the only ones having a hard time grasping this concept, so He reassured them (and us), "I am going away to the one who sent me, and not one of you is asking where I am going. Instead, you grieve because of what I've told you. But in fact, *it is best for you that I go away*, because if I don't, the Advocate won't come" (16:5-7, emphasis added).

Christ dwelled *among us*—yes, no doubt about it, that's incredibly awesome! But do you know what's even better? The Holy Spirit dwelling *inside of us*. The Spirit Himself will not only guide us into all truth, convict us of sin, empower us, and lead us into righteousness—but He will comfort us, assist us in prayer, guard our salvation, renew our spirit, give us wisdom, and fill us with love, joy, peace, patience, kindness, goodness, faithfulness, gentleness, and self-control (Galatians 5:22-23). He is our Friend, Helper, and Spiritual-Gift Giver.

No longer do we have an external list of rules to follow. With the Spirit living in us, God's laws are written on our hearts and instilled in our minds, guiding us in every unique situation we face.

We don't have to wait for three days for Jesus to come to Lazarus's tomb. If a loved one is sick, we have instant access to the Holy Spirit— and, with Him, the same power that raised Christ from the dead.

No wonder Jesus said, "I tell you the truth, anyone who believes in me will do the same works I have done, and even greater works, because I am going to be with the Father" (John 14:12). Just as Jesus was fully God, He was also fully Man . . . one Man. But if every single believer, millions of us around the globe, took Him up on His Word, picked up our cross to follow Jesus, called on His power along the way, and seized this reality of the Holy Spirit dwelling within us? Well, of course we will do greater works! Strength in numbers, yo! Strength in the Holy Spirit, God Himself, Immanuel.

So *"Where do we go from here?"* Always to His Word. Once we hear, learn, and dwell on "for it is written," we can move forward with the Holy Spirit empowering and guiding us every step of the way.

When we do this, we realize that not only has the ending already been written, spelled out for us clear as day in the Bible, but spoiler alert: He's coming back for us soon, and in the person of the Holy Spirit, He's already here today.

I'm glad, Heidi, really I am . . . but WHAT ABOUT MY UNFULFILLED DREAMS? What about that thing I so desperately want? Our desires matter, for sure. Our unique passions come from God, most certainly. And what matters to us matters to Him, you better believe it. But Jesus warned His disciples, "Don't be afraid of those who want to kill your body (or that thing just as deadly); they cannot touch your soul. Fear only God, who can destroy both soul and body in hell" (Matthew 10:28).

And on that positive note . . . the end!

Just kidding. *Almost* had you, didn't I?

But here's the last nugget we gotta dig out before you shut this book and hop on social media to recommend to all your friends and family that THIS BOOK IS HANDS DOWN A MUST-READ and THEY WOULD BE DOING THEMSELVES A BIG FAVOR getting their hands on their own copy . . . *Shameless plug since, you know, I "no longer live in shame" (Isaiah 54:4).*

So much of what we worry about, obsess over, and allow to dictate our thoughts and emotions only has limited, temporary, earthly power. Cancer? Could kill us, yes. Financial debt? Raises the blood pressure, for sure. The state of our nation? Imperfect, indeed. Our parents' divorce? Heartbreaking, no doubt.

But when we get to heaven, there will be no more death, sorrow, crying, or pain (Revelation 21:4). Every tear will be wiped from our eyes, every relationship restored, and all these tragic things will be gone forever.

Do you see where I'm going with this? This ending has already been written. This reality is sure and coming. And our future, our forever home, our standing in Christ? *It's forever secure.*

> Our future, our forever home, our standing in Christ? *It's forever secure.*

So at the end of the day, when our pulse is racing, our doubt is growing, and our mind is spiraling, what if we asked ourselves: *Will this matter when I get to heaven? Will this last for eternity?*

If the answer is no, then maybe it's not worthy of taking up space here on earth, either. Maybe our time really is better spent thinking on "whatever is true, whatever is noble, whatever is right, pure, lovely, admirable, excellent, and praiseworthy" instead (see Philippians 4:8, NIV). Maybe God knew what He was talking about when He said, "Think about the things of heaven, not the things of earth" (Colossians 3:2)—because this earth is full of fear-inducing, anxiety-driven, terribly tragic things. But because of the hope set before us in heaven thanks to Jesus Christ? They cannot weigh us down.

Because they cannot kill our soul.

Do you believe that? Until you do, you'll be tossed to and fro by the circumstances of your life and the atmosphere of this world. You'll continue living as if this world is *it*. The only reason worth existing. The only chance you get for happiness. If you don't get what you want here, then FORGET IT.

But if we live for Jesus—to build His Kingdom—and live with our forever home and eternal truth in mind? We are free . . . *no matter what*.

"It is for freedom that Christ has set us free. Stand firm, then, and do not let yourselves be burdened again by a yoke of slavery" (Galatians 5:1, NIV). "Do not let" implies we have a choice. Will you stand firm in the freedom He already paid for and currently offers? Or will you *let yourself* be burdened by the things of this world, the circumstances of your day, the what-ifs to come?

Jesus paid a high price to secure your freedom, so girlfriend, *be free*. How? **"For it is written."**

It really is as simple as that.

GIRL, YOU DID IT. You clocked in the time, walked a marathon of miles alongside these Bible heroes, and now reached the end of the road where we part ways and say our goodbyes. *I'LL NEVER LET GO, JACK.* I know . . . I feel sad too (and it still hurts 25+ years later since *Titanic* released, doesn't it?).

But great news: While *some* good things must come to an end—i.e., this book . . . did you leave a five-star review on Amazon yet?— it's untrue that *all* good things must come to an end. Exhibit A being God's character and promises.

So keep your walking shoes on, eyes lifted up to the Lord where your help comes from, and whenever you're consumed with your story, go back to His, okay? With every question we think and ask—*What if?*

Why me? How? What about when?—God's Word points to the answer about faith, fear, and all the things, and He will never lead you astray nor let you down.

Although in this world we will face trouble, you now know we have every reason to take heart. Not only does God hold the final Word, but our Savior has already overcome! Someday, we will see.

Yet in the meantime, while we're in the middle of our stories, sitting in the question marks of today, and unsure how God's going to come through, I hope you now confidently believe and see more clearly than ever that no matter how it looks right now . . . it's not only going to be okay, but . . .

P.S. It's gonna be good.

Love, Heidi

FEAR:

"Where do I go from here?"

THE HOW: Instead of lasering in on your anxiety and hard circumstances, focus on "it is written"—what's already been spoken and promised in His Word—and take God up on His Word by trusting it.

HOW CAN WE TAKE HEART WHEN WE FACE TROUBLE AND SORROW? Confidence builds when we remember who our Savior is, what He already promised us, and that His promises will prevail. Go back to the things He has told us and remember, ultimately—while we may not know how, why, when, or where—we know WHO and WHAT: Christ has already overcome.

WHAT TYPES OF THINGS DID JESUS TELL US TO EXPECT IN THE SATURDAYS OF LIFE? When Jesus was sending out His disciples in Matthew 10, He assured them they would be arrested, flogged, threatened, betrayed by their own families, and hated—solely because they were His followers. SIGN US UP, right? "But everyone who endures to the end will be saved" (verse 22). Oh, there it is again! The choice . . . to give into doubt and fear or remain faithful.

WHY DID GOD LEAVE US HERE TO DEAL WITH THIS MESS? *Technically,* we're the ones who created the mess (you know, choosing sin and all). But semantics aside, God has never once left us nor forsaken us, and He's not about to do so anytime soon. Rather, He sent His Son to take the punishment for our sins, restore our relationship with Him, and give us the assurance we so desperately crave in our anxiety—through salvation alone. When we remember the hope of the gospel and Jesus, the Hope of the World, we realize we have every reason to keep believing and moving forward in faith. For surely "we know that God causes everything to work together for the good of those who love God and are called according to his purpose for them" (Romans 8:28)—and someday, we will see. Until then, while living through the Saturdays of life and navigating the chaos of this world, we stand firm in "it is written." For the Word of the Lord stands forever, "and that word is the Good News that was preached to you" (1 Peter 1:25). Keep your chin up, girl . . . **Sunday is coming for us too, and** (say it with me this time)**: It's gonna be good.**

DISCUSSION QUESTIONS

CHAPTER 1: DID GOD REALLY SAY . . . ?

1. God's heart is for us to be united and in community—yet the enemy's intent is to divide and isolate. How have you seen this play out in your life and in the world today?

2. Lions often follow the same hunting patterns over and over. What attack patterns have you seen the enemy use in your own life?

3. How are you tempted to bow to the way you feel? When that happens, what steps can you take to go back to the Word and stand on the truth you know?

4. How do you hear the enemy's question circulating today? Fill in the blank: "Did God really say _____?"

5. Where do you feel as if you're lacking—or possibly as if God's withholding something good from you? How do the principles from this chapter and the truths from God's Word counter that?

CHAPTER 2: BUT WHAT IF . . . ?

1. Would you rather be pregnant when the law demands every baby boy be thrown in the Nile River or when masks are mandated in the hospital with no visitors allowed? I DARE YOU TO ANSWER.

2. What's your Midian? Where do you run when times get tough?

3. God is moving and working and speaking all around us, all the time. We just need to have the eyes to see. Jot down three times you've recently witnessed God at work.

4. We are God's plan A to reach this lost world. Where may He be calling you to go as His ambassador?

5. What kinds of what-if questions are you asking these days? How does God's response "I am" answer them?

CHAPTER 3: WHY AM I OFF-COURSE?

1. How does the canvas of your life look different from what you originally pictured? Has God taken you down any detours?

2. Have you ever thought, *Why am I here?* How does Moses' story encourage you?

3. Instead of giving in to doubt, what does it look like to give God the benefit of the doubt?

4. What do you consider "the glory days" in your own life? How do you resonate with the Israelites pining for what they had back in Egypt? How can you wait expectantly instead?

5. How can you follow the Israelites' footsteps by (1) committing your situation to the Lord in prayer and (2) moving forward in faith?

CHAPTER 4: WHAT IF I DON'T HAVE WHAT IT TAKES?

1. How have you echoed Gideon's question, "If God is with me, then why . . . ?"

2. Where do you feel inadequate? What name has God given you that directly speaks otherwise?

3. How have you based your identity off your past or current set of circumstances?

4. Who or what are the Midianites in your life? Who or what makes you afraid or steals your peace?

5. What does it look like to do what you can do and trust that God will do what only He can do?

CHAPTER 5: WHAT IF I WANT TO RUN AWAY FROM THIS?

1. Jonah had no interest in going to Nineveh. After learning more about this feared world powerhouse, we don't blame him! What does God sending Jonah there show us about His heart?

2. Where have you stood at the same crossroads as Jonah with only two choices available: (1) walk away from God or (2) follow where He leads?

3. "When you're being rocked back and forth by the waves of life, don't ever forget that others are in the boat watching you." Take some time to think of who those others are, and jot down their names below. Spend a couple of minutes praying for them.

4. What would it look like for you to turn right around and extend the same comfort to others that the God of all comfort has given you?

5. When it's fight or flight, we can either run from the Lord or to the Lord. How can you run to the Lord today?

CHAPTER 6: WHAT ABOUT WHEN THE WORLD GOES CRAZY (AND I'M KIND OF TEMPTED TO GO CRAZY TOO)?

1. From your childhood to the present day, how has the landscape of the world changed?

2. The first attack from Daniel's enemy came in the form of assigning him a new name. What labels has the world and our enemy tried to slap on you that God *never* put on you? *Hello, I'm* _____.

3. The second attack came in the form of an invitation from the enemy for Daniel to go against his convictions. What temptation(s) are you facing today? What command from God can you hold on to instead?

4. The enemy's last-ditch effort was to position culture against Daniel and his God. How is the enemy using this tactic today?

5. Instead of copy-and-pasting the behaviors, customs, and beliefs of this world, what are some practical ways you can be transformed by the renewing of your mind?

CHAPTER 7: HOW CAN I HOPE FOR A GOOD FUTURE WITH MY PAST?

1. How do you picture God? Which imagery at the beginning of this chapter sticks out most to you? What's true about your picture of God—and what's false?

2. We can walk along the same paths as others yet come to very different conclusions. How have you seen this happen in your life?

3. How can you allow God to define your circumstances instead of allowing your circumstances to define God?

4. As with Ruth, where we are today is no mistake. How can you keep the faith even when others don't?

5. Whom do you resonate with most—Ruth or Naomi? Why?

CHAPTER 8: WHAT IF I DON'T KNOW WHAT TO DO?

1. The word *seek* defined King Jehoshaphat's reign. Can you think of someone who models that kind of posture? How can *you* seek the Lord today?

2. When is prayer typically your last resort? When is it your first line of offense?

3. Jehoshaphat didn't face the battle alone—he recruited others to pray. Whom can you ask to stand with you in faith and prayer?

4. How can you praise God today, *before* the answer to your prayer comes?

5. What does it look like for you to wait expectantly on the Lord's help?

CHAPTER 9: WHICH VOICE SHOULD I LISTEN TO?

1. Who still uses Miracle Whip? SHAME ON YOU. (Just kidding.) Real question: Where have you heard clashing opinions and wondered which one is right?

2. No actual conversation happened between the giants and the spies about their size and who they thought was bigger. When have you believed a bad report even when that exchange of information never took place?

3. What are you comparing your plight to—your disadvantage or God's advantage?

4. "We will all *feel* fear, but God didn't say don't *feel* afraid; He just said don't *be*." What's the difference between feeling fear and being afraid in your circumstances?

5. Like Caleb, how can you choose your allegiance ahead of time? How can you turn up the volume on God's voice and keep His promises at the forefront of your mind?

CHAPTER 10: WHAT IF GOD'S PROMISES DON'T LINE UP WITH MY REALITY?

1. Where in life have you hit a wall?

2. If not everyone can be trusted with all the details, which people in your life *can* you confide in?

3. What can you learn from both the wisdom *and* mistakes of the previous generation?

4. Reflect on a time you felt led by God to do something that seemed absolutely ridiculous—yet proved to be worthwhile in the end. How can that memory fuel your motivation today?

5. "Jericho is already ours, but it'll take obedience all the way to day seven to seize it." What are those mundane or monotonous acts of obedience God asks of you today?

CHAPTER 11: WHY THEM AND NOT ME? WHY ME AND NOT THEM?

1. You know that prayer *that shall remain unnamed*? Yeah, the one that chipped away at your confidence and caused hesitancy in the back of your mind? LET'S NAME IT. Bring it into the light, girl! How have you allowed your past to impact your faith?

2. When's the last time you asked, "Why them and not me?" or "Why me and not them?"

3. How have you fallen into the comparison trap lately?

4. "You can ask someone about their life story, and every single person will tell you a different one—because God didn't copy and paste with anyone." Jot down three highlights from your story. As you reflect, thank God for the uniqueness of your story!

5. How does Peter's story encourage you and raise your hope quotient?

CHAPTER 12: WHAT ABOUT WHEN THE WORST-CASE HAPPENS?

1. When facing hardships, do you respond more like Martha or Mary?

2. What's that thing here on earth you want so badly, causing your hands to cramp because you're clenching it so tightly? How can you release your grip today?

3. How can you live for crowns in heaven instead of treasure here on earth?

4. "Jesus weeps with you AND still has a plan." What does it mean to you that God is both sympathetic and sovereign over your situation?

5. "While Martha already knew Jesus as Healer, it was time she knew Him as Resurrection, too." What aspect or name of God are you becoming more intimately acquainted with because of your circumstances?

CHAPTER 13: WHAT IF IT'S TAKING FOREVER? WHAT IF IT NEVER HAPPENS?

1. What are you on the verge of spilling whenever someone asks, "How's it going?" THIS IS A SAFE PLACE. Now's the time to spill the tea, girlfriend!

2. Where do you want instant gratification—the blessing TODAY?

3. How does the phrase "Everyone else is doing it" apply to your situation? How may God be calling you to act countercultural?

4. How do you relate to Abraham, who bowed down in respect to God but laughed to himself in disbelief?

5. God's timing may not always line up with ours, but what can you do to stay encouraged, knowing His purpose is coming down the pipeline (and P.S. It's gonna be good)?

CHAPTER 14: WHAT IF MY TIME HAS PASSED?

1. For fun, what makes you feel old? For serious, what do you feel too old to do?

2. What circumstances in your life have you echoing the question "How?" Does your tone reflect that of Zechariah or Mary? How can you trust in the God of the impossible today?

3. "There's no ounce of jealousy or hint of resentment in this sacred visit—just two women in pure joy, celebrating the gifts their good God has given them, breaking out in song, and speaking blessing over blessing over one another." To follow in Elizabeth's footsteps, who is that person you need to bless instead of resent?

4. Because a life yielded to God is always a life that can be used by God, in what area(s) of your life do you need to submit to Him today?

5. Gray hair is a crown of glory! Think back over the years and experiences you've lived through. What nuggets of wisdom have you picked up along the way?

CHAPTER 15: WHAT DO I DO WHEN GOD FEELS SILENT?

1. When has someone else's request felt like an imposition at first, but you couldn't shake it off? How did the situation end?

2. Fill in the blank with a role or title of yours: Who knows if perhaps you were made _____ for such a time as this?

3. "Our world is so focused on following our hearts and building our own kingdoms, but what if the call is actually to follow *Jesus* and build *His Kingdom*?" How can you serve the Lord where He's planted you?

4. What would it look like for you to move forward in obedience to your previous conviction even when nothing encouraging or supernatural has happened?

5. Reflect on a time when God felt silent. Now, with the gift of hindsight, how can you trace His hand through the unfolding of events?

CHAPTER 16: WHAT ABOUT WHEN GOD LETS BAD THINGS HAPPEN?

1. Where would it be easy to look at your current set of circumstances and jump to conclusions about God because of them? What does Joseph's story teach you?

2. Life is full of highs and lows—for both Joseph and us. Are you in a high or a low right now?

3. In what ways has God given *you* success? Has there been a time when someone, like Pharaoh, declared you to be a woman "so obviously filled with the spirit of God?" Why or why not?

4. Instead of holding a grudge and becoming bitter, whom is God calling you to forgive?

5. "Don't put a period where God intends a semicolon." How do you need to reframe your perspective to see yourself living in the middle of your story, not the end?

CHAPTER 17: WHAT ABOUT WHEN EVERYTHING GOES UP IN FLAMES?

1. "God's always called us to unity *with other believers*, but He's never called us to unity *with the world*." Are you in unity with other believers? Why or why not?

2. How are you "in the world but not of the world"? Can you think of a time in your own life when the high fives halted and you had to take the heat because of your convictions?

3. "Notice that Shadrach, Meshach, and Abednego weren't the ones amazed by their deliverance. That was their expectation. It was the king whose jaw dropped." When you pray, do you tend to expect God will show up or not?

4. How have you seen someone else's faith act as a catalyst to spur on others in their faith?

5. "It was only in the fire when the king could see Jesus." Whether it all went up in flames in your life or someone else's, how have you seen Jesus in the fire?

CHAPTER 18: WHERE'S GOD?

1. How have you had the rug pulled out from under you and been blindsided by bad news?

2. When do you feel like the last Christian standing—at work, in your friend group, or when you draw the line on a particular belief or conviction?

3. How are you asking, "What will we do now?" How does Elisha's response encourage you?

4. How can you see both the physical *and* the spiritual reality of your life today?

5. Since you have direct access to God—who has limitless, unending resources at His disposal—how can you pray big asks like Elisha, "knowing *for certain* our God is going to come through for us in His almighty, unique way"?

CHAPTER 19: HOW DO I CHOOSE FAITH WHEN I DON'T FEEL IT?

1. Fill in the blank: How would things be different if I would have (or wouldn't have) _____?

2. Where do you tend to field the most doubts—from others in your life or from yourself?

3. If it's true that 80 percent of our thoughts are negative and 95 percent of them are repeated, what thoughts are replaying over and over again in *your* mind?

4. Where do you need to make the shift from listening to yourself to preaching to yourself?

5. "Your praise is the doorway to your freedom." How can you lift your praise to God and incorporate worship into your daily rhythms?

CHAPTER 20: WHERE DO I GO FROM HERE?

1. At this point in your life, how does the question "Where do I go from here?" apply?

2. "While we don't know when, where, or how, we certainly know WHO and WHAT." How do these two certainties encourage you in your circumstances today?

3. Where in your life do you need to declare "it is written" instead of succumbing to "but what if this happens?"

4. Do you tend to think of the Holy Spirit as a force or a Person? Why?

5. Did you leave a five-star review for this book on Amazon yet? I'M SORRY, I'M DONE—I PROMISE. Real question: Because of Jesus, His promises, and our sure hope of heaven, how can you remind yourself of the truth that it's not only going to be okay, but . . . P.S. It's gonna be good?

ACKNOWLEDGMENTS

To Ty, my forever person: I love how God could've crossed our paths at any point in my 30+ years of life, but He chose the short six-month stint when I desperately needed hope for a future.

You are my favorite answered prayer, and our story continues to be the fuel behind why I talk about the goodness of God like a broken record. Thanks for loving me so well, generously sacrificing and putting our family first, and having faith like only Bible heroes did. I love you to the maximum, okay? Thanks for making my dreams come true—this book included and beyond.

To Oscar, Mabel, Hazel, and Dottie: One of you said, "My mom's job is her Bible studies on Instagram and changing diapers." I'll let you guess who (I'm sure it'll only take one guess) . . . but you nailed it. I have no greater privilege in this life than to tell anyone who will listen about Jesus and to be your mom. Thanks for letting me do both. Alongside your dad, you four are what make this life so fun and so full.

To Mom and Dad: I won the lottery with you two as parents. You were dead set on not breaking the spirit of an (apparently) very spirited child, bringing me to church even when all my friends got to sleep in after a sleepover, and constantly reminding me to dream big. Thanks for always being my biggest cheerleaders and standing by your faith and values—I'm so proud to be your daughter. Oh yeah, and practically speaking—without you (Mom) watching the kids each week, this book wouldn't have happened . . . probably should've dedicated this to you, LOL. Thanks for all the ways you love and keep on giving to me and my family!

To Dustin and Krista: For those wondering why I care so much about that one B+ and a 3.96 GPA, what they don't know is you both graduated with 4.0s as class valedictorians—and that about sums up my childhood. LOL, but honestly, I've looked up to you two all my life (minus the earlier years, Krista . . . I'm still sorry), and your genuine, heartfelt support has meant everything.

To Tammy and Gordy: Somehow, I landed the best in-laws a girl could ever ask for, and I can't thank you enough for not only loving me like a daughter, but knowing this book was coming far before I dared to dream it possible and continually speaking encouragement over me. Thank you for your unending generosity—both in word and deed.

To Grandpa Al and Grandma Phyllis: I know the Lord's hand is on my life specifically because every single day of it has been bathed and saturated in prayer by you two since before I was even born. Thank you for the legacy you have built and continue to build as you faithfully bring each child, grandchild, great-grandchild, and beyond before the throne of our good God.

To my brothers- and sisters-in-law: I've blubbered enough, so I'll leave it at this—I love you guys. Thanks for being on the group text, okay?

To Kara, my publisher: I'll never forget the day I got your email that read, "Have you ever considered writing a book?" It took everything in me not to hit Reply straightaway with "SINCE THE DAY I STARTED POTTY TRAINING AND WOULD ONLY SIT ON THE TOILET

IF I HAD A PEN AND PAPER IN HAND." Thankfully, I had enough composure at the time to respond (a bit) more civilized. But seriously, thank you for seeing potential in me as an author, making a way for me to fulfill a lifelong dream, and being the best advocate along the way. I can still text you every day after this book has been published, right? Or is every hour better?

To Danika, my editor: You're a wordsmith genius—thank you for all your time, intention, and back-and-forth track changes dedicated to this book. We never did use "spill the tea," but we *did* spare the people from many "intense" details. LOL, thank you for your wisdom, research, and gracious feedback!

To Sarah, Ron, and everyone else on my Tyndale team: Y'all are a dream to work with and put your heart and soul into everything you do. From brainstorming titles to conceptualizing cover designs, I can't thank you enough for always being EXCITED about my book. Thanks for inviting me to partner with you in the mission to share God's Word in a way people can relate to and *understand.*

To Cynthia, my agent: You took on quite the novice of a writer, and I'm 100 percent grateful you did. Thanks for catching the vision of this book right away, jumping on board on our first call together, and being a sounding board all the way through.

To Eagle Brook Church: Thanks for taking the chance to hire me straight out of college with no ministry experience (or really any experience for that matter), and for almost a decade, letting me join in the mission, empowered by God, to reach others for Christ. Much of the content in this book I gleaned while, in some form, on staff—and I'll forever be grateful for the friendships made, and in turn, the lessons learned. Always cheering you on.

To my Instagram friends: SORRY I WAS SO CRYPTIC THESE LAST COUPLE OF YEARS. The cat is finally out of the bag, though: the book is here, and I have zero surprises left . . . well, except for **my second book (this time, a *devotional*) coming next!** I can't wait to take you along for the ride step-by-step on social media—but in the meantime, thank you from the bottom of my heart. Whether you've been around since Weekly Devo Shares or just hit Follow today, y'all linking arms with me to reach anyone scrolling with the Good News of Christ is hands-down the best. Never lose your zeal, okay? The world needs His light, and Jesus said that's exactly who you are and what you radiate: the light of the world reflecting the glory of God (Matthew 5:14-15). See you on the gram, girlfriend.

NOTES

INTRODUCTION
1. See Priscilla Shirer, *The Armor of God* (Nashville: Lifeway Press, 2022), 132–33.

CHAPTER 1: DID GOD REALLY SAY . . . ?
1. Rhitu Chatterjee, "Child Psychiatrists Warn That the Pandemic May Be Driving Up Kids' Suicide Risk," NPR, February 2, 2021, https://www.npr.org/sections /health-shots/2021/02/02/962060105/child-psychiatrists-warn-that-the-pandemic -may-be-driving-up-kids-suicide-risk.
2. Emily Paulin, "Is Extended Isolation Killing Older Adults in Long-Term Care?" AARP, September 3, 2020, https://www.aarp.org/caregiving/health/info-2020 /covid-isolation-killing-nursing-home-residents.html.
3. "How Lions Hunt Their Prey," Bali Safari, August 30, 2019, https://www .balisafarimarinepark.com/how-lions-hunt-their-prey/.
4. "How Do Zebras Protect Themselves?" Reference.com, last updated March 24, 2020, https://www.reference.com/pets-animals/zebras-protect-themselves -7adf77e4f896ea6.
5. "Predatory Behaviour," ALERT, January 8, 2020, https://lionalert.org/predatory -behaviour/.
6. Priscilla Shirer, *The Armor of God* (Nashville: Lifeway Press, 2022), 146.
7. Caleb Bell, "Americans Love the Bible but Don't Read It Much, Poll Shows," *HuffPost*, April 4, 2013, https://www.huffpost.com/entry/americans-love-the -bible-but-dont-read-it-much_n_3018425.
8. Conrad Hackett and David McClendon, "Christians Remain World's Largest Religious Group, but They Are Declining in Europe," Pew Research Center, April 5, 2017, https://www.pewresearch.org/fact-tank/2017/04/05/christians-remain -worlds-largest-religious-group-but-they-are-declining-in-europe/.
9. Lysa TerKeurst, "Life between Two Gardens," sermon, Elevation Church, March 25, 2019, video, 21:00 to 24:00, https://www.youtube.com/watch?v=x5kH3SI1nJs.

CHAPTER 2: BUT WHAT IF . . . ?
1. Levi Lusko, "You're No Good Samaritan," sermon, Passion City Church, August 17, 2020, video, 32:26, https://www.youtube.com/watch?v=3jjAQrdHzek.
2. Craig Groeschel, "Praying through the Pain—Anxious for Nothing Part 2," sermon, Life.Church, August 11, 2019, video, 37:26, https://www.youtube.com/watch?app=desktop&v=kag18xv6aMA.

CHAPTER 5: WHAT IF I WANT TO RUN AWAY FROM THIS?
1. Kyle Idleman, "Jonah: Running from God," sermon, Southeast Christian Church, April 21, 2013.
2. Jason Strand, "When Life Swallows You Up," sermon, Eagle Brook Church, May 23, 2021, video, 44:34, https://eaglebrookchurch.com/media/past-messages/when-life-swallows-you-up/.
3. Idleman, "Jonah."

CHAPTER 6: WHAT ABOUT WHEN THE WORLD GOES CRAZY (AND I'M KIND OF TEMPTED TO GO CRAZY TOO)?
1. Jon Miltimore, "6 Statistics That Show How Much America Has Changed in a Half-Century," Intellectual Takeout, May 22, 2017, https://intellectualtakeout.org/2017/05/6-statistics-that-show-how-much-america-has-changed-in-a-half-century/.
2. Jeffrey M. Jones, "As U.S. Pandemic Eases, Fewer See Religion Gaining Influence," Gallup, June 21, 2021, https://news.gallup.com/poll/351329/pandemic-eases-fewer-religion-gaining-influence.aspx.
3. Deyan Georgiev, "How Much Time Do People Spend on Social Media? [63+ Facts to Like, Share and Comment]," Review 42, May 12, 2022, https://review42.com/resources/how-much-time-do-people-spend-on-social-media/.
4. Tony Evans, "Kingdom Parents Know the Power of a Name," Alternative View, OnePlace.com, October 3, 2017, https://www.oneplace.com/ministries/the-alternative/read/devotionals/alternative-view-with-dr-tony-evans/alternative-view-october-3-2017-11719864.html.
5. Chris Hodges, "When Culture Shifts," sermon, Church of the Highlands, April 7, 2013, video, 44:28, https://www.churchofthehighlands.com/media/message/when-culture-shifts.

CHAPTER 7: HOW CAN I HOPE FOR A GOOD FUTURE WITH MY PAST?
1. Jason Carlson, "Faith in the Famine," sermon, Lakes Free Church, November 17, 2019, video, 42:20, https://lakesfree.org/sermons/?sapurl=Lytxd2Y4L21lZGlhL21pLys0bnAzOHZ4P2VtYmVkPXRydWUmcmVjZW50Um91dGU9YXBwLndlYi1hcHAubGicmFyeS5saXN0OJnJlY2VudFJvdXRlU2x1Zz0lMkJkdDM5dXNj.
2. Jason Carlson, "The Lord of Refuge," sermon, Lakes Free Church, November 24, 2019, video, 41:54, https://lakesfree.org/sermons/?sapurl=Lytxd2Y4L21lZGlhL21pLytnamRqOXNzP2VtYmVkPXRydWUmcmVjZW50Um91dGU9YXBwLndlYi1hcHAubGicmFyeS5saXN0OJnJlY2VudFJvdXRlU2x1Zz0lMkJkdDM5dXNj.
3. Carlson, "Faith in the Famine."

CHAPTER 8: WHAT IF I DON'T KNOW WHAT TO DO?

1. Craig Groeschel, "The Peace of God—Mastermind Part 4," sermon, Life.Church, October 1, 2018, video, 36:57, https://www.youtube.com/watch?v=mNLf4tRWXyE.
2. Groeschel, "Peace of God."
3. Charles H. Spurgeon, "The Singing Army," sermon no. 2923, Metropolitan Tabernacle Pulpit, November 23, 1876, Spurgeon Gems, https://www .spurgeongems.org/sermon/chs2923.pdf.

CHAPTER 9: WHICH VOICE SHOULD I LISTEN TO?

1. Tim Dowling, "Everything Gives You Cancer," *Guardian*, September 6, 2001, https://www.theguardian.com/education/2001/sep/06/medicalscience .healthandwellbeing.
2. Steven Furtick, "I Caught a Thought," sermon, Elevation Church, October 7, 2019, video, 44:08, https://www.youtube.com/watch?v=JBH_SudUQoA.

CHAPTER 10: WHAT IF GOD'S PROMISES DON'T LINE UP WITH MY REALITY?

1. "What Should We Learn from the Walls of Jericho Falling Down?" Got Questions, last updated January 4, 2022, https://www.gotquestions.org/walls-of -Jericho.html.
2. "The Walls of Jericho," israel-a-history-of.com, accessed June 20, 2022, https:// www.israel-a-history-of.com/walls-of-jericho.html.
3. Kyle Idleman, "7 Days of Victory," sermon, Southeast Christian Church, March 28, 2021, video, 1:23:48, https://www.southeastchristian.org/sermons/strength -and-courage.
4. Idleman, "7 Days of Victory."
5. Steven Furtick, "Don't Stop: Part 1—'Don't Stop on Six,'" sermon, Life.Church, March 23, 2015, video, 35:10, https://www.youtube.com/watch?v=4b-GNnxOa7w.

CHAPTER 12: WHAT ABOUT WHEN THE WORST-CASE HAPPENS?

1. C. S. Lewis, *Letters to an American Lady*, ed. Clyde S. Kilby, rev. ed. (Grand Rapids, MI: Eerdmans, 2014), 124.
2. Craig Groeschel, "When God Doesn't Make Sense: Part 2—'When God Seems Late,'" sermon, Life.Church, video, 36:14, December 14, 2015, https://www .youtube.com/watch?v=GAUE4PC0seM.

CHAPTER 13: WHAT IF IT'S TAKING FOREVER? WHAT IF IT NEVER HAPPENS?

1. See Priscilla Shirer, *The Armor of God* (Nashville: Lifeway Press, 2022), 135.

CHAPTER 14: WHAT IF MY TIME HAS PASSED?

1. Craig Groeschel, "When God Doesn't Make Sense: Part 2—'When God Seems Late,'" sermon, Life.Church, video, 36:14, December 14, 2015, https://www .youtube.com/watch?v=GAUE4PC0seM.

CHAPTER 15: WHAT DO I DO WHEN GOD FEELS SILENT?

1. "What Is the Meaning of Sackcloth and Ashes?" Got Questions, last updated January 4, 2022, https://www.gotquestions.org/sackcloth-and-ashes.html.
2. Paul Azinger, quoted by Matthew Martin, "Land of the Dying vs. Land of the Living," Faithlife Sermons, accessed June 27, 2022, https://sermons.faithlife.com /sermons/34812-land-of-the-dying-vs.-land-of-the-living.

CHAPTER 16: WHAT ABOUT WHEN GOD LETS BAD THINGS HAPPEN?

1. Steven Furtick, "Triggered: Taking Back Your Mind in the Age of Anxiety Part 6," sermon, Elevation Church, October 1, 2018, video, 53:30, https://www.youtube .com/watch?v=Mi80NIttniU.
2. Perry Noble, "He Never Saw It Coming," sermon, Elevation Church, June 26, 2017, video, 36:01, https://www.youtube.com/watch?v=1MCYdiRZZGk.

CHAPTER 17: WHAT ABOUT WHEN EVERYTHING GOES UP IN FLAMES?

1. Bob Deffinbaugh, "Faith and the Furnace (Daniel 3:1-30)," Bible.org, May 26, 2004, https://bible.org/seriespage/4-faith-and-furnace-daniel-31-30.
2. "Where Was Daniel during the Fiery Furnace Incident in Daniel Chapter 3?" Got Questions, last updated January 4, 2022, https://www.gotquestions.org/where -was-Daniel-furnace.html.
3. Deffinbaugh, "Faith and the Furnace."
4. Craig Groeschel, "Can You Trust God? In God We Trust Part 1," sermon, Life. Church, October 25, 2020, video, 34:08, https://www.youtube.com/watch?v =KS8pdAE3B-c.

CHAPTER 18: WHERE'S GOD?

1. Steven Furtick, "I'm Still Scared," sermon, Elevation Church, March 29, 2020, video, 1:03:04, https://www.youtube.com/watch?v=_rIoV9yaUaM.

CHAPTER 19: HOW DO I CHOOSE FAITH WHEN I DON'T FEEL IT?

1. D. Martyn Lloyd-Jones, *Spiritual Depression: Its Causes and Cure* (Grand Rapids, MI: Eerdmans, 1965), 20, emphasis added.
2. Stephen Galloza, "80% of Thoughts Are Negative . . . 95% Are Repetitive," *Faith, Hope, & Psychology* (blog), The Miracle Zone, March 2, 2012, https:// faithhopeandpsychology.wordpress.com/2012/03/02/80-of-thoughts-are -negative-95-are-repetitive/.

CHAPTER 20: WHERE DO I GO FROM HERE?

1. Kyle Idleman, "The Promise of the Holy Spirit | Wind & Fire," sermon, Southeast Christian Church, January 10, 2019, video, 32:28, https://www .youtube.com/watch?v=A6Ohf5pY0iI.

Heidi Lee Anderson is a writer, speaker, and stay-at-home mom. While crafting Instagram devotionals @heidileeanderson and @thismotherhen, she's a master at cleaning up Cheerio spills, building Lego towers, and simultaneously chugging coffee like a Gilmore. Heidi has a bachelor's degree in marketing from University of Northwestern, MN, and has spent her career in ministry—from teaching hundreds in kids' ministry to writing daily devotionals, Bible reading plans, and small group curriculum as a content developer. After being diagnosed with cancer, Heidi's fuel is now to make sure Christ-followers realize, know, and claim the sure promises God offers—in the mundane, amidst the heartache, and on top of the highest mountains. Visit her online at thismotherhen.com.